GOOD PSYCH - BAD PSYCH

GOOD PSYCH -
BAD PSYCH

& How to Tell the Difference

JOSHUA THOMAS
CLINICAL PSYCHOLOGIST

To order additional copies of this book, contact:
Xlibris
AU TFN: 1 800 844 927 (Toll Free inside Australia)
AU Local: 0283 108 187 (+61 2 8310 8187 from outside Australia)
www.Xlibris.com.au
Orders@Xlibris.com.au
807000

CONTENTS

DEDICATION

This book is dedicated to:

Firstly, my clients who have both trusted and tested me.

Secondly, my little support team of good psychologists who help me build insight and give me courage.

Thirdly, my wife, Dianne, who correctly thinks that psychology is all in the mind.

Lastly, you, the unwitting client or new psychologist, that is about to step into the murky world of psychological therapy.

WELCOME TO GOOD PSYCH, BAD PSYCH

Congratulations on buying my book. You are going to get a look inside the practice of psychological therapy, diamonds, warts, and kryptonite. You will get to recognise and be adept at avoiding bad psychology and bad psychologists, which together produce Bad Psych. You will get to recognise good psychology and good psychologists (Good Psych) so that you can be assured you have both something (psychology) and someone (psychologist) working in your best interests.

This is essential because everyone will need 'good psych' during testing periods of their lives. In our man-made world, your psyche is tested to the limits whilst being weakened and made soft, made obese. You might expect that with help you would get better. But I will demonstrate that 'bad psych' is everywhere, even where you least expect it. I will show how bad psych weakens your poorly mind, sends you backwards, makes you sicker.

You, or someone you love, will need good therapy, so this book is essential to read but also to have on the shelf for when your mental well-being is in strife. If you want to make sure that you get good help—that is, good psych—then this book is your foundation to help you navigate through the myths and the self-serving systems and institutions so you find good psychology.

REASON FOR THIS BOOK

According to Beyond Blue, over 75 per cent of Australian adolescents with serious mental health problems do not seek help from public health services. Have you ever wondered why and even if this was a good thing? Is government spending of over $10 billion of public money on mental health last year, this year, next year, and every future year a good measure of success—or an excellent measure of failure?

You might think that your country will look out for you so that you only get good psych when you need it and don't get bad psych. But this is not the case. In Victoria, the bravest of state governments, has established a royal commission into the mental health system because the mental health system you have is sick and so performs very badly. And I figure they don't know why. It simply goes wrong for too many people because it is bad. I call it bad psych. General practitioners, psychiatrists, public mental health services, insurance organisations, regulation agencies, employee assistance programmes, disability schemes, not-for-profit groups, and hospitals are facilitating your access to this bad psych.

How do I know?

Let's look at some awful societal facts.

Our Australian Scorecard

Mental Health	
Incidence of Mental Disorder	5 million people each year Getting worse
Living with Depression	3 million people Getting worse.

Suicides	65,000 attempts per year 3,000 successful per year Getting worse.
Taking Psychotropic Pills	5 million people Getting worse.
Spend on Mental Health	$10 billion plus! Getting worse.
Cost to Economy	$60 billion/year Getting worse.

As a client, you walk into a room and think that you are getting good psychology from a good psychologist. What if you are wrong? What if the psychology is bad or the psychologist is bad? How would you know?

This book will teach you what is good psych and bad psych. Our world, despite all its promises, has a dark side that promotes, perhaps even imposes, deteriorating mental health, depression, anxiety, suicide, and disordered personalities. You can't avoid it; and that is why in the 2020s, this book might just save your mental life, if not your real life.

I am a registered clinical psychologist working in private practice, but I was first exposed to good psychology about 20 years ago. At around 40 years old, I got myself into big trouble. Awful things had happened that had rocked me off my centre. I couldn't resolve those dilemmas of mind myself; and like a stereotypical man, I didn't ask for help. Suffice to say, I knew I was way off course. I'd wrecked my good life. I was drinking heavily, hurting myself, hurting those I loved, crying a lot, feeling an intense mix of shame and hopelessness.

Some years later, I found myself in a lonely town, on the floor of the kitchen crying, wanting it all to stop. I wasn't off track—I was lost, somewhere in the dark chasm that I had made. I found Sally who took me for the mess I was. She loved me, and I loved her back. She introduced me to Benjamin, a Jungian analyst in Caulfield, whom I spent three years with, working to put myself back together. Anyway, my life started again.

Since 2006, I have formally studied and practised psychology and have earned quality qualifications, and some of my research about body image is published. I have worked in both public and private practice and established a lovely small business in the CBD. I've hired and supervised psychologists in their professional capacity and mentored others, and I've taught master's students.

Along the way, I developed group-based programmes that work in the public and private domains. One was a dialectical behaviour programme for youth. The other was a schema-focused therapy programme for adults. Importantly, I've worked hands-on with, and for, thousands of clients aged from 3 to 83 across the spectrum of psychological difficulties and disorders.

I'm not new at this. I am well-seasoned, perhaps better described as salty, both in personality and humour.

I decided to write this book for you because there is very little guidance for you from practitioners of psychological therapy. Most information you get is from scientists, researchers, institutions, businesses, and today's shows. Unfortunately, this information is almost always wrong, misses the point, misrepresents what we know, or is simply industry dribble. It promotes and leads you into trouble—trouble that you might never overcome. It promotes bad psych with bad psychologists providing bad psychology that destroys good minds.

Now you have this book in your hand, start reading. Time is of the essence. Your mind needs good psych, and even a week with bad psych will do you harm. You can stay optimistic and grateful, and perhaps you can prevent your 'breakdown'; but if not, you will be able to find and use good psych.

INTRODUCTION

There is a lot of good psych out here. But there is plenty of bad psych too. And for the average folk, it is almost impossible to know the difference.

Good psych is when a good psychologist does good psychology. *Bad psych* is when a bad psychologist does bad psychology.

Now, that means there are other combinations of psychologist and psychology. A good psychologist can do bad psychology, which will feel like general, supportive counselling. But it is not equally true that a bad psychologist can do good psychology. Be assured that the good-psych combination is helpful therapy. Some other combinations are unhelpful, whilst bad psych is kryptonite and can kill you.

I've had numerous clients whose mind has been permanently injured and their life spoilt forever because of bad psych. Of course, some have died on purpose to end their misery. Sounds complicated? Risky? A matter of life or death? Don't fret. I will work through the dangers with you, so you know what you have gotten yourself into and can change direction if needed.

But one day, perhaps next month, you will find yourself or your loved children in one of these combinations:

<u>PSYCHOLOGICAL THERAPY</u>

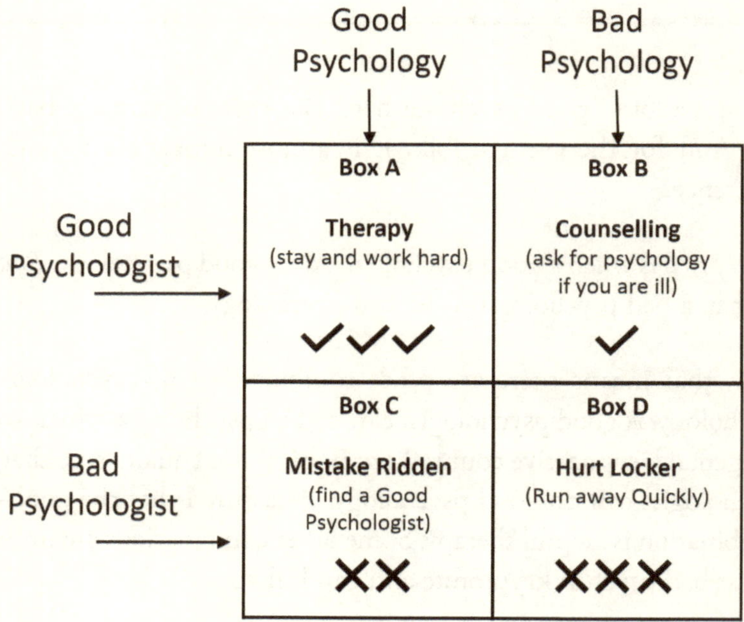

Your job is to make sure you or your loved ones get to be in box A if you have mental difficulties.

Box B is fine too if your mind is working reasonably well but needs some help to 'problem-solve' ordinary life dilemmas. Box C is risky, will confuse you, and send you backwards. Box D is loaded with kryptonite and is dangerous, so I call it the hurt locker. In box D, you will stagnate. You will go backwards. Your temporary difficulties will become entrenched, personalised, and pronounced. Your misery will grow, and you might die.

Unfortunately, there are so many myths about psychology that you won't find yourself in Box A very easily. You will likely languish in counselling for months, if not years, resolving repeating problems but not healing or growing. Worse still, in Boxes C and D, you will be being made worse, getting sicker, becoming more stuck. This happens when you take what could have been a temporary period of mental distress into your deeper personality. You move from having some symptoms to becoming an 'anxious person' or 'depressed person', 'crazy person', 'bad at relationships'—somehow broken.

If you have been seeing a counsellor or psychologist or any mental health worker, and your mental health is not improving, and poor life patterns are not changing, then you are not in Box A. Period!

But remember this:

It is not your fault, and you are not broken.
You have been getting bad psych.

This book is in two parts with plenty of chapters; and once read, you can jump to any bit when you need it.

In part I, I will lead you through the myths of good psychology. You know how Christmastime is full of joy and love? You know how if you send something positive into the universe, something good comes back? You know that when you see a person to help with your mental illness, they will give the right help? Hmmm, really? At least Christmas comes every year, and the universe is actually spinning around. Unfortunately, lots of psychological therapy is unhelpful and, worse, harmful.

Only—and I mean *only*—good psych is helpful if you have mental difficulties. But you carry so many myths with you, stuff you know to be true, that getting good psych will be a game of chance using weighted dice. Like in the first days of spring, we need a refreshing wind. We need to blow the myths away so you can see with a new understanding. We need to illuminate the lack of honesty and truth so you can navigate the terrain of psychological therapy. And we will.

We will polish the mental-health diamonds and find the dull, insidiously dangerous kryptonite inside. I won't be making any friends, more likely putting some friendships at risk. Shining a light on this material is like talking about racism within your family. It never happens without shame, defense, and the bigoted argument—so it never happens.

That is why this book has not been written before and perhaps can only be written once.

Part I would not be complete without some examination of psychological therapy and treatments. Do they work, how do they work, and what does that even mean for you, the client? I hope to treat you as an equal in that part. After all, although I might be the expert in psychological therapy, you are definitely the expert in you. And as an aside, it is a practice that I have at least tried to keep in my work with clients. I was taught that way, and it stacks up as the best way.

You see, since the 1960s, the most promoted model of psychological therapy is called the scientist-practitioner model. And there is good evidence that this is a reasonable, perhaps optimal, model for a psychologist to adopt with you, the client. This model includes you, the person seeking help, in the decision making of how your therapy might progress. It insists that you must actively participate with your psychologist, in your formulation and diagnosis, but especially in the selection and progress of therapy. If you're going to be able to do that, then you must have some of the questions ready to ask your psychologist—or at least know when they are talking gibberish and misleading you.

In part II, I will provide an insight into the good psychologist and what sets them apart from the many bad psychologists. Maybe you already know that the psychologist is much more important than psychology. Our best research demonstrates again and again that the good psychologist is your best help, regardless of the mode of help.

Yes, of all the benefits of therapy and medicines, over half the benefit is explained by having a good psychologist in the room with you. I will explain the competencies and personal attributes that a person brings into the room that allow them to be a good psychologist. I will make obvious the lack of competency and the therapy defeating even dangerous personal attributes the bad psychologist may bring into the room with them. When I do this, I will cover the material regardless of the job title a person is given or gives themselves. For example, people you or your children end up in front of might be called *counselling psychologist, clinical psychologist, mental health clinician, general psychologist, occupational therapist, nurse, psychiatrist, social worker, counsellor, therapist, analyst, sage, guru, mindfulness facilitator, GP, marriage counsellor, priest, pastor, school counsellor,* or *life coach.* Without exception, all these people play psychology with yours or your children's mind.

Except it is not play!

THEORY AND OBSERVATION

True or False?

What goes up must come down.

I want to say yes, do you?

Skip this short chapter if you know everything. My dad knows everything, and I'm sure he will skip it. Of course, he can because he has never been wrong once in his life. When we disagreed—my observation was wrong, or my theory was wrong, or it was my fault—he would point that out. On the upside, it made me resilient to being wrong, you know, I got used to it. And Dad, never being wrong, in a way was kind of reassuring to me, his youngest son. Now I find people are much more scared of telling me that I'm wrong than I am scared of hearing it.

Dad is a confident person, quite safe in what he knows and good at everything. He is kind and great, and I have early and lovely memories of me sitting on the sofa, Dad on the floor, cutting my toenails the right way. Still, his biggest weakness is that he knows, so he can't be corrected. This is not too much of a problem for society. After all, he doesn't go around fixing people and meddling with their minds. Except mine, of course.

So knowing is a tricky thing. It is, I suspect, at the bottom of all psychological disorders. People who are depressed really do know that they are broken, sad, with little hope. Anxious people really do know that it is going to end badly. They have thought about it a lot, and all have their theory on why. They also have observations that prove their theory. They are using what we call the scientific method, just like my dad. The difference is my dad can never become depressed or anxious in a disordered way. He already knows he is not fallible, vulnerable, or

"

hopeless. Because of his knowing, he is inoculated from depression and anxiety. Interesting, isn't it?

Being a clinical psychologist, I'm grateful to have really learnt the scientific method. It is one of the ways we know things, improve our knowing, and most importantly know when to stop knowing. I've had to do the hard yards in research methods connecting observations to our theory of the world, especially the psyche.

What is your take on your psyche?

Do you think you are your brain or your mind? Both? Perhaps your whole body or something spiritual, perhaps the soul? Do you think that psychological therapy helps people who are mentally unwell, disordered? If it is helpful, can it be harmful, or are they mutually exclusive? What is your theory on that? What have you experienced, what have you heard, and what have you observed? Can you even know if good psychological therapy exists and if it really works better than just letting someone recover their mental health, perhaps with support from family and friends? Similarly, how can I know that bad psychological therapy exists, that is harmful, and that it sends people backwards?

It turns out the first question, although not resolved, is well answered. Many thousands of well-put-together studies show that good psych helps most people most of the time. The theory and observations match very well. But those same studies don't show that it works for all people all the time. In fact, in the hundreds of studies I have reviewed, there have always been people for whom it did not produce noticeable benefits, and many people went backwards.

We can wonder why and move on, I guess. Or we can surmise that their mental dilemma was more complicated or incorrectly diagnosed in the first place. Or that their personality traits were resistant to the therapy, or that it was the wrong therapy for them, or that the research itself was inadequate in some way. But the theory of psychological therapy that it heals mental wounds and promotes adaptive ways of thinking and experiencing the world seems quite sound. It is supported by various observations such as changed and freer people, with reduced misery, more happiness, and changed behaviours. Biological observations too suggest it works as expected. For example, changed chemical and neurological arrangements in the brain seem to follow good psych.

Unfortunately, there is a dreadful lack of research into bad psych. In my posh profession, we don't say *dreadful lack* of course. We say *dearth*, which is close to saying *duh*, I think. Anyway, following a sound search of psychological studies, I can't find a single well-put-together study into how psychological therapy done badly (bad psych) affects people's mental health. I am odd, but that seems strange even to me, someone who understands the need to find the whole truth of such matters. To me, it is like we study white and forget black even exists. Many aboriginal folk would say it is exactly like that.

But imagine our world if we had no studies on how smoking cigarettes negatively affects people's physical health. We might still think it was beneficial to our well-being. It was not that long ago that cigarettes were recommended by doctors as good for you. It is actually proven to soothe your throat, suppress your appetite, and relieve your stress. But by looking around, evidence was built to show that, not only was it good for us, but it was also deadly bad for us. And so, we know much better than to promote smoking.

This was a big advance in people's physical health and also their knowing. Of course, we all know plenty of people who still know different or simply refuse to know! Anyhow, what evidence do I have that bad psych exists, is harmful, and damages people perhaps just as badly and insidiously as cigarette smoking?

First, the theory of psychological therapy the same theory that predicts and explains good psych, also predicts bad psych. Just as a mind can be changed for the better with the combination of a good psychologist and good psychology, a disorder can be amplified and misery increased. Psychology can effectively and relatively quickly build observations for the client that become evidence of them being broken and hopeless. It isn't hard to do actually.

Unfortunately, you know a parent or two that have done that by mistake to their children without even trying. Dad and Mam! Certainly, a psychologist can do it on purpose or by mistake. But a psychologist won't because they work ethically, aim to help, and are very competent, aren't they?

But what about a bad psychologist, someone who does not know their way around the mind, the brain, the soul? What if they are 'parapsychologists' without correct education, training, and practice? The theory of psychological therapy would predict a worsening of mental health. And if there was a worsening of mental health, we would, if we look, find observations to confirm the theory of bad psych existing.

What are our observations of bad psych? Because we, as a society, worry about the misery of mental illness, we do a lot of counting of it. We have counted millions of people sick with symptoms that can be, and often start as, relatively mild. We also count disorders that have deteriorated so much that many thousands of people are experiencing severe symptoms so awful that they are trying to kill themselves.

We can also compare counts of mental illness with other blights on our humanity. For example, in January 2021, we are in the middle of a year-long COVID-19 pandemic because of a virus that, as of 1 January, killed about 1,000 people. That number is awful—1,000 lost people, likely mostly dads and mums just like my own. But that is a very small count relative to the harm of mental illness over the same period, isn't it? You know the numbers, right?

The uncomfortable truth is that the biggest pandemic we are dealing with is worsening mental disorder and that our cures do not work as they predict. Worse, all our counts, our observations, show that our psychological treatments don't work very well at all. The fact is that the more treating we do, the worse mental health gets. That really is an odd fact, isn't it? It just doesn't make sense in theory. More therapy and more services should equal to fewer ongoing mental health problems and disorders. Don't you agree?

This is tricky territory. I'm trying to open eyes that might not like to look. Still, let's think carefully about how we know things are working. We mostly look at what we are trying to mitigate, such as death and disease, and look to see if it is getting better when we implement a solution. For example, if seatbelts in cars saved lives, we would expect to see lives lost in crashes reduce as compliance with safety belts increases. This can be represented in two graphs of observations.

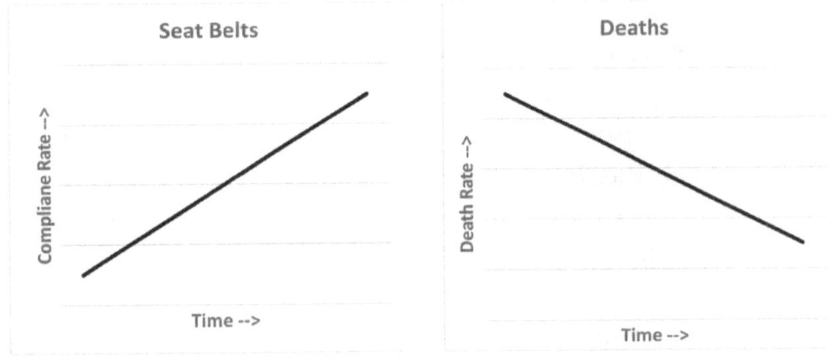

It turns out that observations carefully counted by Abbas and Zidan in 2011 support these two graphs. Further, they were able to say that with less than a 1/1000th chance of being wrong, the relationship was strong, and seatbelt compliance accounted for 70 per cent of the improvement in the death rate—that is, as one went up, the other went down.

Wow, now that is good!

We can be quite certain—we can 'know'—that all our efforts with safety belts are substantially helping to reduce the road toll. Hidden in this good news is that seatbelts do hurt some people, and some people would have been alive today if they had not worn their seatbelts. But overall and clearly, society's investment in seat belts has worked. Of course, there are other factors at play such as less drunk driving and better brakes on cars, airbags, and such; but seatbelts are working for sure.

Do you put your seatbelt on? Do you tell your kids to put them on? Sure, you do, and you're right to do so. Our theory and observations about seatbelts saving lives match really well.

Let's look at another example, a health-related one. It is tricky to suggest that the next person's lung cancer will be caused by smoking. We have all heard of the man that lived a good life into their nineties and smoked like a chimney. However, reviews of large collections of cases matched the theory of how cancer might be caused by smoking. It eventually became accepted that smoking causes lung cancer and triggers many other cancers.

Society appreciates the awful distress lung cancer causes people. Individuals are placed into misery, likely incapacitated, and many die from the illness. Also, the family is distraught and loses that person who was part of their life. It is a disaster and a tragedy that can be avoided. So a lot of society's resources have gone into reducing smoking—lots and lots. After all, it is a big deal.

We have put big efforts in, and we have paid for it. What do we expect? Well, the following two graphs using measurements published in the American Cancer Society's journal in 2020 give us an answer.

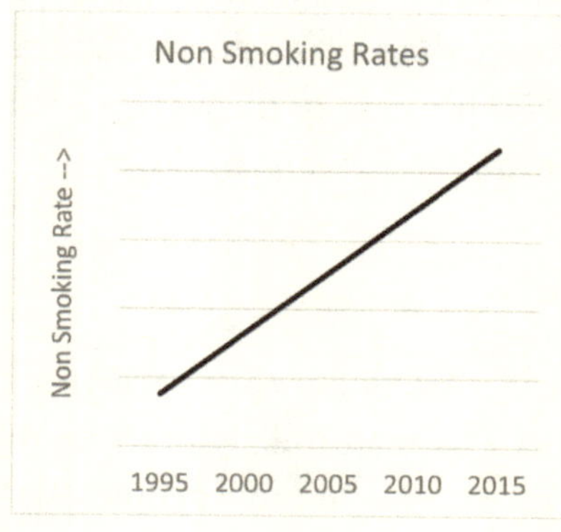

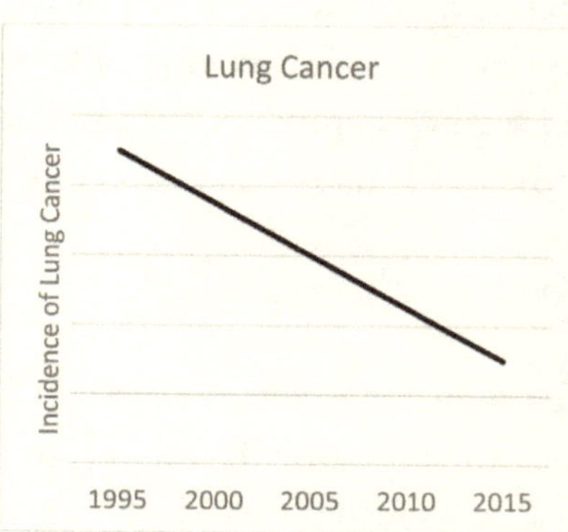

And not luckily, but reasonably, we see that as nonsmoking rates increase, the incidence of lung cancer decreases. These observations match the theory. Now, this is not 'proof' that the public effort to increase the levels of nonsmoking is fully responsible for less lung cancer. There could be something else happening that is unexplained.

Perhaps there is increased popularity of jogging amongst smokers and that jogging protects them from lung cancer. Possible? Well, cigarette companies would be happier suggesting that, but what about you? My idea is that being a thinking person, you know that the solution has worked well. The theory is intact—that is, fewer people smoking equals fewer people getting sick with lung cancer. I too know that the graphs based on real outcomes match the theory and are the right way around. One goes upwards, the other goes down. *Phew!*

Do you suggest to your children that they take the chance and smoke anyway, provided they jog each day? No, you don't! You know nonsmoking is better for their long-term health. And you are happy your knowing is borne out by the scientific method.

Now concentrate hard. Can you think of anything that society does where we have a good theory, but the more we do to help, the worse the outcomes are? And all other things being equal, the graphs are reversed? For example, the more children use toothpaste, the more they get ruined teeth. Nope. Why is that? My idea is that it would be completely unacceptable, unthinkable. Firstly, it is the opposite of the theory. Secondly, society would get it fixed!

Suspend disbelief and pretend the facts on toothpaste bore it out. As kids used more toothpaste, the worse their cavities got. Now, what if the makers of toothpaste said it wasn't their toothpaste that was causing worsening cavities. It was the soft drinks children are drinking. The toothpaste providers are saying that they are part of the solution, not the cause. I guess, simply put, maybe the toothpaste providers were just responding to the increased demand. More cavities sell more toothpaste.

That sounds feasible, and we know that more children are drinking more soft drinks this year compared to last year, don't we?

What if I told you that the natural demand for toothpaste did actually increase simply because there are more children? More teeth to clean. Also, parents are helping their children be more compliant with brushing their teeth. Then, to meet the increase in demand, toothpaste providers started to do their part by making more but cheaper and quicker toothpaste.

But they made more by making their machines more efficient and with fewer chemists running the show. Yes, they promoted lesser-trained people to do the work experts in toothpaste had previously been doing. Unfortunately, new ingredients, unknown to the owners, included hidden sugar. Now, children brushed even more thoroughly; but the more toothpaste they were given, the more ruined teeth they got. An upwards spiral in cavities and toothpaste sales.

What would those graphs look like? They would be like this I think:

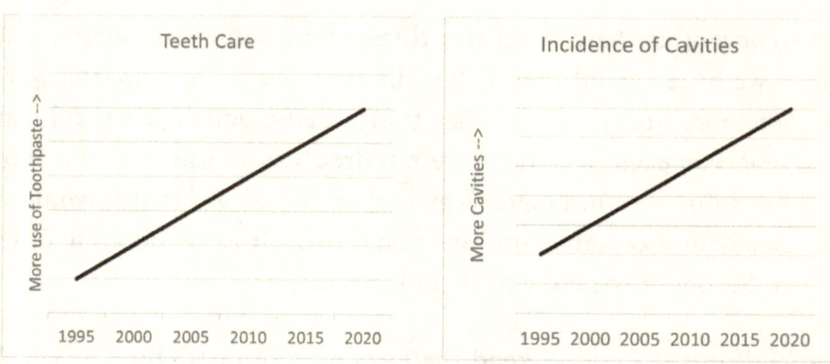

Now, these two graphs are fanciful. Only the conspiracists would expect them, maybe suggesting some sinister neoliberal agenda for big business. Perhaps a confederation of white-coat dentists? But what if I told you the graphs for mental disorders were exactly like this? The more interventions and solutions to mental distress we provide, the more mental distress there is. Yes, really. As far as I know, this is the only example in our society where this is the case, and we keep on making more.

People and institutions can argue the point, but just like the hidden sugar in the fanciful example of bad toothpaste, there must be hidden kryptonite in the help and therapy for mental difficulties. That hidden kryptonite is what I call bad psych.

True or False?

What goes up keeps going up.

I want to say no thank you, do you?

Can you see that the graphs below are the wrong way around?

The first one is the increase in the Australian workforce working in mental health—that is, more of me or people who think they can be me. The second one is the increase in the incidence of mental disorders.

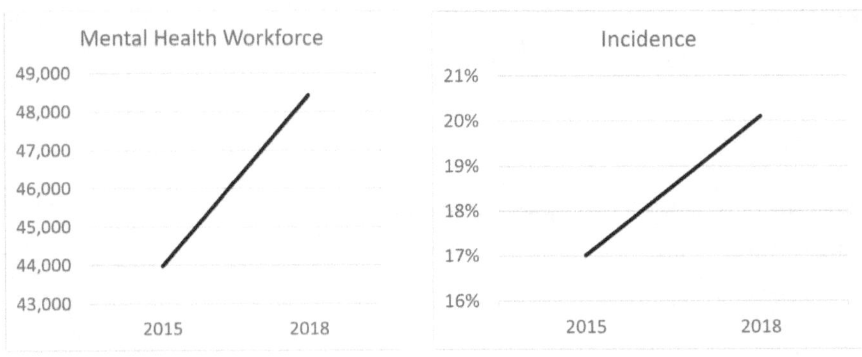

(Australian Institute of Health and Welfare, ABS, 2020)

Actually, it turns out that any graph you make about our solutions to mental health difficulties is this way.

The WRONG WAY AROUND!

The observations don't match the theory that mental health solutions fix mental health problems. In fact, it is worse than that because the more we provide, the worse it gets.

All these are true:

More antidepressants	still,	more depression.
More therapies	still,	more mental disorders.
More phone help	still,	more suicides.
More mindfulness programmes	still,	more anxiety.
More mental health workers	still,	more severe cases.
More self-help books	still,	more worries.
More youth services	still,	more youth with mental distress.

To my mind and yours and everyone's reasonable mind, we would have expected the graphs to be very different. We would think that as our clever solutions and preventative solutions to mental health problems were deployed and increased, we would see a reduction—no, a dramatic reduction—in mental health problems.

Apparently not.

And in fact, as society deploys more and more and more solutions, the worse and worse and worse it gets. You and I have the observations predicted by bad psych.

Wow!

Some of you reading might suggest that it is the other way around just as in the fanciful toothpaste scenario—that is, as mental disorders increase, the more they demand solutions and services. So our efforts and solutions are demand driven, kind of like an economy. That presupposes some other factor is at play. Perhaps increasing standards of living are causing mental disorders? Perhaps iPhones are doing it? Perhaps it's the new generation of children who are naturally disordered? The trouble with these ideas is that they don't stack up.

For a long time, standards of living have increased, iPhones have been around since 2007, and every generation thinks the next one is broken. Nothing has really changed. Despite all the hype and self-admiration of what we call progress, we still use the same car engine designed 167 years ago. And I, along with some clever folk, implemented internet connections to the world in 1990. Yes, 30 years ago! Sorry, millennials. Whatever! And all these are 'slow burners'—that, is slow and gradual in effect. The recent increase in the incidence of mental difficulties and the worsening of them is skyrocket material!

What has changed rapidly, though, is our focus on, and resourcing of, mental health. And we have equally rapidly geared up a whole new industry. Think. What happens when you do something quickly with poor standards and without evidence to show it is working? Answer. It goes badly wrong!

I suggest to you that, just like our explosion of convenient take-away food made some 'bad food', our mental health industry is making some bad psych.

The above counts, in the scorecard and graphs, don't include other huge privately and publicly sourced services. So both scorecard and graphs underestimate the true awfulness of sick people and the efforts and resources going into the mental health industry. In 2021, its likely resourcing is at least double the 2018 numbers and accelerating exponentially. Just like the COVID-19 virus of 2020 could do if we let it loose. This is because governments are rapidly and unthinkingly deploying much more and then even more.

There is also the explosion of health and non-health workers moving into the rapidly expanding and lucrative psychology industry.

Employer programmes, insurance programmes, NDIA programmes, primary health network programmes, public hospitals, private hospitals, Headspace, eating programmes, Jigsaw, child mental health programmes, phone help and telehealth programmes, and children monitoring programmes are all expanding businesses.

I say businesses because the money incentive is there. Budgets are improved, organisations grown, salaries bigger, and more people employed. All are supposed to be supplying good psych. Do you believe that it could really work well like that in a poorly regulated industry where money rushes to change hands at $200 per hour? It reminds me of roulette in a downtown casino.

Today, a social worker, trained in social work, can help people reintegrate into their community for $40/hour. Or they can do psychological therapy that they are undertrained in via the primary health network for $80/hour. A competent occupational therapist can be employed at $60/hour, helping children overcome their disability and do better at school, or they can optimistically provide psychological strategies for children with severe mental disorders via the NDIA for $150/hour. If you are motivated by income, which would you do?

Psychologists, on the other hand, meet the highest of educational, practice, and ethical standards set by the Australian Psychology Board so they can be good psychologists. Relative to those good standards, the new business models hire lesser-trained and poorly equipped people to provide cookie-cutter psychological interventions and therapies. All the while, evidence shows that at a societal level, things are getting much worse, not much better. I personally know social workers, OTs, and nurses who do some good psych. But that is not the point. Most simply are not good psychologists providing good psychology. Our sickest people can become locked into Box D, the hurt locker. Add the stupid and complex labyrinth of pathways and solutions, and we have kryptonite in the system.

You know this to be true as does the Royal Commission into Mental Health, which has endured the outpouring of bad stories, bad outcomes—all bad observations predicted by bad psych.

You and your children can wait for society to change direction and ensure that anybody playing with your mind, the most complex and vulnerable thing you have, is very good at it. But you will be waiting a long time. People will have to 'unknow' what they know is working. They will have to backtrack, like climbers 200 metres from the top of Mount Everest. They will have to admit mistakes, backtrack, say sorry, and make good. But these are all but impossible psychological constructs to overcome. So instead, I urge you to navigate past the kryptonite and avoid bad psych.

Keep reading.

Aside from the societal evidence—which is confronting, to say the least—I have case studies. I have thousands of hours of therapy notes, I have first-hand assessed, formulated, diagnosed, and provided therapy with thousands of ordinary people with mental dilemmas and disorders.

Normally, single case studies, just like one sunny day, are considered within the scientific community as 'weak' evidence. After all, how can a single case reflect what is happening in the general community? How can that case be done over again to determine if the outcomes are predictable? Well, they cannot. That would be like seeing one jet-black wild rabbit and saying lots of wild rabbits are jet-black. We would correctly assume it was an anomaly, perhaps even a baby rock-wallaby!

But what if we saw jet-black rabbits, up close, most weeks, over seven years, and in different places? What if we could point to them and show others the jet-black rabbits? Then each example, or case study, becomes part of a larger sample that makes us pretty sure that there are lots of jet-black rabbits. The collection of examples has become very good evidence, as are my cases, taken together as a collection.

Over my time, I have collected large samples of good psych, bad psych, and 'indifferent psych'. Within our public system, I have worked in community heath, mental health emergency, and a public programme for folk suffering from personality disorder. I founded and made a successful business in private practice. There I worked as a private psychologist, in my rooms providing therapy for the broad spectrum of psychological disorders and difficulties across the lifespan. Every one of my cases is a real-life study with its specific validity, often better than a strictly controlled study, which irons out the intricate wrinkles of human beings.

My cases contribute to the overwhelming evidence that bad psych exists and is highly prevalent. When I work through good psych, bad psych with you, I will provide cases from my practice. Each, although thoroughly disguised to maintain people's privacy, will be interesting but awful reading for you. They will bring tears to your eyes and anger to your belly. They should also make you nervous, 'for the sake of God go I'. Anyway, you will be persuaded by this good evidence that there is bad psych. Science would say that to prove something exists, I only have to show one example. I will be giving a lot more.

Clearly, we continue to make things worse, not better. Advocates for the system, business entrepreneurs, and politicians claim that as more people get sicker, they provide more services. But what is more likely is that as more services and solutions are provided, more bad psych is provided and more people get sicker.

Can that be true?

Can it be that straightforward?

Part I will take you through our myths that support and make bad psych both real and normal. It is not fun reading; but each myth, when debunked, will help you know what to seek out and what to avoid.

The Dangerous Myths
of Psychology

True or False?

Australia is an egalitarian country where all people are equal based upon mateship and freedoms.

I want to say yes, do you?

DICTIONARIES TELL US that a myth is a story, likely without a determinable basis in fact. It is a false collective belief often used to justify a social institution. As a psychologist, I appreciate how they arise, are adopted, and kept true in our minds. I understand that myths are practically unbreakable, that people can't change their minds because they know they know. Like my dad, they would rather know and be quietly wrong than un-know.

You see, knowing things is a clever trick that our minds do to make our lives easier. Imagine the mental effort required to decide everything over and over. Knowing is much easier and efficient. But that knowing makes myths dangerous. What if you really don't know something, even though you know you know? Ouch! That does my head in. Brain freeze! My frontal lobe must be lighting up!

In any case, I'm going to show you that what you mostly know about psychological therapy is, in fact, a series of well-promoted myths. More like excuses for institutions and proud and deceitful people to keep doing what does not work. Those things you are so sure about are really fake news, slogans, and fancy posters. They are impressive statistics that don't prove any point at all but reassure you and spin you in. Unfortunately, it is all but impossible for me to convince you. It will be a waste of my time and your reading of this book. After all, you are grown up, smart, and clear thinking.

But what about this example?

Do you like to gamble?

Imagine, it is your turn to be mentally unwell, the unlucky person to be in a situation where you need good psychology with a good psychologist—good psych if you like.

Now, imagine three doors are leading to psychological therapy. One will take you to good psych. The other two doors take you to bad psych. All you have to do is choose the right door from three choices. That one best correct choice can take you to a good psychologist who does good psychology. Your odds are 1:3, okay?

Anyway, you make your choice! You select Door 2. But before you get to see what is behind Door 2, and to make it even *better* for you, a mental health worker opens Door 3 to check in there. And sure enough, that bad psych lurks dangerously behind Door 3. *Phew* and wow, lucky for you.

So you've chosen Door 2; and because you now know bad psych lurks behind Door 3, you're in with a much better chance. Family cheers you on; and more helpfully, that mental health worker gives you an opportunity to change your mind. You can stay with Door 2, or you can change to Door 1. Your family holds their breath. What will you do? Keep your original choice or change?

JOSHUA THOMAS

You need to
choose a door.

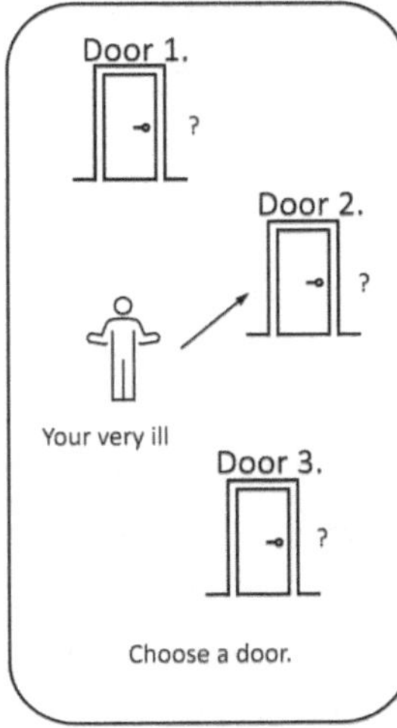

You choose
Door 2 and cross
your fingers.

Door 3 is opened.
Bad psych
is there.

Think about this situation. Think about what you know to be true. Would you really change your choice to Door 1 at this stage? We know that, at the start, the odds were against you. Only one out of three doors leads to good psych, which reflects reality. But now there are only two doors left, and you've already picked one of them. Two doors and your first choice made. Looks like fifty-fifty to me, so maybe keep your choice? Maybe change to Door 1 for superstitious reasons? Knowing this, I certainly wouldn't change my choice. What would be the point? I don't do superstition.

Now I'm going to tell you something you know is not true. You must change your choice of doors to Door 1. If you stick with Door 2, your odds are still 1 in 3. The odds for door 1 are 2 in 3, twice as good. Yes, changing doors will double your chance!

Reading that bit over and over? It's tricky finding out that you don't know what you know, isn't it? I'm forcing you to use your brain and not rely on what you know!

Christmas is a wonderful time. I just love the joy and kindness and how families come together to celebrate and bond. To help keep some spirituality in Christmas, you tell your children that baby Jesus was born on Christmas Day. You bring them up with the simple message that Christmas is about giving and being with the ones you love. The week before Christmas, have you ever found yourself wondering what planet you are on?

Despite all the contradictions and knowing your indoctrination, you continue to work the myth. Christmas is one of the most complicated, greed-ridden, and difficult times for your and your child's minds. 'What do you want?' is the most-used phrase. Who to please, where to go, who to see, which half of the divorced family to miss out on. Should you get your Christmas, the one 'you want', or do you get someone else's Christmas?

Yep, you know what I mean, don't you?

In one psychology practice, I saw a very large photo of Richard Branson sitting in a chair overlooking the deep blue ocean, being at peace with the world, looking mindful. Some caption said that being mindful is the key to a good mind and a good life. Yeah, sure it is—not! For most anxious folk, this is a myth—at best, an optimistic idea. Richard is not a worried working mother, stretching the last dollar, dealing with a big mortgage, wishing she had more time with her daughter who is externalising her insecurities because she is being dropped off for the third time this week. Yet you continue to like knowing that being mindful, even for a few minutes a day, actually improves your life.

JOSHUA THOMAS

Meanwhile, the truth really is that that form of mindfulness simply gives you the old-fashioned peace and quiet that Mum and Dad and Grandad and Grandma used to insist on perhaps so they can rest or concentrate on what they were doing. Did you know there is now a big industry geared to teach you how to have peace of mind? Crock of shit, isn't it?

In another consulting room, there is a fantastic photograph of an iceberg. It shows the peak and the deep depths of the underneath, indicating that there is more under the surface than meets the eye. Wha-hoooooo, kind of mysterious and spooky like. It is a stunning photograph and kind of true, I think. But the photo is a lie because it has been photoshopped to death. That iceberg simply does not exist in the real world. It is a myth created and framed to support what happens next in psychology. Crock of shit, isn't it?

Look, I'm not against myths. I'm Jungian in both nature and practice, and I see myths as a true mirror of ourselves. After all, we made them! But our new myths, the ones manufactured by institutions, aren't there to help. They are there to justify their existence, their agenda, their industry. And these myths all have something in common, don't they? Well, two things actually. Firstly, they are supporting some institution or social need. Secondly, they are a fib. But scientific research, with carefully controlled studies, will show you that the myths are true for you.

Crock of shit, isn't it?

All the new myths are dangerous because they promote bad psych.

Let me take you through the ten dangerous myths of psychological therapy. Just like patronising photos and captions, icebergs in front of the *Titanic*, and next Christmas, they are always around the corner.

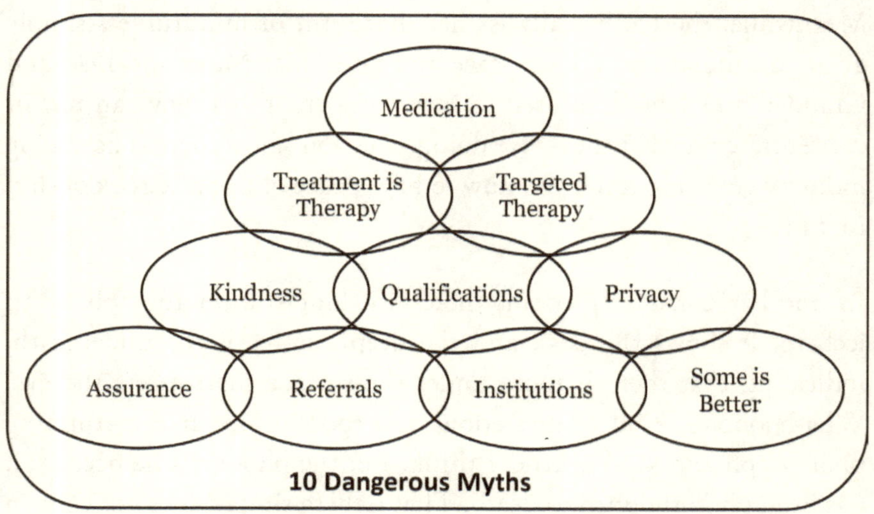

We will look at them one by one and debunk what you are sure you know.

THE ASSURANCE MYTH

DID YOU KNOW that psychological therapy is a regulated health service? This gives all Australians assurance that they are getting good psych. The main purpose of the Australian Health Practitioner Regulation Agency (AHPRA) is to 'ensure that only health practitioners with the skills and qualifications to provide competent and ethical care are registered to practise'.

You can be assured by AHPRA's claim that 'public safety is always our number one priority'. The AHPRA is the Australian government's key instrument in setting national standards for people who want to call themselves psychologists. AHPRA, through the Psychology Board and National Standards, defines essential competencies, sets minimum qualifications, and maintains a register of those people who meet those standards to provide psychological therapy. In my humble opinion, these standards are exceptionally well done. They really are world-class. By the way, my name is on that register. I'm very proud to meet their high standards. As AHPRA should, they take public safety seriously. The last thing they want is for you, or your child, being hurt by poor practice.

This means that it does not really matter who you get to help you heal your mental disorders and wounds and develop new mental capacities and grow as a person. You can be assured that *they* are all going to be 'good'.

<u>**Case of Judi**</u>

Judi and her mother came to see me during school hours one day. Judi was 11 years old, ordinary height and weight, dressed casually and sitting quietly, seemingly content. Her mum, on the other hand, was distraught, talking quickly, desperate for help.

Judi had not been to school for three weeks because she was too scared to go. For two of those weeks, each morning, the parental battle was on trying to get Judi to school but with Judi resisting with all the will a frightened 11-year-old can muster. I'd rather try driving a mad bull to market with my bare hands. Mum explained that Judi might get in the car; but by the time they got to drop off, Judi was crying, shaking, and yelling, begging, pleading to go home. She said that when they did go home, Judi became calm but felt 'bad' about not being at school.

Mum explained that she had rung for help from the public Child & Adolescent Mental Health Service, but they considered Judi's difficulties not severe enough. Mum had sensibly agreed to stop the daily battle and get different help.

In my rooms—now on her own with me, quietly playing with magnets—Judi said that she felt stupid, said that she was broken and no good and that she had been thinking about death—a lot.

Four weeks prior, Judi had been a happy girl, wanting to go to school, liking her teacher and classes. Judi told me that about that time, she had forgotten to do homework one weekend and realised the night before. She said she worried about that a lot because everyone else did their homework, and she would be embarrassed when the teacher asked for it. She felt sick in her belly that Monday morning, so Mum let her have the day off.

On Tuesday, Judi went to school but was not herself, being quiet and reserved, not joining in. Her teacher sent her to see the school nurse. The nurse rang her mum, explaining that Judi was feeling sick likely because she had anxiety in the classroom. The nurse told Mum that she had helped with some counselling, but they decided Judi should be picked up and go home for the rest of the day.

Judi said that she was scared to go to school the next day because everybody knew. But on Wednesday, she did go, with Mum holding her hand, helping. They saw the nurse together, and Mum described Judi's symptoms as feeling sick and scared. The nurse advised Mum that Judi was suffering from anxiety and would do well with some antianxiety medication and some counselling, so she can get through the school day.

This nurse is a nurse practitioner and is authorised to prescribe medications. And she did. She prescribed a common selective serotonin reuptake inhibitor (SSRI) and a drug called quetiapine, sold as Seroquel. Judi had another counselling session with the nurse whilst Mum went to the chemist. About lunchtime, Judi took her first-ever psychotropic drugs, an antidepressant, and an antipsychotic.

By midafternoon that Wednesday, Judi was home again, feeling sick. The nurse told Mum that the medications took some time to work and to see what happens over the next week. Judi stayed home, sick, until the following Monday. But on that Monday, Mum and Judi started the drama and trauma of full-scale school refusal. Each day, Judi became more scared, agitated, and determined not to go to school. At home, she was calm, quiet, but experiencing deep shame and worthlessness and had been thinking about death.

Happy on Friday, broken in seven days. What the crap happened?

Bad psych happened.

The good psychologist thinks differently, contextually, and wisely; finds the gaps; and finds the part of the person that is asking for help. They do this with what was once known as expertise, something you earn over many sets of integrated learning experiences and with practice.

Well, before it went wrong, Judi was happy, perhaps a little too proud of being a good student, wanting to please the teacher and her parents. But that is not abnormal. Neither is being embarrassed when you make a mistake, which is what Judi did in forgetting the weekend's homework. For whatever reason, Judi's second mistake was not telling her mum or dad that she had forgotten the homework, trusting the adults if you like.

                    JOSHUA THOMAS

Without the adult help in processing the emotional content of making this small mistake, Judi is now heading into guilt, shame, and fear out of proportion to that mistake. Still, not a mental disorder. Just a mistake.

There are another fourteen kids in that class. All have done their homework. Self-disclosure is a mammoth task in that group, especially to a teacher Judi likes and wants to please. How could she go to school and face that emotional content on her own? She can't. She is a lovely 11-year-old, and most adults can't do what she needs to do. Judi likely did feel sick that first Monday morning, just the same as you do when you try to own up to your mistakes. It gets you in the guts. Mum did the best thing: let her have a quiet day but unaware of the emotional content that Judi was handling and that she needed her help.

On Tuesday, Judi's teacher knew something was wrong. As a good adult, she sought help—the best help—from someone assured to be the right help: the nurse associated with the school, trained in both physical and mental health. Only she wasn't. It took me the normal eight years of university study and practice to work well with presentations of children. The nurse had at best a university degree where they mentioned psychology as an add-on or area of interest. She also had received a week's ad hoc instruction on cognitive behaviour therapy, something that is often taught quickly as a simple structured treatment. But as part of therapy, CBT can be a sophisticated, complex process of insight building, modelling, mentalisation, and diffusion of mental dilemma.

The nurse in front of Judi was not a good psychologist, and she could not do good psychology. She was incapable of formulation, assessment, and treatment for mental dilemma even this most ordinary one that Judi was experiencing.

But unfortunately, frightened Judi doesn't know that. Neither did frightened mum for the first three weeks, which is all it took for Judi to be driven into a clinical mental disorder with severe symptoms. Judi thinks she is broken. After all, she can think for herself. She is going crazy, full of shame. Counselling doesn't work, medicines don't work, and she knows that she is broken. What can be done?

People will have lots of ideas on what could be done. We can't undo what has happened to Judi, but we can help her do what is needed, whilst we adults take her fears and shame upon ourselves.

It took a bit of arranging and doing, but we planned to tell Judi that the nurse had made a mistake, which had made her get worse (which was true), and to arrange a meeting with her good teacher so she could say sorry for forgetting the homework and receive the obvious love and forgiveness. We also planned to go back to school on a day when Judi's favourite subjects were on. All three of us—Judi, Mum (sometimes Dad), and I—practised good parenting and child skills with role-playing. We played cards, board and games, made promises, and practised making mistakes and saying sorry and thank you.

We also got Mum and Dad to be more in charge of what was going to happen, and all of us got to know one another better, liked one another, and said why. Woven through all that was some cognitive behaviour therapy but not the stuff you learn in a week's course. Woven in the therapy was re-parenting, play therapy, emotional processing therapy, exposure therapy, and psychoeducation for Mum and Dad, so they can be even better at their most important job.

It took four sessions over ten days, and then Mum rang and told me that Judi was back to herself again. We checked in again after another few weeks. All was good, and Judi's difficulties had become hard for her to remember.

Consider this.

Your government is increasing the capacity of nurse practitioners not competent in psychological assessment, formulation, and therapy to prescribe psychotropic drugs to anyone and remove checks and balances.

                    JOSHUA THOMAS

Nursing advocates are pursuing access to Medicare rebates reserved for psychological therapy provided by psychologists. Why? Because they can get paid triple the rate of nursing. It should not matter what nursing advocates say or the career paths they want. My opinion is—and I suggest yours should be—that they are not good psychologists until they meet the psychology board's criteria for a good psychologist.

Question: why are people, not approved by our psychology board providing psychotropic drugs and therapy to our most vulnerable citizens?

Answer: Because there is zero regulation on who can.

There is no assurance.

True or False?

Children are regularly harmed by practitioners of psychological therapy and their interventions.

I want to say no, do you?

Adults often think this is about themselves, but it is very often about our children. The aetiology of mental difficulties and disorders almost always includes a person getting off track in their early years. Lots of things happen for children in an ordinary, good-enough upbringing. Mostly good actually. They adopt good models of the world from their good parents, and they have freedoms to be child-like and unconcerned. They get to practise relationship building and keeping, under the guidance of good adults, and set about becoming a character, a person, a recognisable individual. I guess we think of it as a good start.

<u>**Case of Loki**</u>

Loki, an 11-year-old boy, was referred to me by his doctor in 2016. He had been in counselling all of 2015, but that service could no longer see him. The doctor said that Loki had been diagnosed with attention-deficit hyperactive disorder and ODD. ODD is the diagnosable disorder for disordered behaviour problems. ODD equals oppositional defiance disorder. Kind of means what it says. Boys suffering from ADHD can often develop ODD. After all, they are already in trouble!

Loki's mum was in the room with us the first time we met, and she gave a history of Loki's problems. His estranged father was a perpetrator of domestic violence; and Loki had frequently seen his father argue, threaten, and hit his mother. His mum had her difficulties, and her parenting was at best disorganised. She told me that she wanted Loki to stop lying, stop swearing, stop arguing, and

JOSHUA THOMAS

stop hitting his older sister. She told me that she and the previous counsellors had tried everything, but Loki can't learn because of his ADHD. She said that he was so awful to teachers and children that the school had suspended him for two weeks.

When Loki's mum left the room, Loki and I played Lego with some superhero toys that he brought with him.

My notes describe Loki as a polite, likeable boy. Talking nonstop and distracted in his games. Able to pause only if I helped him. Will not play with me. He makes his games and keeps them to himself. Limited eye contact with me. Said he agreed with everything his mum said and then said that 'I'm bad and can't be fixed.'

We spent the next 15 minutes playing his game. I told him what I had seen and heard today and asked him if he wanted to come back. I told him we can work together on telling more truth and swearing less. I did some contracting with him around his privacy, so he knew I would only break his trust in me if I figured he was going to hurt someone or himself. Loki walked out, turned around, and said, 'I'll show you my Yu-Gi-Oh! cards.'

The next week, Loki and I had the full hour to ourselves.

Loki brought his cards and started to teach me what they were and how to play. It is a complex game requiring both good verbal and abstract reasoning. Obviously, Loki was not dumb. We practised cheating, lying, and swearing and tried to figure out different ways to mean the same thing. Loki liked that. I asked him an example of his swearing at home, and he told me this story:

'If I'm good, my mum buys me a superhero or something. I got all my cards for being good. If I'm bad, I'm not allowed to play with them. I was bad last week, so Mum took my cards off me and let my sister play with them. My sister [13 years old] gets all the attention. She gets to cook with mum. I'm not allowed to even play with Yu-Gi-Oh! because I swore at her when she bit me. And after I swore, I bit her back and made her bleed. Then Mum bit me back to teach me not to do it.'

I checked Loki's arm, and he had his mum's bite marks deep into his skin. I asked Loki what he thought of being bitten by his mum as a punishment. He said quite eloquently, 'An eye for an eye, I hurt my sister, so Mum hurts me.' I spent some time gently evaluating his welfare. Loki, in his living memory, had never had a bed made for him, never had a hot-water bottle, never had a packed lunch ready for school from his mum. You know, the stuff that demonstrates love. I made sure DHS knew of this situation. They did and were assessing Loki's welfare.

After a lengthy assessment phase, I provided Loki a diagnosis that was a better explanation for his difficulties: reactive attachment disorder and major depressive episode (recurring). Essentially, Loki's concepts and ways of relating to the world were badly disorganised. He was living a lonely, sad, angry life. He wants the love of his mum but knows love is unreliable, unfair, and hurtful. He knows that people don't really care—they just say they care. Loki is not trusting anyone, certainly not adults. Over the next two years, I often felt he was waiting for me to drop him too.

By May of 2018, Loki was becoming a different boy. Of course, he had his moments, but boys are not made in a day. At our last session, we played three games of chess. I won two of them and lost one on purpose, and he still enjoyed it. In the ongoing plan for Loki, I noted what had been most beneficial for him. Aside from stable, reparenting therapy with a man, we had built bonding moments with his mum and helped his mum become more reliable in her simple welfare and love for her son. We had moved Loki to another school, where his

JOSHUA THOMAS

reputation did not label him as a bad boy. And we had found other Yu-Gi-Oh! players and gamers that he had made friendships with.

Things could still go wrong for Loki. I remember him threatening to kill a friend because he had broken a game Loki had lent him. Whether or not he meant it, Loki ended up in emergency that day, and it took some time to recover. Slowly, slowly, though. Anyway, with his mum's mental problems in the spotlight, Loki came under stricter care of a DHS 'multidisciplinary care team'. I was asked to provide background and recommendations to that team in the best interest of Loki. At that time, I had not seen Loki for some weeks. You see, therapy lapsed because the NDIA stopped funding for Loki to access psychological therapy. They were, of course, happy to fund him patting horses each week! Crazy, isn't it?

Six months later, I was invited to a meeting of the care team. That week, Loki had run out of his class swearing and screaming that he needed to die. The teacher, in close pursuit, could not stop Loki from running onto the road towards an incoming school bus.

Loki did not die that day, but he could have.

The incident review, such as it was, found that Loki had reacted badly to a 'behavioural intervention' in his class. It consisted of a reward programme for Loki. He was provided with a tangible reward each three days he demonstrated cooperation with the teacher and his class. It was going to be each week, but Loki was a good negotiator. This intervention was recommended and designed by his occupational therapist, which is a normal practice.

Apparently, Loki had regressed quickly under the scheme, which had run for about four weeks.

Going better for a year, regressed within two months.

Can you already see the kryptonite for Loki, the smell of bad psych?

The occupational therapist, exceptionally well-funded by the NDIA, adopted the very approach that demonstrates lack of competence, not that she knew it. Rewarding good behaviour with rewards must have been déjà vu for Loki. He absolutely knows rewards and gifts are instead of real attention and care. Likely, he was waiting for this to happen, and it proved again that love is fake and unreliable. Loki had rigged the scheme too. He knows he can cooperate, so it is a gift to him to play the game. Loki is bright and competitive. He won that arrangement, getting all the rewards he wanted. When the teacher did not pay attention to the rules, Loki let him have it, proving that his life mattered.

I got to see Loki again a few times, but a lot had been undone. I could no longer promise him that he will get ordinary love and care that boys get. If I did, he would know I was lying, just bigger proof his disorganised system needed. So I left him with the relationship we had—a good one based upon trust, care, and attention. I hope that he survived school and, of course, the care team and his mum. My fingers are crossed that someone else finds him and loves and cares for him.

You see, despite the assuring words from our highest governing and regulating bodies, anyone can practice psychological therapy—no licence, no credentials or qualifications necessary. Yes, that is right. You can go out now and start doing therapy, dealing in people's broken minds for money. And nothing will prevent you, except perhaps your conscience. Imagine you having your relatively simple home electrical systems 'rewired' by anyone. No licence required, no study required, no apprenticeship required. Your house would burn to the ground. Just as it did for Judi and Loki. It really makes me crazy that this lack of regulated competence in psychological therapy is quite fine, actually promoted, despite the damage it does to lives. And it is even worse.

It is hard to comprehend; but even if you do get a registered psychologist, they may never have studied any psychological therapy beyond first-year university. They may never have proven competent in the assessment and diagnosis of mental disorders. They may not understand one single psychological theory. They may, however, have attended a four-day course and now be practising advanced therapy on the most disturbed, distressed people we know. Odd, isn't it?

Odd but common. My work has shown me that our health regulations and world-class standards for competent psychological therapy are mostly not applied as society believes. It is simply a myth. Public and private providers perform the old side-step dance to make their services untouchable by the Psychology Board of Australia. Simply call yourselves *mental health workers*, *clinicians*, *counsellors*, *therapists*, *entrepreneurs*, or anything really; and you are magically transformed into being competent to work on the most important and complex organ in the body. This is exactly like giving a cook a new knife and saying 'Surgeons are good with knives and so are you' and then waving a magic wand and setting them off to work fixing bowel cancers.

The person you want in front of you, to be assured they are competent in psychological therapy, should have six years of focused study, master's qualifications, clinical or counselling endorsement from the psychology board, and five years' practice expertise. They should be able to call themselves a psychologist. If they can't, run away.

I have been readily criticised for my firmness on this, my stubbornness not to endorse non-psychologists as competent in psychological therapy. My opinion is that endorsements and approvals is the Australian Psychology Board's job, not mine. Some colleagues of mine tell me that they have non-psychologists working for or with them that are better than many psychologists. Look, I get their point. But doesn't that just prove the state of affairs is awful? If we have people able to call themselves psychologists, and they are bad at it, it makes sense that we have parapsychologists who could be better. But that is like an apple with three worms in it being better than an apple with five worms. One is better, but they are both rotten apples.

How bad is the lack of assurance in the psychology industry? How low do you think we can go? I bet you can't guess or even imagine how poor it is.

In May 2020, on a popular Facebook group, a person posted about their certification in a therapy called EMDR (eye movement desensitisation and re-processing therapy). He said he completed the course so he can help people with trauma, depression, and anxiety, which he wrongly called borderline personality disorder. It was a two-day course; and apparently, he knows all the steps needed and has an eighty-page manual, a clinician guide, and client handouts. What a crock of shit!

It is both mine and your opinion that this man has not earned any certificate. He has bought one—one that may have been better cut out of the back of his box of cornflakes. This is a business model, driven by what you can earn, not a health model driven by who you are competent to help. There is so much money to be made, or saved, often on the growing public purse; but private businesses too are conning you, lying to you.

Training businesses are popping up to cash in too. Right now, you can become a certificated cognitive behaviour therapist for $33. Yep, you watch videos and read some articles and then get your certificate. Apparently, it only takes 60 hours to get competent at CBT, no prior knowledge required. Your lecturer in this endeavour won't be an accredited teacher, university lecturer, or anybody qualified in the simplest of behavioural sciences. But he did go to high school and learn social studies and is a fabulous entrepreneur. And apparently, most importantly, he is an 'influencer' and 'innovator' and seems very rich.

When you finish his course, you can work with people's minds, and you will have a certificate to prove it. The sinister element here is that ordinary good people take the course and start working on people's minds. They don't know any better! They don't know that they are bad psychologists doing bad psychology, putting everyone they work with into Box D.

Then, in 2020, there is an Australian company that wanted to put a device in front of every child at school to record and monitor children's mental and body state. It had a cool name and is promoted by a lovely man and his team. He really thinks this is a really good idea because it provides a monitor of children that teachers and carers can access. But actually, it is really a bad idea and will cause harm to children. It promotes them to purposely, regularly, and unnaturally check their mental state, which is a known driver of anxiety and mood disorders.

It promotes children expressing their emotional state through icons on a screen instead of interpersonally where emotions are supposed to reside and resolve. Awfully, it mines their attention through prompts, then redirects their attention, and asks questions of it for adult evaluation. Is the personal and private attention of healthy children now a resource to be mined, altered, made into information, collated, and turned into profit?

Every good psychologist through their professional registration and practice is bound to protect children. It is the law. But entrepreneurs are not similarly bound by these laws. And remember, children can't consent to potential harm as you might.

How can it be that the people you trust to work with the most important thing your child has forever, her mind, can have no formal credentials to do that work? In any other important endeavour, such as teaching, you might demand someone well graded with four years' university, trained in teaching, plus five years of proven practice experience in teaching. Nope, not in psychology. My crazy uncle can do the work!

No one in charge is doing anything to assure you.

There is NO ASSURANCE.

THE TRUSTED-REFERRAL MYTH

True or False?

When you seek out help through the right channels, you will get referred to the help you need.

I want to say yes, do you?

I DON'T TAKE LAZINESS in my therapy; I work to my capacity, and I expect clients to do the same. Therapy, as I know it, is reciprocal. I love and work hard for every client, and so I expect every client will do something with that hard work and love. Of course, there are the proven and often-complex psychological protocols and practices to cover; but without love and hard work, how good could that be?

Now, when it is your or your child's turn to get serious help, you will find me or someone else that can do this stuff properly. You will get referred to the good psychologist.

Case of Jake

Jake presented by himself in my rooms one day—24 years old, moderately overweight, looking tired and lethargic, seemingly disinterested in being here. Rapport was reasonable. Jake explained that his mum wanted him to attend, but he really didn't think he needed any help. I asked about his referral to me and who suggested he come to psychology. He said his mum had taken him to his GP, and the GP had made a referral under the psychological therapies programme. The local primary health network runs that programme to assist people who don't have ordinary access to psychological therapy perhaps because of cost, distance, cultural reasons, or

JOSHUA THOMAS

minority stigmas. It is a programme that some GPs trust and feel fits their clients well.

In my room, Jake was happy to describe his ongoing difficulties. He told me he often thought he would be better off dead, saying he first tried to kill himself when 16 years old. He listed numerous diagnoses of obsessive-compulsive disorder, attention-deficit hyperactivity disorder, major depression, anxiety, and bipolar mood disorder. Still, he said that right now he was symptom free, and my assessment of symptoms indicated the same. He was doing okay these last few weeks.

I discussed the possibility that sometimes the assessment part of therapy is best worthwhile when we feel well enough to reflect clearly on our patterns of behaviour. When we feel truthful and unpressured. He had never considered that before and did agree that he had 'issues' that could do with some attention. I asked who had helped him before, and he said no one. I took that to mean that I was the first person to offer therapy, but he said that he meant he had seen lots of people over lots of years and no one had helped. Hmm, my ears pricked up a little.

I asked Jake how they had 'tried' to help him. Jake said his earliest memory was when he was about 6 years old, seeing a doctor after he was in trouble with his mother for breaking things. He said he had always been bad at home, always getting into trouble, hitting and breaking things mostly, but shouting back at Mum and not paying attention to what his mum wanted or, if at school, what his teacher wanted. Jake put his bad behaviour down to not having his dad around, his dad having left when Jake was 4 years old. Anyway, after seeing the doctor, he had to take Ritalin every day to help with his behaviour.

He told me that he thought his teacher had suggested Ritalin to his mother but was not sure anymore. In any case, it did not help much. He said he was just as bad; and when he got old enough, he refused to take it. He said he did not like school, felt different from everyone else, and mostly stayed alone, although always feeling lonely. He said that his shouting arguments with his mum continued and still do. Jake told me that over the years he has broken doors with his fists, smashed furniture, and made threats to his mum and girlfriends about killing himself. Sometimes this was because he was angry, sometimes because he was stressed, sometimes because he was depressed, but mostly because he wanted to make the arguing stop.

Jake said that between fights things were calm; but he was always on edge, knowing it would not last. His mum did not know what to do with him so had taken him to get some help. I asked who he had seen most recently.

Jake described going to Jigsaw when he was 17 years old because he was going to hang himself in the garage after a heated time of arguing and fighting with his girlfriend and then his mother. His mum had taken him to emergency triage because she said he needed urgent help. Jake said that after talking with a nurse in triage, he was referred to Jigsaw, where he was diagnosed with a bipolar mood disorder, he said, on his first visit. Jake remembers his mum at the interview telling the mental health worker about how he was crazy with big mood swings. He said his mum had kept a diary of his breaking things along with photographs to prove how manic and awful he was. Jake said that he did not remember seeing a psychiatrist, but that week, he was prescribed medications and assigned to somebody else that he had to see once a week.

Jake told me that they did not do any therapy at JigSaw. Rather, his psychologist explained to him that his problem was not curable, that the medication would help prevent his mood swings. Jake said he saw the person for a while, and they mostly problem-solved each week. Jake told me he took the meds for a few months but that he still argued big time with his mum and girlfriend, with some periods of pretend harmony. He told me, with a wry smile, that he'd explained to his worker that the meds didn't work; but they explained back that if he doesn't take them, they don't work. Anyway, Jake gave up on Jigsaw.

Jake told me that he had been intimate with two girls. His first was when he was 16, and that relationship lasted two years; but it was full of jealousy, worry, and arguments about where she was, who she was with, and if she loved him. Jake remembered physical fighting and being reckless in a car, driving without a licence. He said that his first girlfriend left him and has never talked to him again.

Jake said his current girlfriend of six months is fantastic because she understands him. In the next sentence, he explained that she threatened to leave him three months ago. So, of course, he tried to kill himself again, again with a rope. But after making the noose, his mum found it and got him to the hospital once more, after which he was referred to suicide prevention, a programme dedicated to helping people overcome their crisis and stay alive.

We discussed his life as a pattern. Being lost, being lonely, wanting love but relationships hurting, always feeling anxious knowing the things you care about are going to go wrong and break. We talked about the likelihood that one day he will kill himself. After all, it was part of the pattern. He said he knows people don't believe what he says, that he is misunderstood and quick to be angry. When on his own, Jake describes he'd been mostly sad and scared that things will not change. Jake came back three times for assessment and therapy. He really wanted to understand.

On fuller assessment, including psychometrics, I provided Jake with a diagnosis of borderline personality disorder. Along with psychoeducation, I suggested that he might go back to Jigsaw and participate in their dialectic behaviour programme, or he might complete a different long-term therapy with me over the following year. On our fourth session, which became our last hour together, he brought his girlfriend in with him. They were both happy in the room, sitting close and holding hands. Both wanted to explore how relationships are affected by his disorder. Jake made further appointments to progress a therapy that works for BPD, but he did not attend.

Thirteen months later, Jake shot himself to end his misery.

What happened to Jake?

Bad psych happened.

Let's look at the pathway to help: the referral path.

Clearly, Jake was in distress and trouble at the age of 4 onwards, when his dad left. But there was no referral, no help. I'm presuming both his mum and dad and himself believed his label of being a naughty boy. Two years later, though, at school, a good teacher had seen a 6-year-old agitated, lonely, argumentative boy who did not listen and do what he was told. He was I suspect quite disruptive to the class and teacher.

My sister is a teacher, and I sometimes think she can diagnose an attention deficit disorder and point parents in the right direction. And to be honest, most of the time, she might be spot on. Still, she and Jake's teacher are bad referrers. Not because they get things right most of the time, but because they get it wrong sometimes. And your entry into the complex maze of mental health services can be, in the words of the ex-leader of the free world, *bad, bad, very bad, very terrible.*

For Jake, some good psych at the start, I'm convinced, would have meant a different life for him. But no, he got bad psych at the start. The referral system broken, Jake was headed to the hurt locker, Box D.

     JOSHUA THOMAS

His first port of call was the GP, but he was referred to the GP with a problem to solve, not for a formulation of how his difficulties had arisen. There was no chance for a differential diagnosis that a good psychologist would have provided. All of Jake's behaviours and mental state as a young lad might have been better understood as depression, a mood problem, the externalisation of his sad life. His dad had left, he didn't have the required control of his world, so he acted out that control. That is different from being labelled a naughty boy, disruptive at home and in class, not willing or able to pay attention. But if the referral was for the latter, with reference from the teacher, then the GP, or paediatrician, will often head that way.

I'm sad as I write this because, overall, it is about sadness. Of course, Jake will meet the criteria for ADHD. They are somewhat a subset of common features of depression in young folk: poor attention and concentration, poor organisation, avoidance of effort, easily distracted, forgetful, risk taking, agitated, difficulties staying on task, failing to finish, fidgety, not playing quietly, attention seeking. Yes, children suffer from depression! Jake might have done well with both parents on-board for him, helping him through his heavy and unprocessed sadness about his dad leaving. If they are both not on-board, or if Jake is having ongoing difficulties, then a family counsellor might have been helpful to the parents.

It is tricky these days because you *know* that mental disorders are an imbalance, a biological condition, which is simply never true. The common-day, awful use of science has all but convinced you that the brain is the problem, not the mind. So I understand Mum for seeking a chemical solution. She wanted it fixed. She wanted his brain to work better, have him learn at and enjoy school. Anyway, Jake at 6 years old was prescribed a psychotropic drug, a stimulant, to help resolve his ongoing real-life dilemma.

Hmmm . . . now, how is that going to pan out? I wonder. Even if Jake has enough Ritalin to 'sedate' him, he will continue to be depressed—so sad and lonely, misunderstood, unloved, broken—that it becomes part of his personality. It did. Jake went from 6 to 16 getting worse. In the hurt locker, he went backwards, developing chronic and complex emotional regulation problems triggered by interpersonal interactions that he had little capacity to understand. His behavioural solutions were attention seeking, isolation, anger, aggression, hurting, and self-harm.

Now, at this stage, I find something astonishing. Jake—with all his difficulties, frailties, and behavioural and emotional issues between the age of 6 and 16—had never seen a psychologist. It is simply odd that no one referred him to one. His mental well-being was not a priority at 6, getting him to behave and making him easier to handle was. And Jake knew that. Six-year-old kids think and work things out rightly or wrongly. A medical solution was prescribed and forced onto Jake to fix him. But it did not work; and in Jake's mind, he is at least broken, if not stupid. He doesn't understand that it is the adults that are doing this all wrong.

When the medications did not bring back a happy little Jake, no one checked or backtracked. Despite Jake's mental state and emotional content being disordered and needing therapy, the GP did not follow up with a referral to a well-credentialled psychologist. Jake, starting as a little boy, spent 10 years of his formative development experiencing being broken, unlovable, with his inner world invalidated and ignored.

The second referral pathway was to Jigsaw, a public institution. He got to Jigsaw through an internal referral from the public mental health triage service. He had been taken to triage by his mum because he had made a noose and hung it over a rafter in the garage. Jake had just experienced a period of heightened interpersonal conflict, which he had done many times since 4 years old. He'd been fighting with his girlfriend and mum. He stayed at triage for a few hours, debriefing with a mental health nurse, who I know would have completed a risk assessment before allowing, and likely suggesting, that he go home with his mother.

In any case, during or following his visit to triage, the triage nurse made a referral to Jigsaw.

According to Jake, the first person to assess him in Jigsaw was not a psychologist. I find that quite incredible given Jigsaw is dedicated to youth in serious trouble with their mental well-being. But I believe Jake. Just as I believe him when he doubts, he was assessed by a psychiatrist before being prescribed psychotropic drugs. My experience in public triage showed me that antipsychotics, for example, are regularly prescribed without the psychiatrist or any psychologist doing any assessment. In any case, that week, he was quickly provided a diagnosis of bipolar mood disorder, and he was treated as such with medicine that was never going to work.

Jake and his mum presumably figured that the referral from triage was to a good psychologist, who could complete a thorough assessment of his mental state and difficulties. But no, the idea that the referral is going to get you to see the right person for you is a myth because Jake went to an institution, not a psychologist.

I can tell you for sure that there are some good psychologists at Jigsaw, but that does not mean you will do assessment and therapy with one. You are referred to the institution, the team, not a good psychologist. Those good psychologists that work inside Jigsaw work hard within a multidisciplinary team, which used to mean something quite useful. A young man like Jake would likely have done well with a social worker on his side, perhaps overseeing his real-life adjustments and supports. But he needs a good psychologist as well, 100 per cent focused on resolving his mental difficulties. But he got one and not the other.

You see, the social worker isn't called the social worker, and the psychologist is not called the psychologist. They are both called mental health clinicians, which is a made-up name and there is no such profession. They are presumably called the same job name, so they can both do the same job. But just as the clinical psychologist likely does a crap job case managing and overseeing the client's supports, social integration, and welfare, the social worker likely does a crap job of psychological formulation, assessment, and therapy. They can never do good psych.

In Jake's case, he was likely in Box C—mistake ridden, with a rushed, poorly informed diagnosis. There was probably a good person in the room with him, but they were not a good psychologist doing good psych. Medication and weekly problem solving were not going to help Jake because they had put him in the wrong paddock because of the string of poor assessments and diagnoses.

Jake's story is not uncommon in that younger folk are diagnosed with bipolar mood disorder when it is not a good diagnosis. I spent three sessions with Jake exploring his mental difficulties. We could not find a single instance in his life of him experiencing a manic period. No experience of persistent euphoria, delusions, or overactivity. Yet the Jigsaw mental health clinician did. How? Well, most likely because it was Jake's mum who was describing Jake's experiences. Parental testimony is often taken as gospel during intake and assessment. Jake told me that his mum provided his history of mental problems, diary and photos to boot.

I met Jake's mum. She was at our first session for 15 minutes until I got her out of the room. The first thing she did was to tell me Jake's mental problems and how he needed help. She had the folder of her notes and photographs of the damage he had done to the house. She even had a phone recording of him shouting and swearing at her during a fight. During that 15 minutes, Jake just looked at me, judging what or who I believed. That 15 minutes was a fast forward of Jake's life experience and relationship with his mum. When I got his mum out of our room, I asked Jake if his mum was always talking for him. Tellingly, Jake simply said, 'Since I was born.' I have no doubt that Jake's mum thought Jake was broken and was a maniac, but that is not the same as a mental health clinician discovering mania. Honestly, I suspect the mental

JOSHUA THOMAS

health clinician would not have known the difference. Maniac, mania, and manic are all the same thing, right?

But the result was very bad for Jake. Bad diagnosis and bad medicines that would not work. And no provision of a therapy that might have helped him. For both Jake and his mum, it was simply more proof that he really was broken. I don't blame him for quitting on Jigsaw. His referral to that institution was a mistake. It should have been to a good psychologist who worked there, but perhaps too much damage had already been done to that little boy.

Although I got to know Jake for a moment of his sad life, I was optimistic enough to offer him psychological therapy. We'd already started work on our relationship, a good parental model that was to be the mainstay of therapy. But at that time, he felt well. He was in his connecting phase, loving a girl who loved him back.

One last time I think.

If you are referred to an institution, ask for what you really want. It will dramatically increase your chances of getting well. If you have ongoing mental difficulties, you want a good psychologist.

Unfortunately, despite your trust in your referral, you might not find that good psychologist. There are no signs in the window. There are no advertisements, no way for you to distinguish or choose. Bad-psych pathway was first set, perhaps by a good teacher, pointing Mum in the direction she had seen work before. But Mum cannot be the wiser. She was in the dark as to what good psych is and where the good psychologists are. She never knew that it was important to know this stuff. Isn't it all the same, counselling, talking? I wouldn't at all scold her. She was doing what she knew to do, and we know how useful knowing is, don't we?

Today, on the Beyond Blue site, the stock image used to describe who can help with depression and anxiety is of two medical-looking people.

One seems to be a doctor because they have the computer and seem to be helping their nurse—in uniform. I think worse. In their pages, they continue to call psychological therapy 'talking therapy'. This is an outdated term. It more than hints at 'talking' being the therapy, which it clearly is not. Aside from underestimating and demeaning my profession, it badly misleads the public.

It clearly promotes the knowing that if you attend sessions with someone and talk things out, you are somehow on a therapy pathway. But talking is not the active ingredient in psychological therapy; it is only a vehicle of communication. Imagine calling chemotherapy injection therapy. I suppose anyone with a needle could then cure liver cancer?

Talking therapy—yuck. Psychological disorders are just not taken seriously, so competence is just not taken seriously.

True or False?

If you got a red-hot tip for a horse in the Melbourne Cup from someone who breeds sheep, you would bet your house on it.

I want to say no, do you?

You have lots of individuals, businesses, and institutions bidding for your mental-distress business. But there is no open information that addresses the competencies or successes of a psychologist. Referrals are mostly done through relationships, mate-ship if you like. Often, it is just done because the doctor knows one 'handy', or your child's friend's mum liked her counsellor. Sometimes it is because the referrer has a financial connection to the help. Maybe they rent rooms or take a percentage. Sometimes it is because the organisation paying directs you, like employee assistance programmes and NDIA coordinators do. Public institutions tend to refer to other equally flawed public institutions. At the end of the day, it is just business. People want your or the public's money, better-paid jobs, and empires. Mental health is now big business, and the referral is the easy way to print the money.

It is different for physical health. If you have an infection or chronic illness, you go to a doctor to get better. If you need some medicine to help in your treatment, then you will likely get a prescription from the good doctor. Although not perfect, this system means a person with demonstrated and accredited expertise is prescribing you treatment. In a way, the doctor is not really treating you but is the reliable diagnoser and prescriber of what treatment, if any, is good for you. I'm not sure about you, but I like this idea.

I don't like the idea of my neighbor Robert or my workplace or my insurance company or a nurse or a social worker or an occupational therapist or counsellor prescribing me serious treatments. They have not done the work that doctors have done to demonstrate that they can formulate what is going on, diagnose a serious illness, and prescribe serious treatments with low risk and maximum benefits. You don't want mistakes from the start. You want quality. Although this system is littered with examples of it going wrong when mistakes were made at the start, for physical ailments, the system as it stands has a good chance of doing well for most people most of the time.

Now imagine if the system was not like this. Imagine a silly system where *anyone* can prescribe you any serious drugs at any dose for any condition. Imagine that this is done without them having any competencies to diagnose your condition. Also, imagine that this is done without knowing what the best treatment is, or what dose will be effective. And imagine that in this silly system, this is what everyone did and accepted as proper medicine. Now, increase exponentially the incentive for this silliness to happen by making prescribing and selling drugs over the counter anyone's profitable business practice. Now, when you need help, would you be at risk? Would your children be at risk? Would you accept this risk? No, this is kin to voodoo and back-street drug dealing and would be your worst nightmare.

Well, the referral system for accessing psychological therapy is like your worst nightmare. Anyone—absolutely anyone—can 'prescribe' psychological therapy of any type of any dose for anything. That person might be a doctor, which helps if they know what they are doing and if they can spend hours completing a formulation and differential diagnosis. But many referrers are teachers, nurses, social workers, occupational therapists, insurance coordinators, friends, bricklayers, and hairdressers. For many, the referrer is an institution, for example, an insurance company, employer, government department, the police, or lawyers. The one thing that all these prescribers have in common is that they are incompetent when it comes to diagnosing psychological disorders and prescribing psychological therapy.

Trusting a referral for psychological therapy from them is equivalent to you trusting them on which horse to bet your house in the Melbourne Cup. The difference might be that you are only losing your house in the Melbourne Cup.

Trust the referral myth.

Busted.

Instead, you will take charge. You will ask your doctor for a referral to a good psychologist for an assessment and opinion. Someone who can help work out what is going wrong and then prescribe the therapy you need.

TRUST-OUR-INSTITUTIONS MYTH

GOVERNMENTS BUILD INSTITUTIONS for the good of society. I can't imagine our wealthy, lucky country not having our world-class public hospitals with great, well-credentialled doctors and nurses. Similarly, I can't imagine us not having great schools with great teachers. Living in Australia means I can trust the institutions that oversee and deliver on society's agenda items of education and health.

Did you know that you can't set up your school as you please with pretend curriculum and pretend teachers? Are you aware that you can't set up your hospital with pretend medicine, pretend doctors, and pretend nurses? Well, it's the same for our mental health institutions and programmes. They all adhere to good practice; they all insist that their professionals are well educated in their profession, with registration requiring them to meet the high standards of competence Australian society demands.

This means that we can trust our mental health institutions to provide great mental health programming and great psychological therapy services. Obviously, it also means that just as for hospitals and schools, we can trust that they don't provide pretend psychology with pretend psychologists. We are, if you like, protected from harm whilst being provided top-class education, medicine, and psychological therapy. After all, just like the song with a true first verse, that should be our national anthem: 'I am, you are, we are Australian.'

<u>**Case of Tiffany**</u>

Tiffany was a 21-year-old woman who came to see me to 'work on herself'. Explaining why she came to see me, she said that she was exceptionally intelligent; but when things went wrong, she would react by blaming others and cutting herself. She told me that since middle high school, she had hurt herself by cutting her legs with a razor when 'things did not work out'. After a recent physical altercation with a best friend, she was referred by her doctor to the Western Victorian Primary Health Network's (PHN) Psychological Therapy Services, including for suicide prevention.

The PHN is an institution that funds psychological therapy for people that may otherwise not have access to such therapy. I was an approved provider to that service.

Tiffany presented neatly dressed in loose clothing, appeared stated age of 21, and looked somewhat underweight. Rapport was good but with eye contact often being intense. Tiffany spoke freely and confidently about her 'moodiness' and 'cleverness', which she said annoyed people. Affect flattened, with tendency to smile when talking about her difficulties, as if they didn't bother her. She said that she thought a lot, and very quickly, because she was intelligent. Speech content mostly about being clever, more intelligent, superior to her peers, seeking approval from me. No apparent delusions or hallucinations. Insight inadequate with limited appreciation of emotional content and her impact on others. Judgement fair, cutting an example, nil current suicidal thoughts or intent.

Tiffany told me her awful story. She said she had told it many times before. She had seen a counsellor when she was 13 for depression and again at 15 years old. She had attended Headspace for a while. But Tiffany told me that she did not feel she fitted in with all the different, sad, and multisexed people there. After some repeated

   JOSHUA THOMAS

aggressive episodes and regular cutting, she was referred to Jigsaw, the public mental health service for younger folk. Her doctor had heard of the DBT programme there and thought it would be useful for Tiffany. However, on assessment, she was not found to be severe or urgent enough for their help, so Jigsaw referred her onto my practice via her GP and the PHN service. Headspace to Jigsaw to the PHN. All trusted institutions.

Tiffany told me that from the age of about 5 through to 12 years, she was frequently sexually abused by two uncles. She explained plainly, matter of factually, that her dad left home when she was very little; and whilst Mum worked, she was in the care of extended family, along with her three brothers and two sisters.

Tiffany said that she did not know she should, or could, tell anyone about the sex until she went to high school and other girls talked about sex. She explained it was complicated because she never felt abused, even though she knew it was wrong. She told me it affected her badly when she told her mum and then had to see a counsellor for depression. After counselling, they moved away to a smaller town. Tiffany said she did not fit in anywhere from then on. She knew she was different.

Tiffany explained that she did not like high school because it was too easy and she stood out in class, considered a nerd. She said she first used a razor to cut her leg because she was lonely and other girls had been doing it. She said that cutting her leg felt 'interesting'; and she liked to clean up the wound, looking after it carefully. Tiffany said she doesn't call it self-harm, just cutting, saying, 'It doesn't hurt.'

On completing year 10, she started upper school; and she got various part-time jobs at the local abattoir and Coles. Tiffany said that the local boys liked her, and she could go with any that she chose. When she was 17, she became pregnant; and when her son was born, the family moved to a regional city. Tiffany told me she is trying to get a career in forensic psychology. She said she wanted to work in the prison system, profiling criminals, especially sexual offenders. Tiffany said that she was enrolling at university but had not started any further study at that stage, being sidetracked when her grandad died recently.

Tiffany said that during her three years living in the city, her infant son was living with her mother whilst she shared a house with two best friends. She described not having a connection with her son and that her mum was fantastic anyway. She explained that nothing is working out as she wanted, that she spent most days bored. I suggested that was sadness; and Tiffany said no, she never feels sad or happy, just bored.

Tiffany said that it was too much effort to make more friends or talk with people because she was much more intelligent, and they don't have much interesting to talk about. Tiffany said proudly, 'I was diagnosed with depression and anxiety and bipolar II. But I've read about borderline personality disorder, and I think that is my proper diagnosis.

Tiffany had real difficulties. She was compromised and complicated. She needed good psych.

Okay, why is this case about institutions?

Let me tell you what I have to do to Tiffany.

I have to practise cutter-cookie psychology on her. In fact, it had already started. At the doctor's, she had to complete a screening measure called the K-10. It is designed to help determine if a person might need help for mental distress. It is really a short list of symptoms people experience during an episode of depression or anxiety. It is a self-report instrument, and it is Tiffany's job to complete the measurement—tick the right

 JOSHUA THOMAS

boxes—which makes sense because the GP doesn't experience any of Tiffany's experiences.

Then once at my practice, because it is a PHN referral, the practice must administer another measure called the DASS (depression, anxiety, stress scale). This is also a self-report measure of symptom severity designed for people experiencing high-prevalence common mental distress. Because the referral was 'ticked' for suicide prevention, the practice must also make Tiffany complete a modified scale for suicide ideation (MSSI), which attempts to measure suicidality in the previous 48 hours. Then, after the first few sessions, I must administer the K-10 and MSSI again, then again after another few sessions, etc. etc.

The institution insists on this process and calls these measures 'outcome measures'. By insist, I mean if you won't do it their way, you can't provide the service and get paid. But this mandatory institutionalised use of general measures is bad psych for Tiffany and likely for you if you get caught up in it. For Tiffany, she had spent an hour ticking boxes and filling out forms that have nothing to do with her difficulties or direction of therapy. But remember, she does not know that!

Those prescribed measures are bad measures for Tiffany. They all showed that she is fine, maybe with a few mild difficulties. Yet aside from my clients with schizophrenia, Tiffany was one of my most debilitated clients. She was very sick and had been getting worse, and none of the measures we are forced to use were useful. One of the fundamental ethics in psychological therapy is *do no harm*. And providing a mentally disordered person with bad measures harms them. Yes, it makes them crazy and crazier. Yet thousands of mental health workers, parapsychologists, and psychologists quietly comply and tick their boxes so funding can continue.

Tick, tick, tick—that's all it takes to get the money. Worse, I reckon nine out of every ten mental health workers, counsellors, and psychologists think this is just fine.

Let's look at an example outside of health, so you can appreciate how awful institutionalised processes can be and the effect on a person's mental health. Imagine that your car is coughing and spluttering. After all, they used to do that a lot. When you press your car's accelerator, it stops, goes, goes, stops, and goes again. You know this is wrong and dangerous, and you've put up with it for a week or so with your fingers crossed it would go away on its own. But it hasn't. It is getting worse. Something is really wrong.

You really need 'good mech'. You're going to avoid the dodgy mechanic down the street and instead take your car to a well-credentialled mechanic shop, a business-type shop that deals with your car type, so you can trust that it will get sorted.

They will look at your car's difficulty with a clear standardised process that they use for every car coming for repair, a process that works for you and them, and so they can't be accused of missing something obvious.

Anyway, on your visit, the mechanic assigned to you asks you what is happening, and you describe the problems with the car, the symptoms. He works through his checklist from top to bottom, and he measures your tyre pressure. One tyre reads 15 psi. He says, 'There's a problem here. Your tyre is too soft. Let's run them all at 36 psi and see how you go.' He has given you what we in psychology call a focused strategy. He is paid to do that, and it is bound to help. After all, you can't expect your car to work well with soft tyres. And you kind of know that.

It sounds silly, but a lot of us who know little about cars or might feel shy to question the 'professional' might get in their car and drive it home. We are assured that it *might* be the tyre pressure causing the problem. The mechanic did measure the tyre pressure, and it was astray. So it makes sense in a way to fix that first. Plus, we've a focused strategy to resolve the car's difficulties. But the next day, you go back to the mechanic shop because your car is still embarrassingly coughing and spluttering down the streets.

So the mechanic measures the tyre pressure again to check—36 psi, so fine. PSI is fixed. Tick and record that improvement in the car's symptoms. Then he pops open the bonnet and measures how much oil you have. Lifting the dipstick (no, not him), he sees that the oil is quite low. He says, 'There's a problem here. Let's get the oil right and see how you go.' Another focused strategy, cool. You're not convinced, but maybe? After all, you don't fix cars yourself and he is the mechanic in the certified shop that deals with your car type. And you're in the evidence-based programme that statistically works.

You drive home and sheepishly tell your partner that you're trying adding oil. She looks at you strangely, saying, 'It's a bit more complicated than that, isn't it?' You feel quite silly, but you do what you're asked. Perhaps the mechanic is eliminating possibilities? But the next day we go back to the mechanic shop because the car is still sick, coughing and sputtering worse than ever.

The same mechanic measures the tyre pressure and oil levels again. Tick, tick, they are both better. Good, the process is working. The measures say so. So now he goes on to measure the—well, you get the picture. Sounds crazy, but this is happening every day in our mental health institutions and their programmes and the therapy room funded by those institutions.

Beyond screening, the measuring of presumed difficulties and provision of 'focused strategy' before a proper examination is simply bad practice.

It leads you down the wrong track and, worse, drives the client bonkers. Following my first session with Tiffany, I knew that I can't and shouldn't measure her difficulties or progress with those crock-of-shit mandatory scales. Tiffany will report no anxiety outside her normal range (she is confident) and no depression outside her normal range (she is not sad). The suicide measure will just make her think of suicide, which is a dangerous thing to do as she has never expressed suicidality beyond cutting her legs. But if I did do the measurements, the programme would get the tick. Tick, tick, tick. Apparently, ticks matter to institutions more than good therapy.

This far in the book, you are probably getting a feel of what a good psychologist does here. Well, I told Tiffany that the measures she had completed were a crock of shit and not in her interests. I explained that they were at best misleading but would be bad feedback for therapy—the last thing her mind needs. I let her know that the best practice is for Tiffany and me to discuss what to measure based upon her goals, our formulation and diagnosis, and the therapy we might employ. I let her know that, being a good psychologist, I'm well trained in assessment and psychometrics and that good measurement is a part of that.

We also discussed the ethical dilemma of whether I lie to the institution about filling in the measures improperly. We could try switching funding institutions, but that was problematic for Tiffany. On this occasion, we decided to lie and fill in those stupid mandatory measures for compliance but with non-information. Tiffany was relieved, and she expressed her appreciation that we would work this stuff out together, me the expert in psychological therapy and her the expert in Tiffany.

I did suppose I was behaving unethically in my disdain for institutionalised mandatory methodology. After all, it might be problematic for them, and they are paying me. But no. Firstly, the K-10 measure is a screening instrument, and institutions are using it as an all-purpose outcome measure. To some, it seems the most convenient instrument. The K-10 is the one to use for everyone and everything. But this ignores the purpose

JOSHUA THOMAS

and psychometrics of this instrument. It was designed for screening within the general population. Useful for folk like doctors who can't or don't have time to do a proper formulation and assessment. At best, it is like a thermometer up your arse but not as accurate.

The K-10 checklist quickly screens in people who *may* require psychological help. It doesn't have to be *accurate*; and in fact, studies show it screens well between 50 and 80 per cent of the times it is used. In Australia, 13 per cent of the non-sick, ordinary adult population will score 20 and over—that is, screened in. And interestingly, only about 25 per cent of patients seen in primary care will score 20 and over. This means, for example, that many people 'pass the screening test', go for help, and don't actually need help. It also means that up to 75 per cent of people being treated for mental health difficulties don't 'qualify' for help, according to the K-10.

Now, this rubberiness is quite fine for a screening instrument for the general-purpose, high-prevalence problem category of anxiety and depression. But it is not designed or suitable as an all-purpose outcome measure. It is misused by institutions for this purpose because of its ease of use (tick, tick, tick) and general purpose (tick, tick, tick). What else do you know that goes tick, tick, tick? Max, it's a bomb!

The institutions have at least two problems here. One, once we know that a person is not in that high-prevalence group, we must not treat them as if they are. It is simply wrong and damaging to them and their therapy. Two, the 'outcome' statistics they collect are known by every clinical psychologist who aced research methods at university to be void. The reliability and validity of the K-10 instrument is inadequate for therapy outcomes and is almost always completed by the clinician without input from the client—that is, it is not applied properly anyway.

Mental health workers and parapsychologists, at best, 'guess' the recent experience of their client whilst the client is nowhere in sight, probably in reception approving their payment. Even guidelines and instructions from institutions allow for the client to be absent during administering the K-10, which is frankly ridiculous but indicative of how badly institutions work. Imagine your GP guessing your blood pressure after talking to you and saying you are getting better!

I was present at the very start of a Primary Health Network (PHN) Psychological Therapy Services programme. Some psychologists, but many more pretend psychologists, were briefed on how the programme was going to work. We psychologists were not asked how it might work, just given the option of joining in via some free-for-all bidding battle. A director of a well-respected private provider of psychological therapy said at that forum, 'We are out [not going to bid] because you have set up poor psychology for the poor. We provide quality therapy with good psychologists, and it does cost more, more than you will pay. So you are keeping us good psychologists out to the detriment of mentally sick people in need of our help.'

She was referring to two key elements of the PHN institution's programme. Firstly, the PHN paid the therapy provider $120/session whereas an ordinary rate for a good psychologist is around $160 to $260/session. That meant the better psychologists would lose between $40 and $140 per session and so can't afford to be providers. Secondly, this institution was promoting the cheaper, convenient, and efficient practice that psychological therapy be provided by 'anyone'. That's right. No mandatory psychology qualifications were required. And of course, anyone would be happy with a pay rate of $120/hour to tick boxes.

Yes, poor psychology for poor people.

This meant a big rush towards the money by instant pop-up provider businesses who 'hired' any social worker, occupational therapist, or nurse that they could find. I know because I was there fighting in the opposite direction. This was fierce competition with businesses stealing one another's people and territory. A social worker, for example, could

JOSHUA THOMAS

double their salary; and small alliances of individuals manufactured profitable cash businesses from the flush public purse.

And to what purpose remains a mystery. The vast majority referred to this institution's programme could already get access to a *real* psychologist via Medicare. Aside from providing poorer psychology for the poor, the whole thing continues to be a profitable enterprise for people not qualified in psychological therapy. Yet this is a federal government institution, charged with delivery of the best-available primary mental health care in their region.

Look, it is no one's fault. I met and talked to a doctor well associated with the Western Victoria PHN. He was kind, well intentioned, and knowledgeable. But he was unable to listen when I explained who was delivering psychological therapy to our most disadvantaged folk. He told me that he *knows* that it is a great programme. But there are inherent problems with institutions and knowing.

The example of the PHN facilitating bad psych is an illustration of how things go wrong. Essentially, institutions are set up to deal with populations assuming standardised, cookie-cutter services. But you the client are a unique person, not a bit of bland dough spread through the population. And when they press the cookie cutter on you, you are unaware of the damage they might be doing to you.

Despite what we often say, banks are an example of where cookie-cutter institutions work best in our society. Your dollar is, whether you think it or not, very much the same as my dollar. Therefore, the holding and moving around of that dollar can be the same for every dollar, without much downside. Efficiency is fine here. Likely, the bank's harm rate to each dollar is less than 1:1 million, but I'm sure some do get harmed in the system. Probably getting torn in some bank teller's draw or lost in a computer's memory bank. But what do you care? Frankly, if every now and then a dollar got harmed, I would not care at all. They are not even alive.

But the use of efficient cookie cutters on people with mental disorders is a bit different I suggest. Well, actually I know it is different. If the cookie cutting is well done, then perhaps it might be useful for 50 per cent of people with mental disorders. After all, the cutter was likely designed mostly with them in mind. But what does the other 50 per cent of sick people look like? Remember, these are millions of real Australian people. Well, they look like cut-up, leftover dough pressed through the process that won't work for them. Often, they are cooked, burnt, and irrevocably harmed.

Every good psychologist has spent time with harmed folk—harmed by the help they trusted. Help provided by institutions.

Headspace and Jigsaw are cookie cutters that have the wrong shape for Tiffany. She went to Headspace because that is the institution for her. After all, she is young and having mental health difficulties. But Headspace would not work for her. She put herself into the process and came out like leftover dough. She doesn't know it, but the Headspace cookie cutter wasn't even designed for her.

Actually, it is tricky knowing who Headspace is designed for: youth, I figure, because it says so. But apparently, not youth like Tiffany. And it is hard not to notice, if you're a good psychologist, that none of its executive team meet the standards of the Australian Psychology Board for being a psychologist. Apparently, you know how to do mental health because you know you do? That is not my view, and it would be a reasonable expectation that someone in charge would be a very well-credentialled psychologist.

Yet Headspace attracts everyone of a certain age. And our Australian studies can't find much benefit to their population of clients. Rather, what the studies did find was some young folk getting better on their own, most young people staying the same, and some getting significantly worse. Hardly encouraging! The study also showed that many Headspace clients did not get proper therapy. In the words of Gomer Pyle, surprise, surprise, surprise.

Tiffany was likely not harmed by the very institution she and her mum trusted; but it was not positive, perhaps neutral at the best. But Headspace, just like all institutions, will have measures—tick, tick, tick—that justify their programme, even proving that it works. So you won't find it astonishing that at the same time this damning study was released, mental health leadership was claiming, 'These data provide encouraging evidence that Headspace is an engaging and accessible entry point to the Australian healthcare system for young people and their families. We can now be confident that this national network of youth-friendly one-stop shops delivers access to effective and holistic primary care to those young people with moderate mental health problems.'

Hmmm, more on what works later, but it smells of something, doesn't it?

Still, the facts show more Headspaces whilst more mental health difficulties in youth. And like all entrenched institutions, Headspaces are spreading and growing, coming to your hometown. Would you want one near you?

The Jigsaw cookie cutter is kind of the opposite of the Headspace cutter. Still, being an institution, they must use them. One is their criterion of severity. If the cookie cutter finds you are not sick enough, then you don't get the programme. This is tricky for me, as prior to Tiffany coming to see me, a good friend and colleague rang. She wanted to understand if we were running a programme for people with deep and unresolved emotional difficulties. We were. So I was happy and pleased to see Tiffany in my rooms, confident and committed to providing the right therapy for her. She had found good psych with the help of my Jigsaw friend.

But the obvious question remains. Why did Tiffany have to go through the Jigsaw assessments and cooking cutting just to be told that she was leftover dough and they had nothing for her at that time? This is a well-funded institution with access to great psychologists. Why wasn't Tiffany's pathway assured?

You know her story. You know she has severe mental dilemma and difficulties, certainly disordered. I think harm was done to Tiffany, the least possible thanks to a dedicated psychologist who got her out of the cookie-cutting machines of institutions. Nevertheless, how would your mind be assimilating this experience from the two main promoted and trusted institutions looking after younger folk? Can you see how institutions can't help but do bad psych? They will do good psych too, but that takes us back to the lucky dip of doors at the beginning of the book. You have to make your luck and chose your door.

You will get mentally unwell, perhaps worse, disordered. Then, if you are referred to an institution, beware. They have a Box D, the hurt locker. And you won't know which door it is behind. Instead, fight for your life to see a psychologist who has the credentials, respect, and freedoms to work with you. They must guarantee their work for you being independent of any organisation's cookie-cutter constraints. If you don't, you likely will be falling into psychology for the poor, the wrong therapy for you, poor dose therapy, with a pretend psychologist.

So what happened with Tiffany?

Well, she completed ten individual sessions with me and ten group sessions with myself and my practice partner. Both symptom and outcome measures (not the frigging K-10) improved.

Interestingly, Tiffany told me that the best thing about therapy was that when she thought about her past, she felt sad.

Let's make this personal to you. Will you send your old vulnerable mother to an institution when she needs care? If so, will you simply trust them to give the care your mum deserves and has a right to? Of course not, you'd be all over it, avoiding Box D, the hurt locker! Why would you believe the myth that institutions for mental health are any different?

THE SOME-IS-BETTER-THAN-NOTHING MYTH

FOR MY FIRST time ever, I rang a radio station in Melbourne. It is a radio programme I respect because the host can be incisive and does great interviews with some people who *may* matter. The station itself is part of the Australian Broadcasting Corporation (ABC), which is the most trusted source of information and opinion in Australia.

At the time I rang, some awful bushfires were burning through a quarter of Australia. Many people died. Homes were razed to the ground as were farms and livestock, with families and communities devastated. It was the worst national disaster I've lived through, affecting every state. Much of our natural environment, including fauna and flora, was made dead. Things are different forever. We all know Mother Nature is angry with us because we disrespect her and don't treat her right.

Anyway, I digress a little. The reason I rang the radio was that a regional bushfire recovery coordinator had been interviewed. I really wasn't sure of what the mouthful of a title did, but the person described the harm to Australia in a way that impacted my guilt. He said that the immediate need of folk in the regional areas of Australia was not money, not blankets or food. It was psychological help to prevent trauma setting in. If you like, to prevent posttraumatic stress disorder (PTSD).

As it happens, being a well-credentialled clinical psychologist, I'm quite good at that. So I rang in to find a way to volunteer my help, which had just been asked for. For me, I instantly jumped into how to formulate, diagnose, and help resolve acute stress disorder (ASD). ASD is a diagnosable disorder described very well in the very thick *Diagnostic and Statistical Manual for Mental Disorders*. Strange, though, it might seem to you, I have read that thick book. It is essential to the formulation and diagnosis and, therefore, therapy for mental disorders. I have also studied and taken time to practise the therapies that help people with ASD.

As it turned out, the station could not help with the contact details for bushfire help. No one wrote them down! But as coincidence would have it, the ABC host had also been discussing the benefits of having nurses complete psychological therapy with folk with mental disorders. Also, getting nursing hands on that Medicare rebate for psychological therapy. I remember this full and favourable discussion being with the head of nursing studies at a regional university.

Anyway, as I was on the phone but off the air, I was asked to give my opinion, on-air, on the idea on allowing nurses to access Medicare rebates for psychological therapy. I figured that the ABC host is an expert in journalism, whilst I'm an expert in psychological therapy. So, I presumed my on-air commentary on nurses providing psychological therapy was going to be taken seriously. And if you've worked me out yet or have gotten this far in this book, then you already know I think that it is a crock-of-shit idea and would say so. It would be like letting you loose on someone with a small but growing cancer of the brain. It's only minor cancer, and you've seen the procedure on TV: simply drill, dig, clean, and take the money.

Now on live radio, for some reason, I suddenly became very polite and simply said to the host, 'I heard what the nurse advocate said, but I don't think it is a good idea. If a person was suffering initial trauma, they will do best with a proper dose of psychological therapy from a psychologist.'

The host simply replied to me, live on radio, 'Yes, but a little is better than nothing, isn't it?'

You see, it turned out that the host, after previously giving 15 minutes of thorough and favourable discussion to a head of nursing studies, didn't wait for an answer from a psychologist about psychology. Whilst I was answering her last question to me, she turned off my live on-air stream. And then she continued to talk to people who can't know the answer to her question. I'd sadly been abandoned before any discussion. She'd already figured that nurses with a little training can and should do therapy. I presume because she thought therapy was something nurses trained in or could train in. I promise you, whatever that training is, it is not approved by any psychology board to be sufficient.

Now, given fair time, I was going to explain to the host and thereby her listeners that my answer was a deafening no. That a little was mostly not better than nothing. Just like needing $3 for a loaf of bread and having $2 is not better than nothing. Still, no bread unless you buy the cheap stale loaf. It is true that nurses would help many people with ASD. But it is equally true that nurses would harm many people by accident through mistake.

Psychology is a regulated health service to ensure that we maximise the benefit whilst minimising the harm. I was going to point the host to the Australian Health Practitioners Regulation Agency's website that explains the purpose of registration. The site also makes publicly available the standards and competencies a good psychologist must attain. They are very different from those for nursing, which, of course, makes perfect sense to me.

But the ABC host *knows* that a little is better than nothing. I don't know for sure, but I now presume a little is better than nothing is a good thing in journalism? After all, that is her stated area of expertise. And she was quite unprepared to think about if her knowing about psychology was sound. The myth that she shares that some is better than nothing purposely ignores the premise of 'do no harm'. It ignores the fact that psychology is best done by good psychologists dealing in good psychology. The myth ignores all the evidence that the correct therapy dose is crucial to recovery.

When the ex-leader of the free world said, 'Maybe, you know, maybe just give those sick people with the virus a little disinfectant. That might work,' there was outrage and laughter. It was truly ridiculous. But why is one ridiculous (some disinfectant) whilst the other a known truth (some psychology)?

If you are prescribed antibiotics for a diagnosed disease, you are prescribed the amount that is shown to work best and, with other things being equal, least risk. If your sick child is prescribed two tablets a day for a disease, do you just give them one because that way you will save money but at least you are doing something? If you come down with the mumps after travelling abroad, does your doctor prescribe antibiotics? Of course not, they won't work on that viral illness.

Ordinarily, you appreciate what the right dose of treatment is. It kind of looks like a math formula. Your best chance of recovery relies on it. If you follow it, it is most likely going to help. If you don't, then that potential help fades away quickly.

$$\text{Effective Treatment} = \boxed{\text{Correct Treatment}} \times \boxed{\text{Correct Potency}} \times \boxed{\text{Correct Frequency}}$$

For example, you need the right tablet, don't you? The right antibiotic. You also need that tablet to be at the right potency or strength. You then have to take that medicine regularly over a period. If you weaken any of those parts of the dose, the effectiveness falls away like lemmings off the cliff.

It is exactly the same for psychological therapy, yet it is ignored every day by those who should know better.

Far from a little being better than nothing, a little is downright dangerous.

Loren was referred to me after going backwards in her mental distress. No diagnosis was offered, which is fine. Just that she felt she was 'falling apart' with family problems.

Loren presented dressed smart in close-fitting jeans and jumper, looking younger than stated age of 36. Rapport good. Eye contact good, well engaged, leaning forward, wanting to tell me her story. Affect normal range, facial movements expressive. Said her mood was 'up and down' depending on the day. She became teary as she repeated *down*. Speech, Scottish accent, mildly pressured. Thought process somewhat tangential, moving from example to example. Mostly about her husband's sister and that sister's family living nearby. Nil sensory disorders apparent, alert, memory intact. Insight fair, able to see life dilemma, but less able to see her role in that. Judgement fair. Nil suicidal ideation but impulsive decision making.

Background

Loren told me that she needed help, that no one was on her side, and that she felt crazy. Loren described her situation as feeling trapped and thinking about it nonstop. She said that her family lived in a lovely house near the surf coast. Loren explained that she and her husband, Bill, had moved there to bring up their two young girls (now 13 and 15 years old) away from the city and for the non-pressured lifestyle. Loren said it had been great until Bill's sister moved to the same suburb with her husband and Bill's mum. At first, it seemed okay, like one big family; but Loren said she felt pushed aside from everyone—Bill, her two daughters, Bill's sister, and Bill's mum. She explained that 'they' all got on so well, but she felt excluded from that closeness.

Loren said she knows it is deliberate because she and Bill's mum never got on well, and Bill's sister flaunts her closeness to Loren's daughters by coming to the house anytime she wants to see them. Lauren said it all became too much when Bill's sister started walking the two girls to school every day instead of her. She said that it has been like this for about a year, and now she feels completely on her own. Loren said Bill thinks it is all in her head and that he won't listen to her worries anymore, and they argue a lot. It came to a crisis two months ago when Loren went out for drinks with some girlfriends. She got drunk and was kissing a man she just met when Bill came to pick her up.

Loren said she saw a psychologist last month for three sessions. At the end of those three sessions, the psychologist had concluded with Loren that the only option was for her and her family to move away. But her husband wouldn't listen, and now she is convinced that they should break up.

When she went back to her GP for some antidepressants, as suggested by her husband, the GP prescribed the antidepressants for Loren but said she needed more therapy for her worsening depression. Yes, she was getting worse, not better.

So what is happening to Loren? She has done all the right things to get help by seeing her GP and then a psychologist. Well, if you are like me, you are thinking about wrong dose of therapy. Mostly the wrong type but also wrong intensity and wrong frequency.

The psychologist clearly is not doing good psychology. She did not produce a formulation that explained Loren's dilemma or appreciate Loren's psychological predisposition to these circumstances or the maintaining factors or her strengths. At best, the psychologist was attempting to help, be on her side, validate her, care for her, listen, and give hope and direction. But applying those important but inadequate competencies to Loren sent her backwards. The three sessions made her crazier, sadder, more depressed, more separate from her family, and more positive the marriage with the man she loved was failing. Her last hope was a medicine that might stop all her worries. Thankfully, the GP got her back to therapy.

> Loren is not a rare woman.
>
> She is one of many lovely women who will really love you, values a close family, and simply wants the same back. Her most prized possession in life is the relationship. She is acutely aware of it, watches it, and polishes it every day, like a rare diamond. Unfortunately, Loren also knows that these diamonds dull over time and become more like brittle glass. She knows that intimate relationships start good, get fantastic and magical, but then go bad. And when they go bad for her, the man leaves, and it hurts like a hot knife in her heart.
>
> This paradox of really loving and valuing her important relationships whilst expecting them to go sour, if not today, tomorrow, tears Loren's heart apart. I'm not going to discuss the aetiology of this psychological difficulty, but it mostly starts during childhood and developmental years and is pronounced in late adolescence. My clients tell me that 'most' women feel this tear, which I believe. In Loren, it was heightened and producing lopsided thinking, feeling, and doing. And that was *really* causing relationship problems. Agreeing with her thinking, feeling, and doing would be counterproductive.
>
> To help Loren, we came up with a plan:
>
> 1. Work hard to stabilise her emotional state and lopsided thinking using acceptance and commitment therapy (seven sessions)
> 2. Include couples work to repair and stabilise her relationship with Bill (four sessions)
> 3. Set in place longer-term goals on becoming more aware and accepting of how others are thinking and feeling. Being less naturally suspicious. (two sessions)

JOSHUA THOMAS

Yes, the plan could have been more in-depth or more 'psychological'; but this was Loren's plan, not mine. And that was the deal when I agreed to help her.

So what happened to Loren? To be truthful, I don't know because the crock-of-shit Medicare system stops access to therapy when it decides, not when we have finished. And Loren had wasted some valuable sessions getting bad psych. But when we stopped therapy, Loren was calmer and more insightful about herself. But she and Bill still had to complete the repair work of her unfaithfulness. Loren kissing another man at the pub whilst drunk was a very big deal for Bill. She was sorry, and Bill said he forgave her, but she had yet to make good. Trustworthiness had not been restored yet. It was tricky for them because it meant her going out with the girls again and demonstrating being sober, adult like, and considerate of those waiting at home.

On the other hand, Loren knew she had changed. She knew that repairs of mistakes can be done with the help of the one you love if only you can conquer your fears and stop avoiding normal, albeit scary, feelings.

For now, I'm hoping you can see what is special in Loren's simple plan. It was somewhat effective because we had the right therapy at the right potency at the right frequency—or the best we could produce.

But what chance do you have of getting your plan, the one that works for you, at 100 per cent effective? Actually, very little chance, nil I reckon. Most psychologists and advocates believe the myth that any therapy is good for you, counselling is always useful, and some is better than nothing. For example, that study into Headspace found that only 28 per cent of Headspace clients had up to the very basic minimum dose of therapy they needed. Yet the advocates of Headspace read these findings and find them 'encouraging', even saying that Headspace is a 'unique evidence-based reform in mental healthcare'. Still, my bet is that they don't send their kids there. Certainly, I am unable to recommend it to any of my clients.

You see, the truth is that psychological therapy isn't that simple or safe; and if at the wrong dose, it can be harmful. For Loren, the wrong dose sent her into an episode of major depression and was construed to destroy her marriage.

There seem to be three main drivers that maintain the myth that some is better than none. Firstly, people and institutions like to specialize. For example, they learn CBT, a small part psychology. Then, that's what they do. You get CBT regardless of any psychological formulation, diagnosis, precipitating factors, your personal attributes, or if they only have three sessions with you. Even regardless of if they are good at that therapy. In some simple sense, this seems fine. After all, CBT has been developed as a general therapy, good for some people sometimes. But it takes time too—time that most people won't get. To do a good job in psychoeducation, formulation, time to correct, time to demonstrate, time to work hard, I reckon it would be twenty sessions plus daily practice away from my rooms. Well, your psychologist is going to do all that compressed into ten sessions—half the dose required for it to be properly effective.

Yep, it sucks.

This weakening of the therapeutic dose is everywhere and is described in different ways. In the private setting, it is seen as insufficient funding by our institutions. We private psychologists can charge a lot of money per hour. My standard charge rate has been $160/hour, so not cheap at all. But with funding from Medicare, the out-of-pocket cost to my clients would be $25, which is quite cheap to them, I think. Still, Medicare has zero respect for my professional capacities and ethics and my clients. It thinks I will rip them off, them being Medicare, by providing more therapy than the person needs. I've never done that, and I don't know any good psychologist who has or would. We simply

                    JOSHUA THOMAS

don't need to. But Medicare remains overcontrolling to the detriment of all sick people. The low dose they impose simply means the sick stay sick, get sicker, or give up. Now that's clearly useful, isn't it? Of course, our graphs of sick folk continue the upwards trajectory, and Medicare has wasted billions of taxpayers' money.

In the public system, this underdosing is done in a few ways. The most obvious way is by providing poor therapy via low-competent parapsychologists. Often, you won't see a psychologist even in the most acute setting. More likely, you will see a mental health nurse, who is really simply a nurse division 1 who did a few courses. I've sat next to them and worked alongside. Yes, they have some familiarity with psychological dilemmas and rudimentary practices. But they are parapsychologists in the same sense as paramedics are rudimentary GPs. They have skills, but the gaps in knowledge and ability are chasms. But unlike paramedics, parapsychologists have zero standards of competency. You get whoever wanted the promotion the most.

The other obvious way to underdose in therapy is to stop psychologists from doing their job, which is therapy, of course. A colleague of mine has taken up senior roles in public health because it has less therapy to do. Well, that's not true, but it kind of is. They would like to take on around six clients a day; and in private practice, that adds up to a good middle-class salary. But you are still at your private practice for eight hours each day, so as an hourly rate, it is kind of average. Think of a plumber's wage. Then, when you calculate superannuation, holiday pay, personal development, and zero private business costs, you can get more than that $80/hour in your public health salary. And that job comes with security, prestige, career paths, real holidays, and long service leave. But often, much less therapy work.

In the public system, you're in an organisation, a bureaucracy, which means you have many hours of meetings, paperwork, compliance jobs, training sessions, and such, some of which might be useful, but you do them all. And being part of a multidisciplinary team, whatever that means these days, you have a relatively ill-defined, less-focused role. You might be a well-credentialled psychologist; but you might find yourself doing social work or supervisory work and management reports, all of which mean less time with your poor clients.

One colleague told me that sometimes they do maybe only thirty minutes of real therapy with their clients in any session apparently because of a mixture of ill-defined roles, admin time, and too many clients on their list that they take on because it is public. Now that is bizarre. It is like diluting your tasty cordial until all you have is coloured water.

Still, financially, it stacks up for each individual. Hmm, can you smell more wasted money, sick people staying sick and getting sicker?

But, apparently, some is better than nothing, and we all know it.

Busted.

JOSHUA THOMAS

THE KIND-PSYCHOLOGIST MYTH

PERHAPS THE BEST idea is that psychologists are kind and that you will be with a caring person. Perhaps that this is the best therapy you can get. Someone who really listens. I've lost count of the number of times I've heard, 'He really understands me. I feel so much better after seeing him.'

Isn't it a bit more complicated than that? People often ask for a compassionate psychologist. And this sounds good; you feel listened to, validated, and supported. But what if part of *your* problem is that you overuse the security of people validating and supporting you? How would that compassionate person properly deal with or challenge your insecurities, the ones you don't want to see? What if you could tell that the psychologist was doing this caring on purpose, artificially if you like? Many psychologists choose their profession partly on the basis that they want to feel helpful and liked or have mental health problems themselves. The truth is, we psychologists mostly have our inner problems, and so we feel a kinship with mentally sick folk. You might instantly feel comfortable with me, but what if my drives are a hindrance to your therapy?

This is important because every client initiates the transference effect that retards the ability of the psychologist to do good therapy. This can't be avoided. But this transference, if appreciated during therapy, will be your best mechanism for understanding and eventual healing of your inner scars. But if not appreciated, the transference effect can be the death of good therapy.

Would you rather have someone who makes you feel better or someone who is open and honest with you, helping you do difficult change? I think the right answer is you want both. But the second provides permanent benefit. You have limited sessions with a good psych, so time is of the essence!

Case of Ryker

Ryker was referred to me after an assessment interview within the primary mental health system went astray. He had been referred for assessment following a period of emotional turmoil, especially related to family breakdown and separation. The primary mental health service worked with people with severe emotional dysregulation. His assessment was to include an evaluation of any personality disorder.

In his first assessment interview, the psychologist completing the assessment became too frightened to continue. Ryker had become verbally aggressive along with scary facial expressions and stamping of fists on the table. I was asked (conveniently being the only man) to talk to Ryker and attempt to complete the assessment process.

Ryker presented to me 30 minutes later dressed in home-style casual wear, tracksuit bottoms, sneakers, T-shirt. Moderately overweight, clean shaven, kempt. Looked stated age of 47, tired, and seemingly bewildered. Rapport satisfactory. Good eye contact, mildly intense with Ryker sitting forward in his chair. Said mood was depressed and annoyed, especially after what had just happened. Affect upset, tense. Speech normal, loud when telling his story. Thought process mildly circular, mostly logical and goal oriented. Thought content mostly about why I (me) was there and what had happened to the other psychologist. Also, about bureaucracy, 'drop kicks', and people in authority, saying he would 'shoot them all' if he could. Nil sensory disorder apparent, memory intact. Insight poor, did not know why the other psychologist had to leave. Judgement fair, nil current suicidal ideation, nil self-harm. Nil intent to harm anyone.

Background

Ryker told me that he needed help, that he was living at home, often thinking of dying. He said that he can feel fine; but if he goes out or watches the news, he gets mad and upset with the world. He said he had previously been diagnosed with borderline personality disorder and depression and that he had seen counsellors and such. He told me that 'nothing had worked'. He told me that he had always been angry at people who were drop kicks, and he thought others that tolerated drop kicks were 'pussies'. He said that his temper got him into trouble all the time. For example, he had been sacked from his last job for abusing his foreman.

After ten minutes of tense and easy banter about my work and his Collingwood football club, I explained to Ryker that the previous psychologist had left because she was very scared of him. Ryker was surprised and then apologised, saying he never would hurt anyone. He explained that he thought he was supposed to express his emotions and tell it like it really was, how he really thought and felt. He asked if I was scared of him.

I said, 'Yes, you come across as angry, impulsive, and aggressive. You are louder than most men and talking about killing ordinary people. And your face gets screwed up and intense looking. So yes, I am a little scared right now, and I feel like I need to leave the room. But I'm not leaving you. My job is to work with you and help. You want my help, don't you?'

Ryker was silent for a bit and then said yes. And we had started good psych, perhaps the first time for Ryker.

Ryker was obnoxious to be with. He openly denigrated women. He was dismissive and oppositional with people with some but little authority. He was easily angered. I recall him being furious that a young boy was messing around in the public library with his mum and the library attendant seemingly not making the boy behave properly. Or furious when a young man jumped in front of him in a shopping queue or when a Department of Human Service attendant would not talk to him about his daughter. And when I say furious, I mean like a dark-storm-with-lightning furious, not a cold front with a little wind.

Otherwise, in my room, Ryker could be the perfect citizen: well read, expert in American Indian history, collaborative with the police, unyielding love for his son and daughter. Ryker was an advocate for charity and help for the homeless and would do volunteer work. Until it went wrong, of course.

Still, if you met Ryker and could not manage the transference, you would not be able to tolerate being near him. My urge was to leave the room, not to care for him. Yet we must do therapy if Ryker is to soften his experiences and judgements on the world and learn that not many women are like his hateful and abusive mother.

For a long time, Ryker refused to elaborate on his childhood. I think it was two years before he told me quietly and calmly about his parents and his awful, awful childhood that he had to survive. He did survive; but to do so, he had to develop this equally awful personality. He was overly narcissistic, passive-aggressive, wary of women, and obsessive about right and wrong. He wanted to be a good parent, but he knows he wasn't. He was overly authoritarian yet helpless in corralling his wayward children.

Ryker had never had a break, a streak of good luck if you like. Who could be kind enough to give him that break? At nearly 50 years

JOSHUA THOMAS

old, Ryker was unemployable. Although he could get jobs using his intelligence and boyish, narcissistic charisma, he couldn't stay employed. He was like Freddy Krueger, a nightmare for any ordinary boss. Ryker was unlovable, and even I could not love him at the start.

Because Ryker did not meet the full criteria for borderline personality disorder, and because we only cut that cookie, we could not help him. He was to be referred to community health, which provides some psychological therapy at their service centres. But just prior to him being moved along, I recommended he be further assessed by our psychiatrist, a woman I shared a desk area with, to determine a differential diagnosis for Ryker.

Once the assessment was completed, Ryker and I discussed him getting a disability pension to at least sort out his practical worries of very little money. With the authority of the psychiatrist's report and her recommendation and other boxes ticked, Ryker got that pension, his first break for many years.

Ryker worked with me for about six more years, some in the public domain and then at my private practice. We mostly completed transference therapy and mentalisation, where we explored and built some flexibility around his personality disorder. I did not cure him, but he got to like and respect me, and it was reciprocal. During the therapy, we traversed the whole range of what it meant to be alive and be a good man. By figuring out the motivations of George Custer, Shane, and the ethics of superheroes, we worked on healing his burnt soul.

Three years ago, I became aware that I was no longer scared of Ryker. He had become easy to sit with. I had grown to like Ryker. He had his moments, but he was no longer scary all the time with everyone. The last year or so, he would walk into the reception area, be good with people, smile more.

The last time I saw Ryker, he was upset and despondent about his two adolescent children. It seems they did go off the rails. Bad peers and stuff. He knows he played a part in their path and how they make choices. He wishes he had never been rough with his son and so permissive with his daughter. One of the truths of his change is that he now knows how awful he was. Ryker feels the sorrow that flows from the life he had lost to his personality disorder.

So what about Ryker, and why is this case about the kind psychologist?

Well, prior to me, Ryker had seen lots of kind people, often women as it happened, likely because women make up most of the caring, and now, psychology workforce. Psychology has recently become a gentle, caring profession; and perhaps stereotypically, this has opened psychology as a woman's career. Or it may have been the other way around? But the assumption that anything not kind is not good therapy is misdirected because kindness is mostly not the active ingredient people need in their therapy.

The term *honest regard* is a much better explanation of the position the good psychologist takes. This stance allows kind gentleness when needed but also authoritative firmness when needed. This stance demonstrates to each client that they can be loved but also held to account in some way. In time and in turn, they will take this model inwards for themselves. The aim is to develop a balance of self-love and self-discipline. The stance of the good psychologist requires ordinariness and authentic engagement, protected from the transference effects from the client. It promotes a healthy therapeutic relationship that accounts for over half the benefit of psychological therapy.

For Ryker, his interactions with psychologists had been spoilt by the transference effect from kind people. Ryker grew up to be overly wary of women. The kindness he got from them as an adult did not feel like kindness. It felt patronising, making him the little boy and the

　　　　JOSHUA THOMAS

psychologist his mum. Each interaction proved his untrustworthiness of women was justified. On the other side of that transference effect, fear and disgust is what I felt when I met Ryker, as I suppose had all other psychologists. But I had to hold my stance of honest regard and resist my natural response to leave him alone and let him suffer.

With Ryker, I have used a case that demonstrates how the capacity of the psychologist to manage and use the transference effect in therapy is clear, even though it is a bit ugly. The trap you, my reader, are more likely to fall into is that you will be nice, the opposite of Ryker. You likely are sensitive to the world around you, sensitive to the needs of your boyfriend, girlfriend, family, and friends. What is it that you do automatically when you meet someone nice, who is sick? You want them to feel better and relieve their distresses. That is what your psychologist might start to do without noticing it or thinking about if it is in your best interest. If they can't point out and discuss things that make you hurt and upset, then how can they really be demonstrating that honest regard for you?

Good psychologists are kind. No, they can be kind and they can be gentle with you. But they must also be straight with you, ordinary, authentic, hold you in regard enough to work hard with you.

If your psychologist is always kind, and you feel great after each session, run away.

THE QUALIFICATION MYTH

True or False?

Your psychologist is properly qualified and competent to provide psychological therapy for your mental difficulties.

I want to say yes, do you?

I HAVE ALREADY EXPRESSED my worries about the parapsychologist—those who practise psychology on you without being a psychologist. Yes, I mean practise because they can't know what they are doing. The Australian Psychology Board has no powers to stop them or insist on any competency. Typically, they are those folk with job titles of mental health worker or similar, divining from the job title that they are both credentialled and have permission to mess with your most important asset: your mind.

That parapsychologist problem can easily be solved by giving them all a month's course in Monopoly. Presumably, then we could give them the job title of moneymaker, and they could look after our superannuation funds with all the skill and expertise of a chartered accountant. I'm being serious!

But this particular qualification myth is about real psychologists, those that can legitimately call themselves that job title. These real psychologists do have both a qualification and permission to mess with your mind, screw you up, deliver bad psych, and make money. But who are they? Who are these real psychologists?

Well, to be honest, they could be a good psychologist and be good at psychology providing good psych. But mostly, they are not. They are what is approved as general psychologist, which I think is an interesting

JOSHUA THOMAS

title. I presume it kind of copies the doctor title, *general practitioner*. Kind of good at everything but not a specialist? And therefore, them being a general psychologist is a good start for you. Or is it?

Anyway, the general psychologist—who are they, and importantly, how did they qualify for that board-approved title?

One way is the recommended way. The psychology board hopes that prospective mind healers will complete a four-year degree in psychology, with honours—that is, a progression from dead-easy psychology, to moderate psychology, to hard psychology. But the board knows that is still not good enough. You are still a baby in your understanding of the human mind and the practice of psychological therapy. And remember, society wants us to be really good at this stuff. So after those four years of undergraduate study, the board wants you to register as a provisional (trainee) psychologist and complete two more years of postgraduate study and practice. On successful completion of the last two years, you can register as a general psychologist and do complex therapy with our most vulnerable and disordered people. You can call yourself a psychologist! And many people do.

That's the path I took to becoming a general psychologist, although I did take a longer road and traverse a few muddy trails along the way. I also spent three years with Benjamin, an analyst of the Jungian kind. There, we delved into the various complexes of my mind and discovered overused, misplaced, and unused capacities. And we made a better, plainer jigsaw of myself. I already had a degree from the University of Western Australia and a decade-long career in organisational development, applied organisational psychology if you like. But I had done little formal reading in psychology. So I went to a university in Burswood and did undergraduate units in various parts of psychology, proudly including developmental psychology.

It was at university where I met, in a face-to-face way, my first general psychologist. He was my worst lecturer. He was supposed to be taking us through Freudian concepts about the unconscious constructs of our mind and how they both instruct and affect behaviour. During a lecture on the 'superego', Freud named the function *super* because, connecting our unconscious and conscious processes, it held us accountable to our deep beliefs, values, and moralities. If you like it produces guilt, shame, pride and stuff like that. This function of our mind helps moderate our base drives by considering our civilised understanding of good and not so good. If you like, it stops me from cheating on my wife or using violence to get my way. Unfortunately, I've done both and carry the associated shame and pride.

Anyway, the lecturer blurted out, 'Why do I have to teach this load of shit? I don't believe that my unconscious mind is doing anything I don't know about.'

I guessed that he didn't want to admit he was only human and has done things he could not stop. The term *goodie-two-shoes* or *psychology clergy* comes to mind. Anyway, that bad lecturer was a general psychologist. In his résumé, it did not include any practice in actual psychological therapy. Let's call him an academic. Would he be helpful to anyone with mental difficulties? No, ironically, he would be that 'load of shit' he blurted out.

After my Jungian therapy and undergraduate work, I completed honours at Deakin University. Now, that was tough. I had to learn and get good at counselling techniques, how the brain worked, and how our autonomic nervous system intersects emotions, thoughts, and behaviours. All sorts of things had to be learnt to a higher level. My maths and research skills had to develop to be top class too. After all, aside from philosophers, we psychologists are the other folk who know how you know. So we have to be really good scientists too! Some of my research from that year was published. It was about body image within women and how circumstances—who they were with, for example—affected how they felt about their body. It turned out that a major driver of concern over their body image was when they were with other women. Who would have thought? Yes, an obvious finding, but most research is set up to

JOSHUA THOMAS

find the obvious because it makes money. Anyway, it was important to get familiar with what good research was and understand what bad research was. That's so I know what works, and what doesn't, and why.

Following honours, I could only be a provisional psychologist, still incompetent and unable to practise therapy with people without a good risk of harm to them. I thought I could do it, but the Australian Psychology Board said not. Anyway, I pressed on and applied for entry into a master's programme either in counselling psychology or in clinical psychology. You see, only those two programmes properly cover the education and practice of psychological therapy. They are both very challenging. One focuses more on therapy formats and types. The other includes a ton of work in formulation and assessment and pharmacology. Swings and roundabouts, I reckon.

My preference would have been for counselling psychology, but the only one near me was clinical, so I did that. The master's programme was gruelling. It was hard work; and we had to demonstrate practical competence in front of assessors, not just through exams. In one assessment, phase I remember half of the class failing the first time around. There were tears, tantrums, and complaints that month. Apparently, hardly anyone had failed any part of their study so far, which is an indication that it had been far too easy. Anyway, completing that two-year Master of Clinical Psychology programme just got me to general psychologist. Ouch, that is a lot of learning and practice just to get a basic ticket. But now, after six years of study, I at least could start working and earning a living. I was, at the time, very short on cash. Some weeks, no cash.

Now, on reflection of that time, I realise I did not know what I did not know. In my fourth year of study, I was not ready; but I didn't agree until I'd finished my sixth year. The board was right to hold me back and insist on being competent and expert in therapy before they let me loose on gullible and vulnerable clients. So it does seem that your psychologist is properly qualified and competent to provide psychological therapy for your mental illness.

<u>**Case of Anne**</u>

Anne was referred to me by her GP for help with anxiety. That is all the GP wrote on the referral, which is actually fine. But in the printout listing of previous conditions were three other instances of anxiety, one just eight months earlier. The associated K-10 screening measure indicated severe mental distress. Anne likely was not in good shape.

Anne presented dressed casually, overweight and a little unkempt, with hair not brushed, looking very tired. Appeared stated age of 32. Anne was shaking as I closed the door behind us. She was hyperventilating, trying to stay in the room and become calm. I suggested we go for a walk around the block and chat about what was happening to her. Rapport was satisfactory. Anne was having trouble holding herself together, but we were able to walk around the block and back into my rooms. Stated mood as awful, saying she was depressed and hopeless, and this was her first day outside her house since booking the appointment five days earlier. Speech normal, thought process focused on not panicking, talking mostly about this getting worse every week. Nil sensory disorder, nil delusion, hallucinations. Memory seeming mostly intact. Inadequate insight. Knew she was getting worse, not able to understand her role in that. Judgement fair. Some suicidal ideation but nil intent.

Background

Anne told me that she had a history of being a worrier, mostly about how people judged her or if they liked her. She said it was apparent at high school where she said she was very shy and quiet. But it had gotten better when she left school and got her first real job in a retail shop. Anne said she met her husband when she was 24, and they were married two years later. She fell pregnant when she was 28 and now has a 3-year-old girl.

Anne said her life should be good as she has everything she wants: a supportive husband and a new family. But Anne explained that she put on weight whilst pregnant; and after her girl was born, she found it hard to lose. She felt embarrassed about her body and started to notice comments about how she still had to get her pre-baby body back.

Anne said she felt like that schoolgirl again. She worried a lot and became more shy around people, often saying no to offers of going out and meeting up with people. She said she feels quite lonely now as she gets asked less to go out. Two good friends come around each week to her house, often with the shopping done, which makes it easier, she said.

Anne said that about a year ago, she experienced a panic attack at the shopping centre. She was coming out of the checkout when she saw a friend walking into the shop. Anne explained that she tried to look the other way and hide behind others, but she got scared. She said she felt crazy but had to leave the shopping behind as she got out of the shops and into the street, where she was able to calm down. That day, she knew she had to see the doctor.

Anne told me that she was prescribed anti-anxieties (medication) and referred to a psychologist. She said that over two months, the psychologist helped her learn mindfulness and how to combat negative thoughts. I asked her how that helped; and Anne said it did, especially at home where she could practise her mindfulness, be calm, and replace negative thoughts with good thoughts. I asked her how it helped with her embarrassment with others judging her. It hadn't. In fact, Anne told me that she had gone to the shops again a few times. Made herself go. But each time, it got the better of her. She quickly got panicky and had to go home. After all, she said, I'm still overweight and people are going to look.

Anne started to cry and said that now she doesn't even like to get in the car and go anywhere. If she does, she gets jittery, short of breath, and feels like she is out of control. Anne said that even after psychology, she went backwards.

Now, sitting still with Anne, I spent some time discussing her objectives, such as getting her life back and shopping with a smile on her face. She also wanted to lose weight to get back to a more natural range for her. Following the psychoeducation about anxiety that Anne deserved, we explored the parasympathetic and sympathetic nervous systems and learnt to trick them into turning up and down.

We did do thought management via socratic questioning and thought cards to develop alternative streams of thought and behaviour that Anne could test for reasonableness. For example, Anne, although embarrassed, decided to talk to her husband about her extra weight and ask for any help he wanted to offer. She also made up some cards to manage thoughts whilst being at the shops.

Mostly, though, we worked through exposure therapy, allowing her fear and alarm systems to become distressed at the shops, then waiting, practising calming, reading some of her cards, until calming started. Then she could stop and either stay to do the shopping or go elsewhere for fun. We did that one with measures of distress and calming many times. Actually, until Anne got quite bored with it. Did you know that when you're bored, it is hard to be panicky?

At the same time, Anne told her friends to stop making it too safe for her by coming around, especially doing her shopping. Things started to change quickly for Anne. After three weeks, she was back shopping, feeling confident she would not get panicky. Anne had already started to lose weight with her husband's involvement in food selection and reduction of drinking in the evening. Instead, they walked each evening with their daughter.

Anne's anxiety disorder had not been helped by the previous psychologist. In reality, that psychologist had created a worsening of symptoms. Bad psych. Not on purpose, but because they did not know enough, did not know how therapy works or which therapy to apply. How can that be? They weren't a parapsychologist; they were a board-approved general psychologist. They had done their six years of study and practice to a demonstrated level of competence.

Well, every psychologist's credentials that count towards their registration are listed on the Australian Health Practitioner Regulation Agency register of practitioners. Simply click and view. You can see them and check their recency, course content, and such. Anyway, Anne's psychologist had attained general registration, not the same way as intended but through a convenient loophole. It turns out that many general psychologists never studied personality, neuropsychology, cognitive psychology, emotional processing, assessment, pathology, aetiology, symptoms, diagnosis, or therapy. I find that quite astonishing as the board is very concerned about the public good. Nevertheless, it is true. Now, for Anne, this mattered a lot.

True or False?

Your psychologist knows how psychological therapy works.

I want to say yes, do you?

Let's look at what the psychologist provided for Anne. I know there is some, but limited, evidence for mindfulness being useful for anxiety.

But I'm not sure what was the mindfulness actually delivered in therapy, and I did not ask Anne. For many, it is a help for relaxation, take your mind off your worries and focus on something tangible—'being in the moment'. For other psychologists, it is a sophisticated process to build an observing self that can see and understand what is happening but remain unharmed.

I have a friend who says it is her iPhone app. It apparently dings every now and then, interrupts what she was thinking, so she can notice the ding? Hmmm, she is a psychologist too. And I was part of a group therapy programme that used to ding the 'gong' at the start of quiet time. Makes me laugh a bit to think of that. If only it was that simple to treat a runaway anxiety disorder.

Anyway, my main problem for Anne is that she was practising both mindfulness and thought control. They are contradictory therapies working against each other. How to confuse a mind? Give it two opposite ways to solve a problem! Or we can politely call it eclectic therapy, where anything goes.

Maybe mindfulness was working? I don't know, but I doubt it. The psychologist was also having Anne capture negative thoughts and replace them with positive thoughts. Many general psychologists *know* that is a good idea and teach it to their clients. I can tell you that is not in any therapy—zilch! It is simply a common but serious mistake in the application of cognitive behaviour therapy.

I suspect it would work when Anne was at home. She could pretend to have negative thought whist she pretended to be at the shopping centre. Then Anne could make a pretend positive thought about the same pretend circumstance. She could then pretend to be doing much better. But no, it turns out the general psychologist did not know what they were doing. And the pretending they did, did not actually work!

JOSHUA THOMAS

Bluntly, I've not yet met a general psychologist who I would have confidence in treating severe anxiety. It is a body-mind dilemma and an awful and complicated disorder. It takes the hard work of the client guided by a psychologist who learnt and applies good therapy—that is, someone who knows what they are doing!

I know Anne's previous psychologist did not understand the aetiology, physiology, and maintaining factors of anxiety disorders. They absolutely had no understanding of how the therapies worked. As it happened, I knew the psychologist and had seen them practise, and I was aware of their learning path to become a general psychologist. They had completed a bachelor of arts, a diploma in psychology, and a master of community psychology.

I've already explained and admitted that the bachelor's degree gets you nowhere in your understanding of psychology, especially psychological therapy. It gives you some foundation material, but you end up knowing that you know very little. After all, it is not like maths or science or english that is taught in high school in years eight, nine, ten, eleven, and twelve. The first years of university study teach you the equivalent educational difficulty of high school. It is just not very hard at all. As a consequence, and I being a bit cynical, undergraduate psychology is very popular. And remember the adage 'Cs get degrees'? That obvious university truth is that you only have to get basic passes to end up with a bachelor's degree. In reality, knowing about half of the stuff taught will get you your degree. In the case of undergraduate psychology, half of very little.

Then there's the neat sidestep people can take, the convenient loophole. It tuns out that you don't need to complete the two-year master's programmes that do hard yards in the pathology and therapy for mental disorders. That's right. You don't need to understand mental illness at all or learn or practise any psychological therapy. You can simply turn left and do a number of other nontherapy-related courses. Studying community psychology, organisational psychology, or health psychology will automatically qualify you to apply for general psychologist registration. Wow.

Am I saying that your general psychologist approved by the psychology board, ticked as okay to work with your mind and make buckets of money, might not know anything? Yes.

That general psychologist is now approved for doing therapy to unsuspecting clients, who rightly presume they are properly trained to the standard the profession proclaims. But they are not. Another crock of shit.

They have been able to get access to a lucrative job, providing psychological therapy, often fully funded by the government at around $90 per hour. Some general psychologists work eight clients a day five days per week and charge $150 per session. That can be $4,000 per week after costs. And money, of course, is an ultimate incentive.

It's just annoying that folk can earn this amount when they can't do the job properly. I have to moderate this by saying that some general psychologists get their qualifications and registration this easy way but go on to become good psychologists. But many don't; and how can you, the unsuspecting client, know the difference?

Your psychologist is qualified and competent because they are registered?

Nope. Definitely not!

THE PRIVACY MYTH

True or False?

What is said in the therapy room is private, between the two of you. So it is safe to talk openly.

I want to say yes, do you?

I T SEEMS SUCH a long time ago when the biggest thing on people's minds was the government's centralised medical record system. Should you opt out? Does it matter? What is privacy for anyway? Does it matter that another health professional can see my records? Well, we were assured, and are assured, that our privacy remains intact. That they are our records and the information will be used to our advantage. Certainly, a big part of psychological therapy is the privacy of information shared in the room, the safe place, the place where you can safely talk truthfully. Without that assurance, secrecy if you like, how could we speak of our demons? In therapy, your personal and private information remains safe. Psychologists, especially, adopt strong ethical boundaries to look after you.

Well, I can tell you that at least for medical information, your information is spread far and wide as a normal practice. Most of my referrals from doctors include your history, whether or not it is related to your current mental dilemma. I had one referral for a woman who wanted some help for her parenting anxiety (yes, that is a real thing!). She worried a lot and was arguing with her ex-husband over ways of helping her daughters overcome persistent emotional problems. Rather than bring her daughters to me, she wisely thought that the best help for her children was her. And that meant sifting through all the poor advice she was getting from an ill-informed family and an adversarial ex-husband. I introduced a good parenting model to her, and we practised in my rooms.

She would go home and practise, rate herself on improvement, and come along the next week. As her confidence grew, her anxiety resolved, and her parenting became more effective. Kids can pick a nervous mum, you know. Anyway, it was enjoyable therapy, helping out a mum and family like that. Oh, I forgot to tell you that the referral indicated that this mum had suffered from acne, slipped disc, and streptococcal infection. Why did I need to know that? I did not. It is simply part of most doctor's systems that they print out everything of your history without your clear permission. Interesting, isn't it?

But luckily, your mental information, sick mind, disorder, personality quirk, craziness, dark past, failed life, abuse, and harms are safe with the psychologist. Well, not quite.

<u>Case of Mary</u>

During my time as principal psychologist at the small business I established in 2013, I've had many requests for 'patient's files'. Some from the public-system parapsychologists who want to know the background of clients I'd worked with. Some from lawyers, some from insurance companies, and, of course, from the clients themselves.

One day I got a subpoena for Mary's files, a client I had been working with for a few months. It was from her husband's lawyers. Mary had told me that he was seeking to have her declared as unfit to parent her three girls. Mary said that their legal conflict had escalated since she filed for divorce after leaving him earlier in the year. I'd been working with Mary to help resolve emotional harm caused by what I unfashionably call battered-wife syndrome. In many ways, she was not the best parent that she could be at this time; and she knew it. After all, her mind was scattered, hypervigilant, enduringly scared of him. But he was not living far enough away, and Mary had to interact with him often because of the child-sharing arrangement figured out by dumb lawyers.

When I started therapy with Mary, she was quite a mess. Her mental state exam, in my notes, was as follows:

Mary presented in her workclothes, tall, athletic build, kempt. Looking state age of 36. Rapport difficult to establish, eye movements to the door and windows, flustered motor activity, jittery and unsettled. Stated mood as good. Affect incongruent with mood with rapid change. Nervous, then smiling, then teary. Smiling with laughs of embarrassment whist telling her awful circumstances having recently left her husband. Speech pressured, few gaps, little silence. Thought processes circular and tangential, repeating herself, changing topics with little linkage. Content mostly about her being very busy, doing daily chores, her work, and her children's timetable. Memory mostly intact, Mary says she has lost her memory, telling me, 'I can't remember anything these days,' but no evidence of that. Nil perception difficulties, delusion, or hallucinations obvious. Insight difficult to determine, judgement difficult to determine. Mary found it hard to answer questions about her life and state of mind succinctly.

During our assessment phase, Mary explained that she met her husband in her twenties following the breakup of a year-long relationship with an older man. She had done well at school, finishing her HSC; and Mary said that if a university had of been nearby, she would have studied teaching. In any case, she stayed in town and met this older man through school friends. She told me that although now it seems silly, at the time, she really loved him, and they had a good relationship. Mary said the breakup came when they started talking about the long term. She wanted children of her own, and he did not want any more children. So they parted ways.

Mary explained that she met her current husband because she was very good at netball, and he was very good at football. Living in a regional area, these clubs shared facilities. Mary said it was common for footballers and netballers to date because they all knew each other.

She said that on her second date with her future husband, she was with a group of other young women; and as a group, they went over to a group of footballers. Her future husband was at the bar getting some drinks and talking to some other men.

Mary explained that a man started flirting with her a little and pulled her dress strap down off her shoulder. She moved away back to the safety of the group of girls. She said her future husband saw what happened, and he walked towards her. She thought to stand next to her and be protective. But instead, he stood within a few feet of her and shouted at her for being a slut, flirting on their second date. Mary said he threw his pot of beer just past her, with the glass shattering over the clubroom floor.

Mary said that everyone around her moved away, and no one stood up for her. She told me that she remembers feeling an intense mix of fear and shame. She was scared, but she blamed herself for talking to the other man. Later in the carpark, he again told her that she was a slut, flirting like that, and pushed her across the car bonnet. Mary said that she went home with him that night and tried to make him happy, make things okay. She said she had been doing that for fifteen years.

During the months of therapy, Mary explained that her estranged husband would 'accidentally' cross paths with them at a park. He would play with the children and then send some nonverbal intimidating message to her. She told me that he had recently attended a series of school meetings because he could. And in the quiet corridors, he baited her in front of the children on how stupid she was, how unfaithful she was, and how he should take the kids away. The very next day, she might have to leave the children with him because of the child share roster, four days with her, then three with him, rotating.

JOSHUA THOMAS

Mary told me that the children had walked home at night back to her house on three occasions because they were upset about their dad drinking and shouting at them. She said that her husband normally drank every night after work; and the more he drank, the more worried she would be about the children.

Mary had left her husband, but the danger had not passed. It had worsened. Mary told me during one difficult session how he had pushed her into the window with one hand around her neck, swearing that he would kill her if she left him. Another time, he had pressed her into the lounge chair by her head—so hard that she couldn't breathe. She told me that this violence started on their second date when she was just 20 years old. She was now in her midthirties. She could not give me a count of the number of physical alterations against her. She had lost count. But now, she was trying to escape, with all the dangers that come with, including having a court take your children off you.

Her mind was awful. Damaged, sick, and disordered. Symptoms of anxiety were severe; depression measures indicated moderate symptoms. Positively, she was holding down a new job, paying her way, and caring for her children. I don't know how because my notes describe her mind as 'severely disorganised'. Certainly not in a fit state to bring up two children in an optimal way. To assist with the assessment, I'd completed a number of appropriate measures, one for PTSD, a diagnosis that well matched her multiple difficulties. I also worked with Mary to create genograms, family trees if you like, that helped explain her predisposition to accept blame more easily than others. We also explored how her tendency to be warm to and permissive of others might be problematic in her personal life, also in her parenting style.

In my notes, there is more but not all that Mary had said or experienced. That's because I don't write down everything. Notetaking can get in the way of listening, feeling, thinking, and participating. Anyway, my notes are objectively damaging to any case of her being fit as a good parent. Of course, my notes also include damning insights into her husband's cruelty. But Mary could not give an instance where he had been cruel to the children. Tellingly, he is very well liked and respected, has great references and resources to draw upon. His mind is not frazzled. He can think with stealth, with his goal in mind.

Mary told me his case against her was that she was psychologically unwell, emotionally unstable. She actually was and had been for 15 years. Years of doctor appointments and medications show it to be true. But Mary had never disclosed her horrible life to anyone, never made a police report, never left home, or ran away. Rather, in her private and public life, she had maintained his lie that they were a happy family. Her accusations against him now had little substance in objective evidence. Mary told me that his defence against her accusations was that she was emotionally unstable and was motivated to lie.

Anyway, when I got the summons, I spoke to Mary and asked what she wanted me to do. After all, I was working for her, and she was my concern because I'd agreed to be her psychologist. You can probably guess that Mary said, 'You decide.' My response was 'Mary, you are really bad at asking for help. You are extra good at self-sacrificing. Your mind is sick from the 15 years of being a hostage and victim to a mean man. But if you want my help, you will need to figure out what help you want and ask me for it.' Three days later, she popped in after work and asked for my help both about dealing with the court case and about finishing off her escape. We chatted for an hour or so. I was quite late home that night.

A few days later, I got an email from Mary's lawyers seeking an expert report on their client's psychological state, how it was caused, any maintaining factors, and prognosis of therapy. They also asked for my opinion on her capacity to parent her two children. I wrote that report, it was straightforward. I had done a thorough assessment, completed psychometrics, provided a diagnosis, sought supervision over the case from my peers, and I was fluent in the criteria for understanding the needs of the child. Mary could not afford to pay, but that seemed fine at the time. After all, I can self-sacrifice too when people sincerely ask for my help.

The report I wrote became a subject of challenge during the court case, and I was asked to speak to it and provide other expert advice. During cross-examination by the husband's well-paid lawyers, I fielded a series of attacks on my credentials, my experience, and my motivations. Being a good psychologist, I had good and appropriate answers, including that Mary did not pay any money for the report. Then they provided me a copy of a report on my report. Their report on my report—I hope you're following this—had cost Mary's husband a lot of money. And it was overtly critical of my assessment process, and therefore any conclusions. Their report had been written by a professor of psychology with an impressive list of achievements, especially in forensic psychology. He'd been on this-and-that committee and was a lecturer at a big university, and he was well published. I was just a lowly clinical psychologist. The judge looked at me and asked me to respond to their report. I felt fearful for myself, sensing a glimpse of Mary's eternal state of mind.

I was allocated only a few minutes to read his report. He had many hours to read mine, so it was never going to be a fair arm-wrestle. I pointed that out to the judge. She simply said, 'Mr Thomas, you are here as an expert in psychology. You will not need much time to read that report and give us your response.' Hmm . . . got me. So I calmed myself and read his assessment process. How exactly did he assess my methodology? Also, I considered, was he a good psychologist? I noticed myself not liking him, but I had to use confidence, not disdain. My response was in three parts, quickly put together on my feet, so to speak.

Firstly, I pointed out that I was well trained in psychometrics and the validity and reliability of processes and that I could not see any note in this professor's report as to his direct observation of my assessment process—that is, he was not there to see what and how I did my work. I noted that a simple phone call from him to me, and I could have explained in detail how I had completed the assessment. Given he was missing the most important information he needed, his report lacks validity. I pointed out that, comparatively, I had directly observed my client over eight separate occasions, thereby increasing the validity and reliability of my processes.

Secondly, I noted that of his exhaustive list of achievements, none referred to any work in therapy or pathology—that is, he may be good at forensic psychology, even report writing, but is he any good at mental pathology? If not, then is he able to comment with any authority on my processes? Lastly, I suggested that the professor was motivated to write a critical report rather than an objective one. The judge told me off for suggesting biased motivation. But I pointed out that motivation does matter and that I had noticed he had not reported on the obvious thoroughness of my work.

I thanked my lucky stars that the professor was not in the room and was not on the expert witness list to appear. Going home on the train, I felt that I'd held up the flag for good psychologists and their clients, especially those doing good therapy.

JOSHUA THOMAS

Cutting to the chase, Mary was awarded primary custody of her children and her husband was visited by the police. And when we ended our therapy, she had regained some of her mind.

But why is this about privacy?

Well, it just is, isn't it? I wrote an objective report that helped Mary's defence. I explained the symptoms of battered-wife syndrome. And I made a compelling case of how she makes a good parent—she does—now and in the future. On the other hand, I did not provide my notes to the husband's lawyers. I provided a very redacted version that omitted significant private and personal information that Mary had provided me in the course of therapy.

I decided that Mary's mental state examination was private and personal information, so that never went in. To me, my description of her severely disorganised mind was private and personal information, so that never went in. And so on. Basically, they got a list of appointments and therapy formats. I imagine they were quite disappointed. Of course, I never mentioned to them that the notes were redacted.

So this is really an ethical question. What would you do if you were a good psychologist? What would you want if you were Mary? It is a question that each good psychologist will consider prior to meeting you and then forever afterwards. I'm not sure about parapsychologists and psychologists in public health. Your public health unit record number means that the thousands of people with the right logon ID can see and use your personal and private information.

I've spent time in public hospital triage and community health. In both environments, your details, history, and presumed truths are on display and accessed by anyone curious enough. And I promise you, people are more curious than you imagine! Thankfully, a good psychologist won't conform to 'session-record procedures', 'form filling' and completing of 'templates' that collect and spread your personal and private information. The good psychologist has more respect for you, the person, the unique individual we have the privilege to know and understand.

My experience, though, is the opposite. Psychologists, for whatever reason, are fearful of looking after their clients' personal and private information or are simply compliant with the bureaucracy. When asked by any insurance company or lawyer, the bad psychologist simply prints out or photocopies or emails and sends their records and notes. In the public system, it is worse because the psychologist's notes become public property. Psychologists simply can't protect their clients' personal and private information. This is what we call a third-party ethical dilemma. Does your psychologist's boss own the notes about you? Or the does the insurance company? Or DHS? Or Headspace? Or the lawyer? Not if you are working with a good psychologist.

Simply put, only the good psychologist will protect you; otherwise, you are put second to the fears or motivations of the parapsychologist or bad psychologist. They will give your info away in the blink of an eye and justify it by saying it's the rules. A good psychologist is confident in knowing when to act outside of the rules to look after you.

Make it your rule to insist that the psychologist protects your privacy. Demand it from them. They can all do it if they are brave and independent enough. And if they can't, make a formal complaint and then walk away.

JOSHUA THOMAS

THE TREATMENT-IS-THERAPY MYTH

True or False?

The treatment you get for your troubled mind is psychological therapy.

I want to say yes, do you?

YOU KNOW THAT when I get a headache that lasts a while, I might reach for the Panadol. Panadol is the brand name, and the treatment is the dose of paracetamol in the tablets I take. It is simple to understand. The treatment matches my illness. It is the same for psychological treatments. You have a mental disorder (illness), you seek out a matching treatment. And most of the time, what works for me works for you.

Do a quick internet search for psychological treatment or just jump to your friendly Beyond Blue, private clinic, or public hospital website. You will find a plethora of what are called psychological treatments. Sometimes they are called treatments, sometimes interventions, sometimes therapies. But to you, the ordinary good person, they mean help from a psychologist or risky help from a parapsychologist. Often, you will find them linked to a specific disorder. For example, eating disorders might have a treatment called cognitive behaviour therapy enhanced for eating disorders (CBT-E). Sometimes they are just brand names and don't even mention the treatment type. LEAP, for example, is a private hospital's inpatient treatment for people with eating disorders.

Most treatments are therapy styles, defined by their theories, protocols, and stages. For example, IPT is interpersonal therapy and is defined by your thorough analysis and relearning of your capacity to engage in and work relationships. Sometimes treatments are psychotropic drugs that affect the availability or potency of neurotransmitters.

Neurotransmitters are chemicals made in neurons to transmit messages within the brain. For example, some drugs retard the natural reuptake of serotonin from within the synaptic cleft. By doing so, they artificially make more serotonin available to the dendrites on adjacent nerve cells, likely making those cells fire more often.

It is really cool that there are so many treatments. I certainly can't count them on two hands. According to a Beyond Blue pamphlet, there are around sixty just for depression, and they are listed by some senior folk who know what they are doing. Oh my god, we're so lucky to have a plethora of treatments for depression. Does that sound right to you? Sixty treatments, interventions, or whatever they choose to call them for the one illness?

Case of Michelle

Michelle was referred to me by her GP for persistent depression and anxiety. When we get these referrals, we feel confident that we will figure out what to do that helps. After all, they are our bread and butter, most common, although often our most challenging.

Mental State

Michelle presented looking stated age of 40. Kempt, dressed neatly, moderately overweight. Trembling leg and knee on left side. Rapport was difficult to attain with Michelle mostly concerned about what treatment and strategies I would provide to give her relief. Mood stated as depressed, affect congruent with mood, distressed and worried. Speech normal. Thought processes goal-oriented, fused with an awful feeling of sadness, loneliness. Thought content mostly about relief from depression and worrying all the time. Said life not worth living if no relief. Nil perception abnormality, nil evidence of delusion or hallucination. Memory seeming intact. Insight fair understood mental disorder. Judgement good, suicidal ideation present but no intent.

Background

Michelle explained to me that she periodically experiences awful depression. Four or five times per year. She said the depression was always just under the surface, and she needs a strategy that works to keep it there.

Michelle told me that she was married with three children, financially well-off, and that life should be good. She described being estranged from her dad since early childhood, and growing up meant always helping her mum and siblings who seemed to have ongoing difficulties. Michelle explained that her mum was permanently on antidepressants, and her dad also likely had depression.

She said that as a teenager, she had boyfriends but started a long-term relationship when she was 19 years of age. Michelle explained that he was emotionally controlling and physically abusive to her and described several fearful, life-threatening events involving that abuse. For example, at her birthday party, he had dragged her by the hair into a room and then shouted at her because she had embarrassed him. Michell said she stayed with him for three years because he loved her, and she wanted that love more than she feared him. She said that she eventually left and was fine being single for a while. Then she met her current husband, who was much different, kinder, although he had his issues with depression, which meant he was often emotionally unavailable to Michelle, especially for her persistent sadness and loneliness.

Michelle described a happier period of her life, building the family she wanted. Michelle told me that she never felt like a natural mother and did not have that maternal instinct all other mothers have. Following her third child, Michelle said she experienced a severe period of depression; and although she had felt depressed before, she put this episode down to postnatal depression.

She explained that the depression further eroded her confidence in being able to give her children the warmth that they needed from her. Michelle explained that when they need her love and attention, it felt overwhelming and draining, making her connection artificial. Still, she has provided well for them, building up her business and helping in her husband's. Michelle told me her girls have gone to good schools, travelled the world, and have everything they need. She understood that her girls, especially one of them, acted spoilt and needy and that perhaps her parenting had been on the permissive side.

Michelle told me that she takes antidepressants daily and diazepam some nights each week. She had been on these medications for over five years. Michelle also explained that she had seen a number of doctors, counsellors, and psychologists who had treated her for her depression and anxiety, but her mental health difficulties remained a constant in her life.

She was asking me for 'strategies' to keep her depression under control.

Okay, obviously, there is more to Michelle's depression and anxiety than her symptoms. Let's frame four important questions:

1. What can you see in this woman's life experiences that predispose her to depression and anxiety?
2. Can you see any precipitating factors, things that triggered or retrigger her mental difficulties?
3. In her story, what is it that keeps the cycle of depression and anxiety intact, coming back again and again?
4. Sitting back, are you able to imagine her inner strengths, perhaps external supports?

Do you think any of that matters? Presumably, I could, like many psychologists, simply ask Michelle to pick from Beyond Blue's list of sixty treatments that work. Well, actually no.

     JOSHUA THOMAS

In my humble opinion, Beyond Blue and all the other claimants of treatments and interventions are wrong. All those hospitals, parapsychologists, doctors, private programmes, and businesses selling treatments are wrong. There are only four treatments that work for depression—in fact, for all mental disorders. Four! There is therapy, drug taking, electronic, and just waiting to get better. Of these, only one works well for most people most of the time. And that's because that treatment addresses all the four questions above. If any remain uninvestigated, unresolved, then Michelle will perhaps get 'relief'. But that relief will be temporary, fleeting, and Michelle will know that.

Michelle will come to know falsely that she has 'depression' or 'anxiety'. Treatments and strategies being the lie, the falsehood, the dog whistle of false hope from moneymakers, money savers and do-gooders that promote their institutions. Treatments, interventions, and strategies are not therapy.

Anyway, in my room, I explained to Michelle that therapy was my offered 'strategy' because I don't prescribe drugs or wave around electronic mechanisms stimulating brain cells. Neither do I electrocute brain cells to shock them into a mode where they provide artificial and temporary relief. I explained that she had become stuck, living her life a long distance from the one she was designed to live. The bigger the difference, the more symptoms.

I remember her being quite confused. After all, every one of her previous counsellors had treated her with CBT or IPT or mindfulness therapy or exposure therapy or behavioural therapy. 'Aren't there lots of different strategies that you can give me?' Michelle asked. Well no, there aren't lots of different strategies, except on the radio, TV, and pamphlets.

Each differently named therapy or named strategy is just a part of proper therapy. They are best thought of as 'bits'. CBT is a bit of psychological therapy. IPT is a bit of psychological therapy. Art therapy is a bit of psychological therapy, behavioural activation is a bit of psychological therapy, and EMDR is a bit of psychological therapy. Therefore, they can all be a bit useful, but none are sufficient for most people most of the time. Certainly, they are not a list to trust as things that work.

That is why most people don't get better. That's right. Most people stay sick. Remember the graphs at the start of the book? Shall I go on?

If we were to attempt a Venn diagram of what therapy looks like, it would look a bit like a bunch of poached eggs laid across one another. When someone or some institution tells you they have a treatment, what they really mean is one poached egg, a bit therapy—some bit that has been picked out to make it more, well, easier for them.

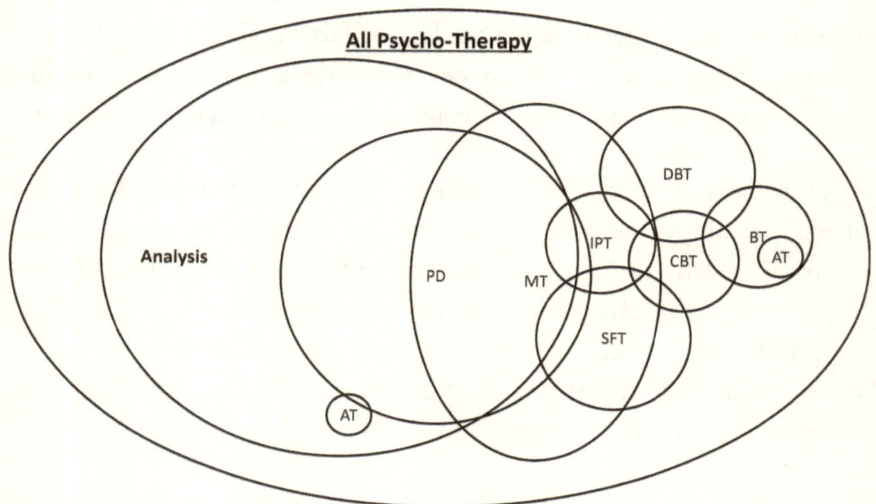

AT = art therapy, PD = psychodynamic, MT = mentalisation, IPT = interpersonal therapy, SFT = schema therapy, CBT = cognitive behaviour therapy, BT = behaviour therapy

In this Venn diagram, I'm trying to arrange logically what can't really be arranged logically. Psychotherapy will always break the boundaries of logic, which is just one way of thinking and knowing.

I've put analysis at the far left. It overlaps psychodynamic psychotherapy but also includes art therapy. Notice how art therapy can sit in behavioural therapy too. Why not? But the takeaway is that when

   JOSHUA THOMAS

someone or some institution tells you they provide dialectic behaviour therapy (DBT), for example, you automatically know they are providing you some particular poached egg. There is a lot more therapy left out than included in DBT. That is why if you join a DBT programme, you might get better, but you might not get well. There is a big difference.

To use a fruit analogy, eat that pink lady apple—yum. Have you eaten a fruit? Well, yes, you have, but one bit of fruit, actually a part of a part of a fruit. It's exactly like that. There is a lot more fruit out there than in the pink lady apple. And you likely need more than an apple a day to stay sane.

Why have we done this cut and slice of therapy? Well, it is to make it more sensate or information based. And more thinking based, less involved with intuition and feelings, perhaps perversely, more scientific. The first people to demand this were insurance companies, and they have lots of money to save. They only want to pay for something that can be counted (information based) and time limited (fixed decisions). And people just like you are more inclined to pay more money for something more tangible, time limited, and branded. You need fruit, but you buy four pink lady apples, perhaps prepacked and prewrapped.

These treatments are akin to bad cookie cutting, where you have all the dough but cut out one neat circle so it fits into your very neat round tray. Making cookie-cutter treatments was never based upon being better for you. It just suits their trays.

And, unfortunately, modern folk like to do something called reduction— that is, getting very curious and then obsessed with the parts of things, forgetting the whole. Once we find that part, we really enjoy seeing what's inside that part, the parts of the part, often done under the banner of research. I can easily make you laugh with an example that shows just how far we go reducing things to meaningless but profitable dribble.

This is true. 'Research' has found that the stimulation of brain cells with magnetism can reduce the symptoms of depression. They have given this an important name, transcranial magnetic stimulation, so it has a nice Martian-like TLA (TMS). Now TMS has become big business with people using your private insurance premiums to both sell and access this new treatment for depression. I've had three clients who had previously or concurrently undergone TMS. Below is their combined description of the TMS treatment.

TMS (Transcranial Magnetic Stimulation) Treatment

You go into a private hospital, and you can stay for up to five days or come and go to suit yourself. They measure your depression before the treatment and again afterwards. You are provided with information about TMS and how it helps you. A doctor in neurology administers the treatment daily over five days. It does not hurt and takes no effort on your part. You repeat this for up to five weeks.

For each treatment, you will be seated in a reclining chair and mostly asked to wear earplugs. Then an electromagnetic coil is placed against your head and switched on and off to provide brain-stimulating pulses. The doctor tunes the amount of magnetism for you by turning it up until you start to feel your fingers twitch. Then it continues its work for around 40 minutes. Afterwards, you can stay around in the private hospital, eat, watch TV, and get a good night's sleep. Or if your insurance does not stretch to that, you can drive home.

Importantly, the doctor will explain that relief may take a few weeks of treatment. Also, if the treatment does not fully resolve your depression or if the symptoms come back, you can repeat the treatment with no known side effects.

The doctor will also tell you that they are 'unclear' on how this all works.

They tell you that they will bill your health fund directly, so few out-of-pocket costs for you.

　　　　JOSHUA THOMAS

Here we are, TMS. Usually, a man doing little but holding a magnetic coil, stimulating your brain with magnetism. Directly affecting the internals of your nerve cell's body, dendrites, axons, and perhaps the neurotransmitters themselves. We are at the microlevel, the smallest particles of our brain, trying to control and coerce the very atoms that breathe consciousness into our lives. It is truly wonderful. No need to know why you're depressed, no need to change behaviours, and no need to heal any internal dilemma. And when you study this treatment, you can be statistically 95 per cent confident that some people with some depression have some of their symptoms reduced sometimes.

But unless we are completely mad, we have forgotten something, haven't we? Are we completely unaware that going outside and walking in fresh air stimulates your brain cells? As will swimming, shopping, talking to Dad, watching a serious movie, cooking your dinner, and doing a day's work? Not only that, but psychological therapy that included you walking in the fresh air for 40 minutes per day five days per week for four weeks would have the same or greater effect. You would likely also build some good behavioural habits, feel good about your accomplishment, maybe buy a dog, meet a friend, and get some pleasure looking in folk's gardens or rubbish bins or stealing some figs. But no, quite a lot of doctors would prefer they stimulated your brain with a machine instead of real life.

Crock of shit, isn't it?

I really do wonder why. Perhaps they are mad as I presupposed. Maybe you are too. Perhaps it's the $1,000 repeat business model. What I'm pointing out is that TMS is not a psychological treatment. At best, it is a 'strategy' mostly for those that don't actually want to resolve intrapersonal dilemma and change how they experience the world. Unfortunately, psychology has fallen into reductionism, looking at smaller and smaller and then even smaller parts until you're working with a Petri dish, not a person.

By definition, all treatments are reductive because they focus on particular elements of our psyche. For example, cognitive therapies focus on your disordered reasoning, the theory being that you are incorrect in your observation and evaluation of information being received. Your thinking is disordered, and that directly affects levels of fear and mood, the neuroses of anxiety and depression.

Each cognitive therapy session investigates how you observe and evaluate situations. You become, if you like, your best scientist, illuminated and guided by the bright and clear-thinking psychologist. Because this is a very structured process, it is easy to measure, research, and evaluate its benefits. And sure enough, just like TMS, it works for some people some of the time. It was always going to work a bit; cognitions are, after all, a bit of the psyche. But they are just a bit.

So we have room for more treatments or, more honestly, more separate rooms of treatment. If cognitive therapies work via cognitions, then behavioural therapies work via behaviours. Sure enough, what we do happens to be part of our psyche. It turns out that doing things brings consequences, experiences if you like. If those consequences reduce our distress or make things easier or bring a reward, then we tend to do more of those things that brought about the consequences. If the things we do bring distress or don't bring us rewards, then we tend to do less of those things, the theory being that we learn by doing or not doing. It is actually called learning theory.

For example, withdrawing from ordinary activity can be learnt by avoiding doing things that bring distress, like getting to work when we are tired. In fact, most things we do bring distress of some form. Effort is distress if you don't feel like doing any work. In behaviour therapy, you will investigate what you do and what you avoid and the consequences of that. You will practise doing less of what makes you depressed and more of what makes you feel useful.

JOSHUA THOMAS

And, sure enough, just like TMS and cognitive therapy, behavioural therapy works for some people some of the time. It was always going to work. After all, what we do is a bit of our psyche. But just a bit. But don't forget that just like TMS and CT, behavioural therapy doesn't work for most. People tend to stay relatively unwell because it is just a bit—a bit of therapy that leaves out huge portions of other potent therapy.

I could explain the same for every one of the sixty treatments listed by Beyond Blue or those provided by your eating disorder clinic or your institution's parapsychologist. Or your local yoga centre for that matter. Yes, yoga is proven to help relieve symptoms of depression. Kind of obvious when we understand that yoga is a behaviour-and-attention management practice that brings various rewards to some people, like the people who do yoga. Duh!

I'm doing some randomised control trials of live-your-life treatment for depression and anxiety. Martian LYL for short. I'm sure it will work. And I can get well known, perhaps even rich. The truth is there is an infinite number of what many call treatments. But they are all bits of therapy, leaving much more out than they include.

So back to Michelle. What did we do? I'm hoping that you can see that she did not need another treatment, another strategy to manage her symptoms of depression. In fact, that would have been bad psych, further committing Michelle to hopelessness. It would have been another treatment that did not work for her. But her legs really were trembling because she was addicted to benzodiazepine and experiencing withdrawal every week. And she had emotional healing to accomplish—had self-sacrificed too much and felt inadequate and different relative to other women. Michelle was bringing up her girls like they were her friends and found it hard to feel and give genuine warmth.

She had some hard work to do; and as it happened, she entrusted me to start that work with her. Still, it used to bug me heaps that she always wanted to know the parts of the therapy and why that bit worked.

I got over it.

We did psychological therapy, not treatment. Michelle wanted things to change, and I explained that the treatments that she had been provided did not change her. And if things were going to change, then she would have to go first and change. A leap of faith if you like. But what to change? What to leave behind and what to keep and what to add to her psyche? Deal with her distorted thinking, emotional dysregulation, patterns of behaviour, addictions? Sure, but what is behind all that? What is it that Michelle is? How does she experience the world and herself, and what capacities does she have as a person, as a woman? What needs healing, and what needs doing over? We kind of need to know all that before we choose any direction of therapy.

The first step is to never choose a strategy or treatment or direction. The first step is always to spend effort wondering and figuring things out, asking why, probing those answers.

We psychologists do ask quite a few questions and are interested in what some of the answers are. But mostly, the good psychologist is curious about how questions are answered. We also use questionnaires that, although never give us an answer, illuminate the tricky areas of life for the client and provide labels to abstract complexes of the mind. The good psychologist must read not only the lines and the answers but also between the lines and between answers, the gluey messy bits that don't have real words to describe them.

We good psychologists carefully help craft what has become to be called the therapeutic relationship—that relationship that transcends any treatment or strategy, the golden road to a person's true centre:

JOSHUA THOMAS

their self. We first craft one within our rooms, only to then have the client take it inside of themselves to become their relationship with themselves.

I liked Michelle, and she knew it. I gave her genuine love and care and provided her with the safety and feeling of competence that she had not felt since her infant years. I also told her to get going with her life, that she can't allow the scared little girl inside her to dominate her adult life. She would have to heal all that and take charge of herself and her future. I am about 20 years older than Michelle; and it often felt that I was her father, sometimes encouraging her to try, sometimes holding her together as she tried, sometimes just enjoying her accomplishments.

When we stopped working together, it was difficult for both of us, especially for Michelle I think. It was easier for me because, from the start and all along, I knew there would be an end before the finish, the way it should be. And I always figured that it would be my job to make that end. Michelle still had a way to go; but I'm convinced—and she believed—that she was getting closer to living her life as Michelle, closer to her centre. She had fewer symptoms less severe and less often, but she had a way to go. She was still on benzos, and those feelings of loss and emptiness were still going to haunt her from time to time.

If you see a sign 'psychological treatment', run away.

If your psychologist says they can provide you with strategies, run away.

If they give you a Martian TLA, run away.

If you do enter such a 'programme', at best, all they can do is provide some relief for some symptoms for some time. Programmes are designed for the statistical ordinary. And I guarantee you that neither you nor anyone else is ever that statistically ordinary.

If you have not worked hard on yourself for a long time and changed from inside to out, if you're not freer, experiencing the world differently, more authentically, then don't call it therapy.

Treatment myth busted!

THE TARGETED-TREATMENT MYTH

True or False?

Targeted treatments work best because they are more potent.

I want to say yes, do you?

WE PSYCHOLOGISTS DON'T have any Hippocratic oath or such. I'm an endorsed clinical psychologist, and that means I have done thousands of evaluations of scientific studies that show if things work as expected—or not. I know my way around multivariate statistics, experiment designs, studies and meta-studies. I understand theory, operational definitions, standardised measures, and tests. I just get off on understanding and measuring psychological constructs.

I could have chosen something more practical and easier for my master's thesis, but I researched process measures for their suitability in therapy, such as the achievement of therapeutic objectives scale. I'm not a geek, I promise! I'm just really interested in if, and how much, and how things work. Perhaps equally importantly, how do we know if and how things work.

It's got a name called epistemology. How do we know we know? Ouch, brain freeze! There goes that frontal lobe again.

But it is kind of important unless you are happy with ignorance. I can be. From time to time, I like to sink into that comfy sofa of ignorance, that velvety blanket of knowing. Yes, ignorance and knowing is the same thing! Didn't you know that? It's kind of nice not to know, stay with what you already know, even in the face of new truth. After all, you can't see most truths because you know so much, and unknowing produces anxiety. You don't like anxiety, do you?

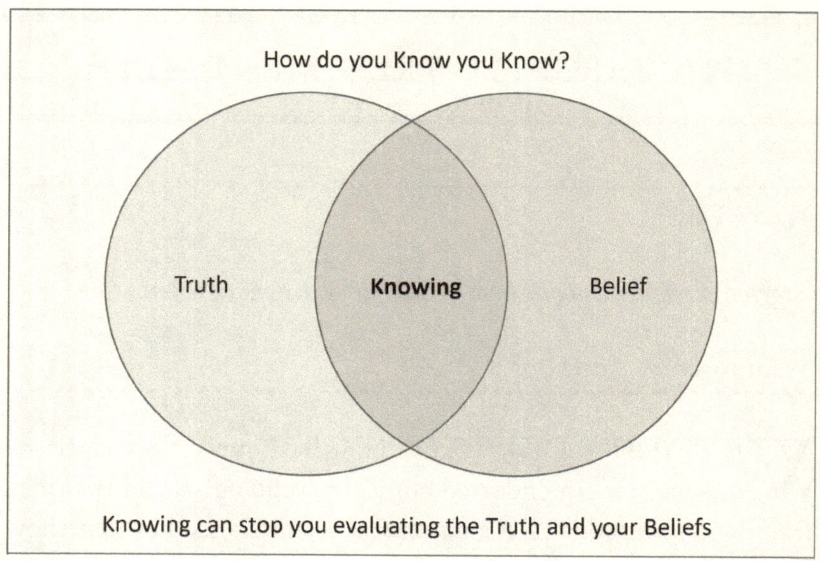

If you look at the above diagram, it raises some questions, some easier than others for you. Is truth that important in our society? If truth was hidden or disguised or misrepresented, would you worry or be content with ignorance? Are you willing or even open to the idea that you believe things that simply are not true? Or harder for you to believe that you know things, depend on things, that simply are not true?

As a society, a civilised one, we have adopted science as a way of knowing. It also means we have adopted science as a tool; and just like any tool, it is as good as the tradesperson. My dad's most enjoyed lesson was 'Josh, a good saw is only useful in the hands of a good carpenter.' Yep, Dad was a carpenter, and he enjoyed hammering that in. I'm pleased to report that this tool we call science has been used to find more truth and work out what works and what does not. Unfortunately, I have to report that the tradespeople—in this case, researchers and users of research in psychology—have reported on truth very badly. They often have misrepresented the truth and instead played on your beliefs. The result is that you know stuff that is plain wrong. Worryingly, you won't change your mind.

JOSHUA THOMAS

I do hope you are okay with some maths, perhaps some nice graphs first? You don't have to be okay with big numbers. Stay with me. I'm going to make it easy for you. I'm going to do the maths whilst you have another coffee and relax. Get that coffee or tea or G&T and keep reading. I'll explain how, using a simple but clever statistic, we know if something works and how much it works.

What we are hoping for when we work with clients is beneficial change. For example, we meet with people with various mental dilemmas. We then provide therapy, which results in beneficial change. In the picture below, the bell curve A, on the left, represents the spread of ordinary folk suffering before getting our help. In this case, I've drawn it so people are sicker the farther to the *left* of the chart they are. There are some really sick folk in bell curve A. The bell curve B, on the right, represents the folk that were suffering but have now gotten the help they needed.

Note to self: the little people are not really piled up on one another. I've just done that to show how most people are middle folk and fewer are unusual folk. So there are more people in the middle of each curve, right? We can call the middle of each bell curve the average because most people are closer to the middle in the curves.

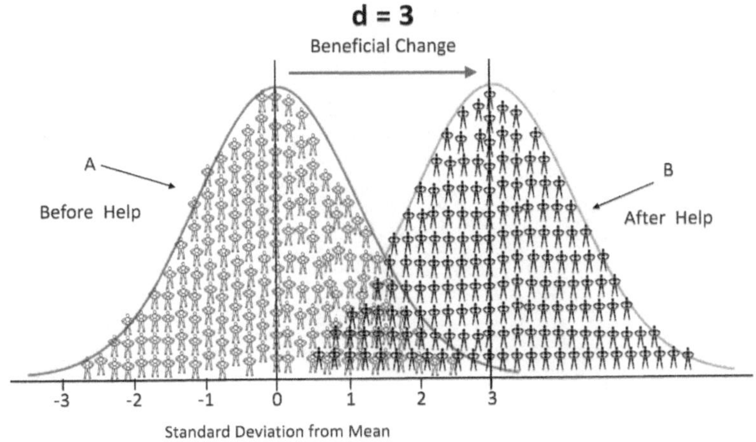

One way of thinking about how much things work is to see how far the bell curve moves to the right. In this case, it moves heaps, which means most people got a lot better. Looking at the centre of the chart, you can see, though, that the two curves overlap. So not everyone got better, and quite a lot are still a little sick. That's life, folk. Our best help just does not work for everyone. But it looks like a treatment that works to me. The overall benefit can be indicated by how much the bell curve moved, specifically how much the average moved. In this case, a good result!

We use a number called the standard deviation to measure distance on these bell curve charts. And the average moved three standard deviations. That little letter *d* at the top is a statistic and is the result of careful measurement of the effect of the help provided. It gets calculated almost all the time in research about making a difference. It is called Cohen's *d*, but you don't have to remember that.

Just remember that the value of the *d* is a reasonable estimate of beneficial change. In this case, $d = 3$.

Let's take out the little people standing on top of one another. They must be quite uncomfortable. So now the chart looks like this. A lot cleaner and easier to use maybe? But don't forget those little folk, even though I've made them invisible. It is about them after all.

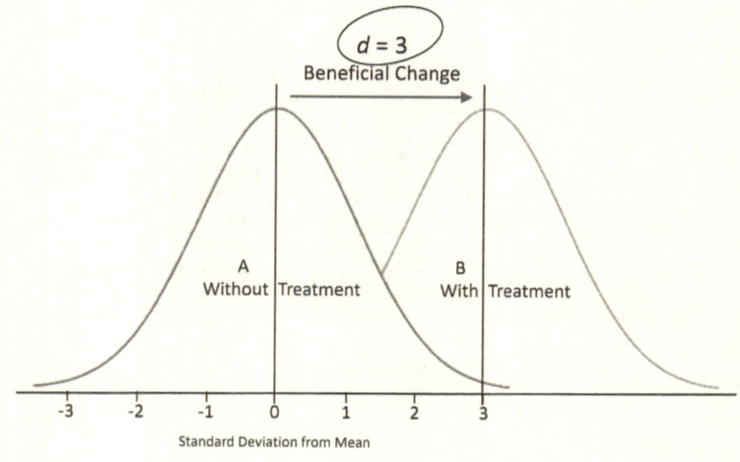

JOSHUA THOMAS

Let us imagine that the above chart represents the effect of a course of antibiotics on people with pneumonia. Knowing that $d = 3$, if I got pneumonia, I'd certainly take the medication even if there were some unpleasant side effects. I'd want and expect to move from bell curve A to bell curve B. Happy days! Now, I can hear you complaining that the bell curve B should be farther to the right. Wishful thinking. Even whilst taking antibiotics, some folk won't respond, maybe even go backwards and get sicker. So there will always be an overlap. The less overlap, the better, of course.

Now, Cohen's d is really cool because it lets us communicate about if something works but, more importantly, how much it works. And now we know Cohen's d, we can also calculate some really cool stuff. Given $d = 3$, we can estimate that the probability of the treatment being superior to doing nothing is 98 per cent. That's really good to know I figure. We can also estimate that the number of people we need to treat before being confident of success is 1.27. Hmm. . . who is the .27 of a person? If I were a GP, I'd probably just say the antibiotics work well for almost everyone. Of course, I would have to know and explain the downside, the side effects of the treatment. But that is okay to do.

Now let's look at a not-so-good example, so you can see how we psychologists use this information. Go on, test yourself. Study the two graphs in the chart below and work out if it is a good treatment for depression. Yes, like before, there are two bell curves; and you're looking to see how far the curve has moved following treatment.

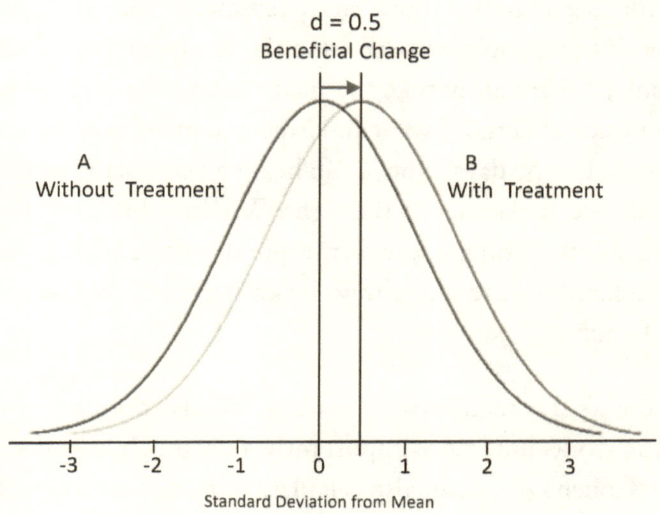

Okay, you've spotted d = 0.5. So maybe I've exaggerated a little by changing from a large effect at d = 3 to a small effect at d = 0.5. At d = 0.5, there is only half-a-standard-deviation difference between those with no help and those that got the help.

Still, I should give you the other statistics to complete the exercise. The overlap is a massive 80 per cent, and the probability that the help is superior to doing nothing is only 64 per cent. Ouch! And the number needed to treat is now at 6—that is, we would have to treat six people to feel confident that one actual person might get this little benefit. Better than nothing, I guess? Unless the help provided causes other problems, side effects if you like, or is very expensive or burdensome. Or if completing this treatment delays you getting help that actually works. In which case, it would be much better if we avoided the treatment and went straight onto plan B!

Okay, maths teaching all done for today! You now know that a big d equals big beneficial effect for more people. Yes, you can smile.

And you know that a small d equals small effect for a few people. Stop smiling.

 JOSHUA THOMAS

But the *d* fails to count any harm within the treatment. It is quiet—in fact, deadly silent—out there in research land about harm caused by psychological treatments. Still, if you know *d*, this simple, clever, statistic, you are ahead of 90 per cent of psychologists and 100 per cent of parapsychologists. Yup, awful but true. Most psychologists refuse to learn about *d* because it takes brain effort. Hmmm . . . but good psychologists look at these numbers and take them seriously. They help us figure out what works and how much they might work for you. It lets us be honest with you about your chances of getting better. In general, practical science, a number of *d* = 2 or better is considered worthwhile reporting on and getting excited about.

But let's forget the maths for now and think about what works and how we know. Here are two clear examples of targeted treatments:

Example 1
Ear Candling

Ear candling is a well-practised therapy to improve ear hygiene and hearing capacity by removing excess earwax from the ear canals. Hundreds of thousands of people swear by it because it has worked for them.

Ear candling works through 'candling', which is a process of burning carefully rolled, unbleached cotton, which has been brushed with high-quality honey extract. You hold the bottom end of the hollow candle to your ear, whilst the top end is slowly burning. The heat causes an updraft of condensation, which draws out the excess earwax from within the ear. You know it worked because, afterwards, the excess earwax is clearly visible in the bottom of the finished candle.

If we graphed the earwax present in the bottom of the candle before and then after candling for hundreds of people, we would see a graph like the one above with *d* = 3. A big effect, proof of it working.

So there is a strong theory, a structured and repeatable technique and measurable outcome that matches the theory precisely. On testing, ear candling works every time except for human error or quality of materials used. Not only does it work nearly every time, but it also works a lot. Let's say $d = 3$.

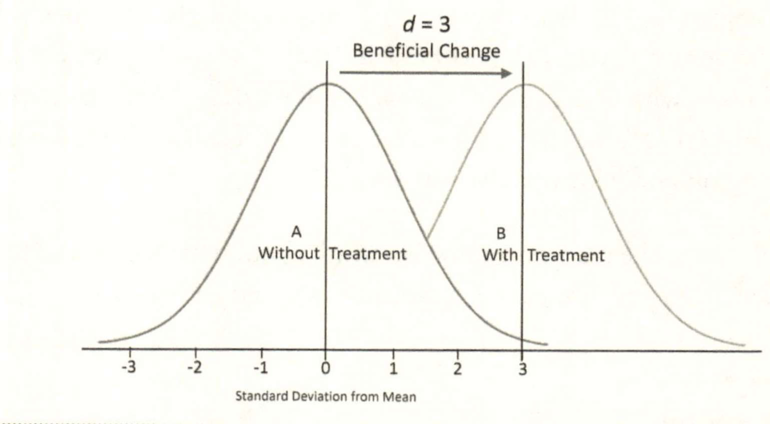

Example 2
Times Tables

Learning the times tables, up to the twelve-times table, by the age of 10 can be done by rote learning. It has worked for millions of children within the school system.

The theory is that learning through repetition is powerful because it works directly with memory. Children, therefore, memorise their times tables; and this can be accomplished by almost all children with an IQ (intelligence quotient) 85 and greater. To remind you, 100 is the average IQ. So ordinary children with a low-average IQ through to smarty-pants children can do this.

JOSHUA THOMAS

This learning is completed by following a teacher and chanting each times table aloud several times most school days. Children start with the two-times table and, once learnt, move to the four-, five, and ten-times tables as they progress through middle primary school. When those tables are learnt, the rest are completed one by one.

A good test of learning is to ask twenty random combinations of the tables. If the score is fifteen or more correct, then moderately good learning has taken place. The teacher can repeat this test and keep a measure of each child's progress towards 100 per cent correct, 100 per cent of the time, which would be full learning.

This rote learning of the times tables is very reliable when the teacher is diligent in ensuring frequency of repetition and the adherence of the children to chant the tables aloud.

On testing, rote learning of the times tables works every time except for human error or personal difficulties of the child. Not only does it work nearly every time, but it also works a lot. Let's again say $d = 3$.

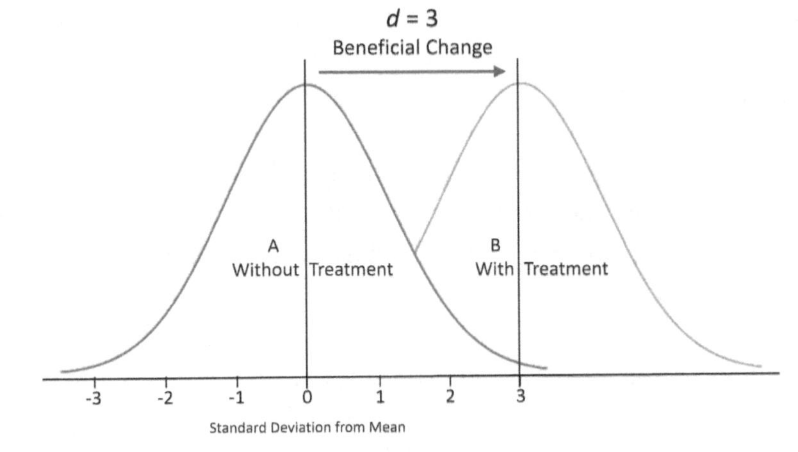

Clearly, both examples 'work'. There is a theory, a procedure, and there are real observed outcomes that the theory predicts. Aside from the reliability of the procedures, the graph, and the big *d* value, means there is a proven large improvement. A large beneficial effect. Both examples are intrinsically good. They both help.

I'm not sure about you, but I have a few difficulties with the first example, ear candling. One difficulty relates to the wax observed at the bottom of the candle following the candling procedure. It is always made up of honey compounds and burnt cotton not found in the human ear. An explanation for this could be that the candling process converts human ear wax into honey compounds. I'm not convinced because this seems to go against the laws of chemistry and physics. But hey, I have an open mind and no harm done, right? As long as the person feels better and thinks they can hear better, no harm done so no problems. Unfortunately, my second difficulty is that many people are harmed by this therapy every day. They either get burnt and scalded or else end up with foreign material in their ear.

In clever Australia, ear candling is quite a thing. People know it works and often pay to have it done properly by an expert! Perhaps you too seek out such experts for things that work. In other cleverer countries, it is banned, much the same as selling alcohol to drunk people is banned.

What about the second example, though? It does seem intact and doesn't go against the laws of nature. I did rote learning of the times tables, and I did advanced maths and achieved honours at university. Clearly worked. What if I told you that at high school I was in the 'ordinary' stream for maths? Well, maybe it didn't work for me after all, but it did for everyone else I figure. Let's not argue. Let's instead agree that it does work as described. I guess that is why so many people favour it. I know it is still very widely used and parents love chanting along with their kids. It simply works and is very efficient for all concerned.

JOSHUA THOMAS

But consider all this learning from a different perspective. Children can learn through other mechanisms too. Instead of straight-line, rote procedure, they can learn through complexity, although ironically very simply. You just have to trust that their mind is inherently clever and will make all the useful connections itself, just like yours did—that is, trust that they are ordinary human beings.

For example, there is a school in the Blue Mountains where children learn their maths differently. To be honest, there are schools everywhere where children learn maths differently but stay with me. At this Blue Mountain school, they engage the children in multiplication through simple, moderate, and then complex play, work, and concepts. Blocks of all sizes are used, as are rainbows, water gauges, pieces of rope, cake recipes, pizza making, fingers, toes, games, and money. The activities are orchestrated to elicit sharing, adding up, taking away, dividing, and multiplying; but they are also to be immediately useful and practical.

Along the way, the times tables are introduced as examples and proofs of their minds' manipulations and interpretations of their imaginary and real world. Tables are not an end or an achievement. When you ask the children what 6 x 8 equals, they might not know. But they can work it out relatively easily because they have been working on even harder things. They might ask you, 'Eight what?' and come up with some bigger answer than you asked for. Like, 6 times 8 cows equals 48 cows and enough milk every day to fill the vat.

Now, I can tell you for sure that the first way of learning times tables is straightforward, easy on the teachers, measurable, reportable, predictable, and easy to proceduralise. It is therefore easier to research and provide evidence for. Evidence—that magic elixir of modern science. But it has to be easy evidence, doesn't it? And easy, convenient factors please institutions and parents. Times tables seem to be a big milestone, and I've heard lots of parents tell me that their child is 'advanced' and that they can do the nine-times table. Hmm, but which way is better? Do you want your child to be a memory bank or a ponderer?

One is directly observable, one isn't. One is heading for the outcome learning; whilst for the other, the outcome is not significant. The process is key. At the end of the day, all can do their times tables; but one group of lucky children have developed a better and more sophisticated neuron network, more ready for abstract reasoning, a predictor of applied intelligence. I have been told by teachers and parents alike that no harm is done by learning rote. I'm not convinced. If harm includes being set backwards relative to peers, being made less than your innate capacity, then harm has been done. Yes, you harmed your children. Sorry for pointing that out. But no harm done.

Throughout the profession of psychological therapy, both examples of ear candling and times tables are in play—that is, some therapies don't work, but people think they do, and they cause harm. And there are therapies that aim to target outcomes in simplistic ways, but you will not have developed any new capacities. They also incur harm but perhaps less observable harm. But some therapies work in the arena of complex adaptive processes, where outcomes, the relief of symptoms, are not an end but a permanent product of improved mental capacities.

Seek that out maybe?

It is the good psychologist that works simply with the complex, helps develop capacity, and enables better models of experiencing living; and through that, symptoms resolve. It is never the other way around. It is never satisfactory for a good psychologist to straight-line the symptoms, hoping that somehow the person's real and internal life will be better in the medium and long term. If the person is not changed, then they will be back; and millions of real Australians are repeat clients, trapped in symptom reduction. That damn graph again!

Now, let's work through an example of 'proper' psychological therapy and look inside to see if and how it works.

     JOSHUA THOMAS

Eye movement desensitisation and reprocessing, or EMDR for short, is a powerhouse of therapy. It has evidence that it resolves symptoms of PTSD and is now one of a few listed treatments for that mental disorder. As such, it is now widespread and commands a premium price in psychology rooms around the world and one near you. There are also regular certification training programmes that clinicians must complete at their expense to become an EMDR-certified practitioner.

Eye Movement Desensitisation Reprocessing

EMDR is a 'discovered' therapy, one that was brought about by the insight of a single person, a person who apparently suffered from disturbing thoughts.

Let's look at how this evidence-based treatment was developed into the powerhouse it is today. Hundreds of thousands of people have been treated with EMDR for posttraumatic distress syndrome, a horrible mental disorder that can bring misery to folk who have experienced, up close and personal, a near-death experience. PTSD can be thought of as the aftermath of the awful intense fear of dying when there is no escape.

Over 30 years ago, a woman said to be experiencing symptoms of PTSD—in particular, disturbing thoughts—noticed something when she walked in a park. When her eyes moved around, her distressing thoughts seemed to ease. Then, when she talked to others about this phenomenon, they recalled similar experiences. She then set about making a treatment for people experiencing disturbing thoughts. She called the procedure eye movement desensitisation (EMD).

Her theory was that having a person bring up disturbing thoughts whilst they moved their eyes from side to side allowed the emotional content associated with those thoughts to be desensitised or normalised in some way. Her measures of client progress showed that this was done very quickly, often within a single session. She later theorised that the effectiveness was due to the bilateral stimulation of the brain—that is, moving eyes from side to side repeatedly stimulates alternate sides of the brain.

To standardise and promote her treatment, she established an organisation dedicated to disseminating and selling EMD. Her targeted patients were people experiencing symptoms of PTSD, especially disturbing thoughts.

The first independent studies of this treatment showed that it did not work any better than maybe destressing, taking those walks in the park and looking after yourself. However, undeterred, she added potent features, mostly cognitive and exposure therapies. Then it started to work, and many quality studies have since measured its effectiveness as like those other therapies.

Because she had added new potent protocols to EMD, she renamed the treatment EMDR, *R* for reprocessing, recognising that her upgraded treatment reprocessed thought and emotional content, much the same as other therapies might do. Still, she stayed with her theory that it was the moving of eyes from side to side that was *the* active ingredient.

Related studies of the biology of the brain offer support to the theory. The imagery of the brain does show the areas dealing with memories and fear being activated whilst the treatment is being administered. They also show the bilateral nature of the brain being active with each side seemingly stimulated by the side-to-side eye movements, again supporting the theory and practice.

To maintain the high standards and effectiveness of EMDR, an international association keeps strict control of training for clinicians, treatment manuals, and materials. To become an accredited EMDR therapist, you must complete training courses, use EMDR in numerous clinical sessions with real clients, and engage in hours of learning with an accredited EMDR consultant. You then must complete re-education every two years. Those that practice EMDR techniques without that certification are thought to be less effective, presumably because they are taking shortcuts.

So here we are in 2021 with EMDR often named as a separate and potent targeted treatment for PTSD.

Interesting, isn't it?

Now, you probably have not read any manuals or training materials, but I have. I've also participated in many training practices given to students of the therapy as the client. The discoverer's original insight into her eyes moving around whilst in the park and the initial one (session effect) have all but disappeared. Instead, EMDR is a crafted series of carefully selected protocols that can be taught to providers and then delivered to clients in an orderly way. The treatment might take 16 weeks or more to complete. You might not even wiggle one of your eyes for the first month.

Why?

Organisations and those invested in the treatment are dedicated to getting their treatment out there. Still, many psychologists don't appreciate EMDR because of its kookiness. I'm one of them. And moving eyes side to side to resolve PTSD does sound kookie to many folk. I have a colleague that practises EMDR, and she describes feeling like a fraud whilst administering that part. Sorry for the fun with TLAs, but EMD(R) reminds me of EFT, the tapping therapy that the good psychologist won't use. They are very similar, but instead of eyes, they suggest other parts of the body to stimulate. Simply think of your problem thoughts, tap away, think of those thoughts again, and notice how they are less problematic. Now, that does happen. Yes, it really works like that.

Now I can tell you tapping has worked for many people with problematic thoughts. They know it works and have a theory and lots of evidence too. Apparently, making something work for someone, having a theory and lots of evidence, is all you need to make a treatment true. And, by the way, make lots and lots of money. EMDR is a very big business, being taken up by every trauma hospital and therapy clinic in the western world. It is—and I agree—an evidence-based treatment. It is easy to proceduralise, easy to administer, and easy to measure results. Again, just like both ear candling and the rote times-table example, it has easy and convenient evidence.

But when you map the protocols within EMDR to other established therapies, you discover good doses of hypnotism, cognitive therapies, exposure therapies, and behavioural therapies. In fact, much more of them than eye-moving therapy. If you are curious and somewhat sceptical, you might think that the moving-of-eyes bit is the excuse to engage you in all the other therapy protocols. If you critically look at the bountiful evidence for EMDR, you might also become sceptical of the logic behind all this.

Firstly, the studies of the EMD part—that is, the eye-movement part, the part that is said to stimulate alternate sides of the brain—show an immediate effect. The same effect as hypnotism, where you feel better after thinking about something, especially under the direct suggestion of the therapist. But independent studies also show that EMDR works the same with or without the EMD part. That might indicate that those short-term effects don't create permanent, useful change. Perhaps people just feel better after each session. Wow, that's great, isn't it? After all, feeling better after each session is proof. Uh, no, it isn't.

It seems likely that the kookie eye-moving part has nothing to do with the therapy's applied success. That just leaves the cognitive and behavioural components as active agents, along with the therapeutic relationship, of course. Perhaps that is why research really can't determine any real difference in effect between EMDR and cognitive behavioural therapy. In our graphs, the *d* value of the difference between

EMDR and cognitive therapy is typically less than $d = 0.2$. The bell curve graphs overlap by 92 per cent because they are 92 per cent the same. Just you might pay 92 per cent more for one than the other.

Then there is the genesis of the idea itself: walking along and noticing your thoughts becoming easier on you whilst your eyes moved around. It may sound kookie to you, but maybe the walking around was the bit that worked for that woman suffering from disturbing thoughts. After all, getting off your backside for regular walks and thinking through your difficulties would be immediately helpful and is a common practice in most therapies. If it was the walking-around bit, then perhaps the whole E thing is really a mistake. The original, ipsative assessment and observations mistaken, the theory broken, the therapeutic ingredients really being the assuring psychologist and cognitive behaviour therapy. Of course, with a dose of suggestion thrown in to get within session effects.

But EMDR works, and that is apparently all what matters. Only it doesn't work because there is no *EMD*, only the reprocessing (*R*). Sick people accessing EMDR therapy for serious psychological difficulties are being told that the eye movement is a key potent ingredient. Those practitioners that use sound via earphones or tapping instead of eye movement are telling their clients that it is the bilateral stimulation that is the key potent ingredient. Well, that is not found to be true; and the evidence is that it is likely a mistake in understanding. If it were true, then I will promise you that juggling three balls whilst you thought about your nightmares will resolve your PTSD quicker—it's just that it won't. It seems that even psychologists can ignore the fact that it is the brain that moves the eyes, not the other way around. You are not stimulating anything!

So one way of looking if a particular therapy works is to figure out the active ingredients and have a sceptical stance. The good psychologist holds their sceptical stance with pride for the benefit of their clients. It would be much easier for me to naively listen to and accept what we are told by industry 'experts'. It would also be lucrative for me to differentiate, perhaps be called a specialist, and to have my clients flicking their eyes and listening to beeps. My view is that EMD is akin to rote learning. It is a simplified path to obtain a result, regardless of how it is achieved, regardless of any opportunity to develop real psyche capacities. I'd rather be real—rather, work hard, rather, work with the natural complexity of your dilemmas. I'd rather do therapy.

Another way to consider if something works and how it works is to look at the numbers. With the EMDR example, we looked at the construct of the therapy, theory, observations, and protocols. We looked inside and sniffed about with our magnifying glasses on to decide if what we were being sold was worth the money spent. But what's next? What if it stacks up, a therapy that is real, does work and the theory, practices, and all observations are congruent with the claim of being a therapy? Well, we use those times tables, of course. We use the good maths that has been provided by the folk who have done the hard yards in studying and then researching the therapy. We call it research methods.

Many, I would say most, psychologists say 'research methods' was the hardest and least-understandable subject in their qualifications. It is akin to mathematics, so they do not use it. EVER!

That is a big mistake, not using something because it is difficult, not putting in the effort to learn more and get familiar with the numbers. I can see my colleagues cringing at the thought of having to use their mental capacity. Anyway, remember when I reached for the Panadol and antibiotics? Why would I reach for them with confidence, and would you like to be that confident when you reach for psychological therapy? I think yes!

True or False?

Man's best weapon against feminism is the mirror.

I want to say yes, do you?

     JOSHUA THOMAS

To investigate the idea of potent targeted treatments, let's look at a popular and typical example where we have a psychological treatment that targets a particular set of disorders: the eating disorders.

Even if you won't look properly, it is hard not to see the complex world women navigate regarding her looks and weight. An objectified world made up by men for men but perpetuated by all. In my private life, I deal with inner conflict as I watch how my family, extended family, and friends treat and relate to their kids based on gender. It is like chalk and cheese. But we all seem to join in, wanting it that way, at least in the moment. It seems no one is thinking it through, thinking ahead. Are we that unaware that what we sow today, they reap later on? Perhaps we are all simply unwilling to change our modelling of being a good person based upon gender roles. Boys wear blue, and girls don't get to unless they ask when they are a bit older. I feel quite mean if I point to it. You will too.

And I can easily point to myself and my family, but I'd like it if you can look at yourself and yours or, if it makes it easier, that family down the street.

If you can see it, is it that little girls are enjoying pretty dolls, caring for baby and wedding dresses and nail varnish, ironing wardrobes, and cooking? Are the little boys doing that? You can see some non-gender-informed stuff like completing jigsaws, riding bikes, looking at shells on the beach, and, of course, chasing seagulls. But you get the drift.

On those children's most memorable, excitable days, you might watch them open and play with birthday and Christmas presents. And sure enough, the adults they love, look up to, and trust regularly buy the girls cooking stoves, skinny dolls, pink dresses, hair ties, clothes, and makeup. Yes, all the stuff they need to be a successful woman when they grow up.

What? Hold on! That is what a successful woman is and does, isn't it? Are you aware that by the time many of our girls reach mid-adolescence, the mirror on them is the most important judge of their self-worth?

As a result, in our great egalitarian society, women bear the brunt of psychological damage. It is daily, it is insidious, and it is relentless. In my very typical practice, women account for more than two-thirds of clients. It makes you cry really. To bring that home, based upon our scorecard, that means 2 million women are living with depression in Australia.

It is much harder and, therefore, rarer for a woman to feel truly free, authentic to herself. Many endure rigid conditions, cold-pressed within them, about what makes a good woman and their role to serve and please in a successful society. Aside from instutionalised subjugation, worry, and guilt, one result of this is eating problems and the emphasis on weight and shape control, moving to disordered eating.

If you are a daughter or have a daughter, then you already worry about this. My experience is that no family escapes, and it is getting worse, not better. There is no part of a girl's body that they won't highlight, feed, starve, build, hide, ink, manipulate, and photograph in the search of self-love. After all, their prospective date has asked to see the body shot before they are interested enough to spend time with the person.

But don't worry too much because there are targeted psychological treatments for eating disorders.

<u>Case of Sandra</u>

Sandra was referred to me for mixed difficulties in 2015. The referral noted recent panic attacks, deliberate self-harm by cutting of arm, anorexia, features of depression and PTSD. She had been prescribed antidepressants and diazepam.

When a good psychologist gets referrals of this mixed set of difficulties, we get very nervous. But we harness those nerves and hope that we are one psychologist that might make a difference for them. But the odds are against us.

Mental State

Sandra presented looking stated age of 37. Kempt, dressed neatly, long-sleeved shirt, obvious use of makeup, looking underweight. On writing her details, would not use my pen, rather taking her own from an office diary of sorts. Rapport was difficult to attain with Sandra using her intelligence and wit to avoid uncomfortable subject matter. Sandra mostly complaining that the help she was getting in the public system was 'shit'. Mood stated as depressed, affect seemingly annoyed. Speech normal. Thought processes goal-oriented, fused with a sense of disadvantage, focused upon personal distress. Thought content mostly about needing relief and proper help. Said that her life was shit and that she had OCD and everything revolved around that anxiety. Nil perception abnormality, nil evidence of delusion or hallucination. Memory seeming intact. Insight fair—understood mental disorder. Judgement good, self-harm ideation present but no current intent. Stated that as a single mother, she would never let her son down.

Background

Sandra explained to me that she has to live with her parents for financial reasons. She said that they help out by looking after her son, Jackson, who has his mental dilemma and needs significant support. Sandra described a dysfunctional relationship with her father, who 'sees me sexually', and a conflictual relationship with her mother who is overly critical of her. Sandra explained that it had always been like that at home, and she had developed ways through OCD to handle it.

Sandra remembered 'the moment' when she took control of things by restricting her eating. She described riding a horse during her adolescence, with her shirt open and the refreshing, cool air against her neck. She had not eaten lunch that day and instantly made the connection to feeling stress free and vital. Sandra explained how it all seemed to work well together—OCD, not eating, looking attractive, in control, also rebellion.

That combination of traits took Sandra on a journey in the seedier side of life. Nightlife, exotic dancing, risky behaviour, and into a relationship with a man who rode with a motorcycle gang. She lived with and had her son with him. Sandra explained it ended when he was targeted in a shooting outside their house. Sandra said at the time she thought she and her infant son were also going to be killed and there was no safe place to go. She explained that it was then that she developed symptoms of PTSD.

Sandra described a current long-term relationship. She said it was often very good, especially sexually; but it was also conflictual and going nowhere because he behaved immaturely, hardly worked, and was mostly bludging and unreliable.

Sandra described ongoing conflictual relationships with various GPs. But she liked her current doctor who seemed to care a bit more for her. And she did care, phoning me now and then to see how Sandra was progressing with therapy. Sandra was also familiar with psychologists. Being a bit clever, maybe too clever for her good, she had run rings around them, essentially giving us psychologists up as pathetic and a 'load of shit'.

Anyway, Sandra described being referred to the local eating disorder programme at the start of the year. I think every major and regional hospital has one. After all, it is a mental disorder that destroys lives, and I think, as I said, is in every Australian family. These programmes do seem to hire good psychologists. At my local one, they certainly do, although I suspect some of them are mental health workers, parapsychologists as I call them. In any case, Sandra described the programme as 'fucking useless'. She had attended her sessions, done everything they asked, completed all the practices. But for Sandra, it made her worse.

Sandra explained to me that before going into the programme, she had her anorexia under control, whatever that really means. When she left the programme, it had her under control. Her eating was severely restricted, and she lost way too much weight. Anyway, as Sandra described things, 'they were useless, pathetic'. 'I went for help, and the help was stupid.' Then again, Sandra was mentally disordered. Perhaps she was wrong in her assessment.

Sandra and I did therapy. We started in the middle somewhere, built a foundation relationship, and Sandra made progress on some life goals. We did do some good work together. She got well enough to have a baby with confidence, and another lovely boy came into the world. I'm not suggesting it was well planned. Sandra was still unconventional to say the least.

My last words with Sandra were kind of dumb. It was a reply message. I was in the middle of taking a year off to do some project work when I got an unexpected contact from her via my business Facebook page. She hinted that she needed help, and I know she does. But I replied that I was not available and that she should make an appointment with her GP or another psychologist. She was very angry and told me that I was useless and a load of shit.

Perhaps that particular day I was a load of shit.

One conclusion is that Sandra couldn't be helped by the eating disorder programme. Perhaps she was too sick, too complex, too angry, too something or other. That is what Sandra told me after she got over her blaming of the people there that had tried their darndest. But she simply reached out for the help, the help that works for eating disorders. And Sandra is a classic, ordinary case in that respect. When your daughter is diagnosed, you will probably tell her to reach for the same help. Sandra's mistake is that she assumed that just like antibiotics, it would work. But the programme providers never explained that their best maths showed that entering the programme, more likely than not, was not in her favour at all.

Let me explain.

And please don't get scared of working the sums here. They are simple enough. We've done them before, remember?

The reported mathematics for eating disorder treatments is typically as follows: 'The effect of the psychological treatment on eating disorders is beneficial, significant within 95 per cent confident limits.'

Reading that, you might then think that if you have a problem, and you take the full dose of the treatment, you can be 95 per cent confident that you will get better. But it doesn't mean that at all! It means you can be 95 per cent confident that something will happen. But that something can be nothing, often going backwards as for Sandra. For you and your daughter, nothing is the most likely result. You or your daughter getting better is against all the research.

But institutions and individuals sell eating disorder treatments, just like boxes of Panadol. The popular ones are cognitive behaviour therapy enhanced for eating disorders (CBT-E), interpersonal therapy for eating disorders, and family therapy for eating disorders. Many doctors, psychiatrists, and private clinics just make their treatments up. You know, a bit like when you make minestrone soup or spaghetti bolognaise for dinner with leftovers. Anyway, do you think a psychological therapy targeting your eating disorder is going to be as good as Panadol is for your headache?

Let's look at some good research into these targeted treatments. A quality analysis by Jake Linardon in 2018 of CBT-E evaluated whether this targeted treatment resolved the psychological dilemma behind eating disorders—that is, do those ill people change their disordered dilemma around control of eating? They found that we can be confident of a real benefit in applying CBT-E. That's the 95 per cent confidence-limit thing again. But that benefit was only $d = 0.36$. You know about Cohen's d. Big is better, right? And 0.36 is tiny in the scheme of things. Just like before, let's graph that possible benefit.

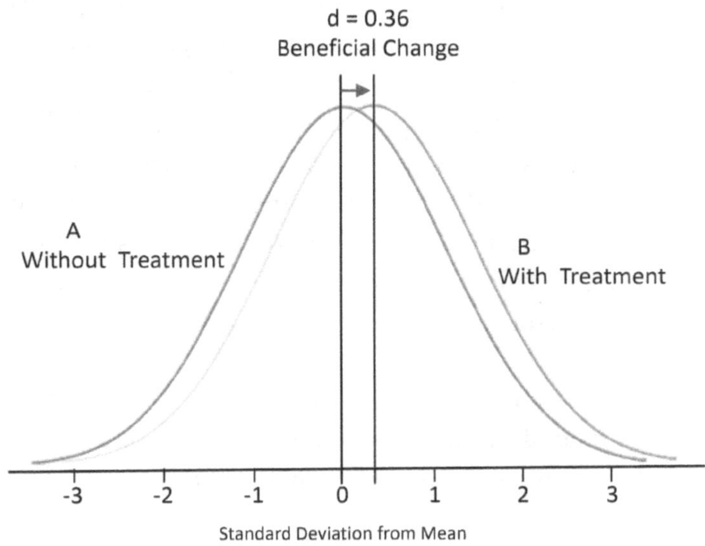

Can you tell any difference in those two graphs? You have to peer quite hard to tell the difference. They are very much the same, and they overlap by 86 per cent! The likelihood of the treatment being superior to doing nothing is only 60 per cent, almost the toss of a coin. And to be confident that one person is getting better, you would need to treat seven first!

Now, agencies that promote CBT-E have done their reviews and conclude that fewer than half of patients who complete the CBT-E programme get better. But they are not telling you that about twenty-five out of each one hundred patients don't even finish the programme. It is, after all, distressing and awfully hard work. Still, what it means is that our institutions know that the targeted treatments they promote and deliver won't work for three out of four people who give it a go. And when it does work, on average, you only get better by a tiny amount.

They forgot to tell Sandra that!

I think that is a bad treatment, not a good one. What do you think?

Does this stuff matter? Does it matter at all that so few people do well with targeted therapies? As long as we are helping some, all is good, yes? After all, there is no hypocrisy in the Hippocratic oath. Well, yes, it does matter. It matters heaps. Under those statistical bell curves are real people, not just convenient numbers. We are forgetting to care about the vast majority that don't get better and the lots who actually go backwards. What, backwards? you say. Yes, therapy is not like Panadol, a very safe treatment. Therapy, when it fails, will compound your psychological disorder or resign you to the scrap heap.

Women regularly walk away knowing that even the world's best potent targeted treatment does not work for them. Only nobody told them that this world's best treatment doesn't actually work!

All good psychologists know this. It is not a secret that targeted treatments are a myth. We simply got them because institutions and private and public insurance companies need a name for something they are paying for. Apparently, the name *psychological therapy* is not enough; and we had to add *targeted, programme,* or *focused* to it. And anything that is targeted, programmed, and focused is simplified, automatically reduced in available potency. Targeted treatments are typically designed to be procedural, ordered and made easy to administer. Just like rote times tables, we all know it is dumb, but we join in anyway.

The problem is that our modern reductionist constructs have brought about a dissecting of therapy into bits. We love to list ailments and then in the name (only) of science, make a dissected therapy for that ailment. But in doing so, we always take out active ingredients of therapy that

JOSHUA THOMAS

would work for the individual client. The treatment-works myth is wrong because we are not treating an ailment. Rather, we are doing therapy with the person, and the person is not an ailment.

Targeted-treatment myth busted.

If your institution, psychologist, or parapsychologist tells you they have a targeted psychological treatment for your difficulties, run away. There is a good chance, just like Sandra, that you will end up in the hurt locker.

THE MEDICATION MYTH

DID I TELL you earlier that good psychologist keeps notes? Why do you think that is? Most psychologists do keep notes, of course, for three reasons. Firstly, they think they must, which I'm not sure is a good reason. Secondly, because it helps them keep track of what has been going on in therapy. Thirdly, it is in case the client or someone like a lawyer asks for them. I've found that none of these reasons are all that persuasive or often useful to a good psychologist.

It turns out that I don't have to take copious notes and that keeping track through detailed notes is an indication that I've got too many clients and I'm forgetting who you are. Yep, that's right. Many psychologists have over sixty clients on the go at any one time. Of course, they don't remember you or what you wanted or what was happening to you or what you are like to sit with. They quickly read the last notes; and bingo, to you, it's like they had you in mind all along. Only they didn't. You were eminently forgettable.

Clients do ask for their notes; and from time to time, lawyers ask for their client's notes; and on rare occasions, courts demand the client's notes. It seems to me that there is a lot of misunderstanding going on here. It seems that my clients, and others, actually thought that the notes I take about the therapy we do are their notes when, in fact, they are my notes. I always know some folk may be wanting those notes

JOSHUA THOMAS

down the track for proof of disability or for family law evidence or such. It has always been tricky for me to tell them that their notes are the ones they took and the ones I took are my notes.

Yes, my notes are my notes, and they are for me. They ask, 'What about my files?' I tell them, of course, they can have them; but my notes are not in the files. Of course, being a good psychologist, I did explain how that all worked at the beginning; but they seem not to register it sometimes. Oh well, I agree with our Ben: 'Such is life.' I have disappointed many a lawyer and folk trying to con their workplace; but for some reason, I don't care much.

There is the fourth reason to keep notes, of course. The reason only a good psychologist would keep notes is to understand and improve their practice. By reading back on my notes and reviewing both therapy and outcome, I can get a bit of a guide about if I'm any good at my work. Am I being useful? It seems something I should know. Late in 2016, my notes went digital. I got myself a Surface Pro; and from then on, I could both hand-write and type my notes in a pre-organised format, including a simple table of if the client thought our therapy had been 'useful' or 'not useful' or if they were 'not sure'.

At the end of our therapy, I always asked that question and discussed it with the client. Also, at the start of the therapy, I always asked my client if they were taking any medications for their mental difficulties. And I asked them if that medication was useful or not useful or if they were not sure. Then I put their answer in the table in my notes.

The table looks like this:

	Yes / No	Useful	Not Useful	Not Sure
Meds				
Psych				

Since going digital, I have worked with over 300 clients. And what I have is over 300 sets of measures about my work and the same about any medications my clients were taking. Three hundred is a lot of observations, a lot of counts. Unfortunately, some clients just don't turn up one day, perhaps after three or four sessions of seemingly good therapy. For them, I decided to tick *not sure*. That ticking has biased my results a little. And I have no way of proving in which direction, positive or negative, my therapy is being useful. Oh well, not foolproof. But on the medications measure, it is accurate because all my clients answered at their first session. It was part of my initial conversation with them about how they had been trying to help themselves or had gotten help from others.

My client's score on our therapy turns out to be 91 per cent—that is, nine out of ten told me our work together was useful to them. Nine per cent told me that they were not sure, and no one told me it was not useful. Well, Sandra told me I was full of shit a year after therapy, so maybe? Okay, room for improvement. Anyway, one in ten of my clients was not sure our work was useful. I've been looking at my files; and to be honest, I would have scored more of our work as not useful. Some clients just did not improve, develop, or could not stand the therapy. After all, it is very hard work.

I remember a lovely man who drank way too much every day. He wanted to stop drinking, so he could see his two daughters again. But it was too hard for him. He had such a low opinion of himself that inside he didn't think he was worth my and his efforts. Then there is Joseph, another fabulous man with schizoaffective disorder. A great musician and a lovely, caring person. He held down a part-time job and was trying to be a good partner. He knows that I admire him. But it would be hard to say our work together was useful, although he said it was.

Anyhow, I suspect the score of 91 per cent is kind of representative of what most good psychologists would be scored. I hope so.

But what about our client's medications?

It is easy for me to tell you because I don't even have to add up the tables and do the calculations for a percentage. That's because only 5 clients—yes, 5 out of over 300—said they thought their medications were being useful. Of those 5 clients, 3 were taking benzos, an addictive drug, which, by perverse definition, is useful to them to reduce stress and distress. One client was taking an antipsychotic after a psychotic episode related to severe stress and depression. And one client said that their antidepressant medication was useful. Almost all clients taking antidepressants said they were not sure.

Isn't that interesting, at least surprising?

Well, it should be surprising if your doctor prescribed them for you. Surely, they are prescribing something demonstrated to be obviously helpful. It turns out that answer is no. In fact, it is more likely that they are harmful. Yes, that graph is the wrong way around again.

In Australia, suicides of people up to the age of 24 rose from 279 in 2009 to 458 in 2018. At the same time, the proportion of younger people taking antidepressants rose from 2.9 per cent to 4.8 per cent. This is despite clear warnings on the packet that antidepressants increase the likelihood of suicide in that age group. Yes, your doctor actually knows this and could tell you. What your doctor can't tell you is that every good psychologist has to try to undo the harm from the drugs your doctor prescribed.

Remember how we reach for the Panadol? Let's guess what happens to your worries, your mental state, when you give your child Panadol for a bad fever, but the fever continues.

It didn't take you long to get more worried, did it? It didn't take you long at all to think something badly wrong is going on. Well, this happens for every client when the doctor tells them to take antidepressants, and nothing happens. They get more worried, feel more broken, and their mental state deteriorates. They develop a belief that something really bad is happening. Perhaps doctors are simply unaware that rumination and skewed beliefs are the ingredients for worsening depression and anxiety.

Many of my clients told me that their doctor explained to them not to expect to feel better for a few weeks. That the drugs might take that long to 'kick in'. What rubbish. The SSRIs break through the blood-brain barrier within minutes and immediately affect the natural mechanisms that complete serotonin reuptake. The only thing that is happening a few weeks later is that the client is doing something for themselves to resolve their symptoms, hopefully under the guidance of a good psychologist. But just because serotonin reuptake is slowed, do antidepressants work on depression, and do you get better? Well, we have to guess that bit.

Look, the research did show that antidepressants work, although with severe side effects, early suicide being one of them. And most types of published research until about 2008 were positive for antidepressants, telling doctors to prescribe. Actually, the first antidepressants were drugs developed in the 1950s, really for tuberculosis and schizophrenia. Doctors noticed that people felt better when their symptoms receded and so started to prescribe them to people with depression. Yes, I can see the crock-of-shit logic in that thinking too. There was then a boom in the acceptance of taking pills for depression.

This boom was despite minimal research into if they actually did make people with depression better. And these first classes of pills were often intolerable for people, with the side effects making the pill worse than the depression. But in 1987 came the miracle of the SSRI (selective serotonin reuptake inhibitor) drug, said by companies to treat depression without many of the side effects of previous pills. We love miracles, don't we?

JOSHUA THOMAS

These SSRIs, which we now call antidepressants, were said to work by slowing the reuptake of the excess serotonin neurotransmitter residing in the synapsis gap. The theory is that even more serotonin in the synaptic gap than our brain demands means more is available to trigger improved mood responses. The companies promoted SSRIs as a miracle drug; and doctors, initially and mostly in the USA, set it as their first line of treatment. With the market expanding because of the doctor prescribing and more people diagnosed with depression, more SSRI-type drugs came onto the market.

Aside from antibiotics, antidepressants are now the most-taken pill in the western world. For some reason, Australians and our Australian doctors have taken up the antidepressant pill with earnest. So now we rate second in the world behind the USA. By 2011, 7.8 per cent of Australians took SSRIs on prescription. In 2018, it was 10 per cent and climbing. Still, more people are experiencing worsening depression and are staying depressed.

This is in the face of substantial proof that the first flurry of published results of trials for SSRI were purposely biased. Yes, surprise, surprise, they were fibbing. In 2008, a doctor of the Harvard Medical School demonstrated that more than thirty-five drug trials of SSRIs submitted to the US Food and Drugs Administration (FDA) failed to show any worth to people suffering mild and moderate depression, the vast majority of people diagnosed with depression.

In fact, placebo, or sugar pills, worked just as well. Also of fact was that the majority of trials to approve SSRIs as a medicine showed that SSRIs had no beneficial effect. Apparently, playing around with the levels of available serotonin within the synaptic gap did not have the effect claimed. Those fewer very sick people who did suffer from severe depression did feel better but only a little. They did not get cured because the SSRIs did not recede symptoms sufficiently. Hardly the miracle drug, likely not even an antidepressant at all!

The positive spin on publication meant that the measured effect size was not clear. Do you remember the *d* statistic and our graphs? Well, it turns out that the most optimistic interpretation of the research is that the effect size for SSRIs on resolving depression is just *d* = 0.3, not *d* = 3, not *d* = 2, not *d* = 1. Just *d* = 0.3, a number so small that it is considered by many to be negligible, unnoticeable. That's not a surprise to me. Most of my clients said exactly the same, 'I'm not sure!'

And considering the downside of antidepressants, the side effects that make life worse, why are Australians taking them?

Remember our graphs? Well, below is the one for pills they misleadingly call antidepressants at *d* = 0.3. Do you think this makes them worthwhile perhaps if they don't do any harm?

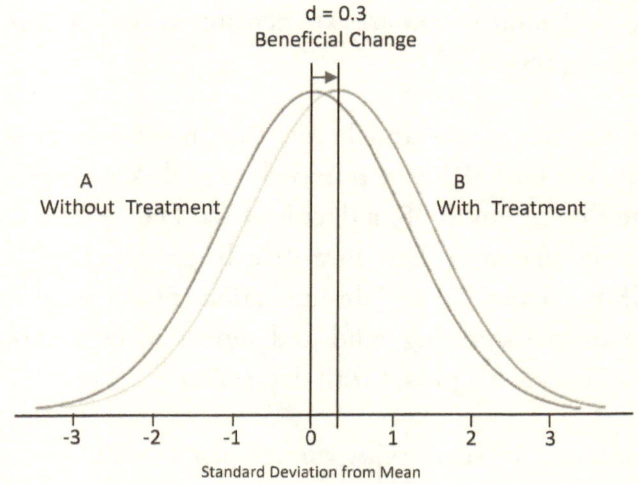

Estimated Beneficial Change at *d* = 0.3

An objective assessment would conclude that Australians are taking antidepressant pills with some misguided notion that the effect is significant and worthwhile. I presume our GPs think the same. Well, that's the only explanation I can come up with unless I go to stupidity, mass delusion, or big money. Considering the known side effects from taking antidepressants—premature suicide, sexual dysfunction, weight gain, and nausea—why else would a doctor prescribe them?

Perhaps it's because they are on the PBS; and you, just like most modern folk, prefer pills that might work, relative to the inconvenience of hard work that does work.

Now, I know by now you are screaming at me, 'Josh, they worked for me!' Or maybe you have heard that from a dear friend of yours. And maybe they did but maybe not. The available unbiased non-paid-for, nonprofit-based evidence is that they did not; but if they did, it was such a small amount you really aren't sure. Did you know that major depression often just gets better doing little about it? Did your doctor forget to tell you that? Today, we have millions of people taking pills that likely don't help but actually do harm, but people are too scared to stop.

It is an awful situation. Even if you really believe that they helped you, would you, in the face of the overwhelming evidence that it is a pharmacology farce, recommend others to start?

PART ONE SUMMARY

True or False?

In Australia, anyone anywhere can harm others by providing a regulated health service to anyone regardless of their competence and credentials.

I want to say no, do you?

UNFORTUNATELY, WE BOTH have to say yes. That is the state of affairs in our *lucky country* where expediency and profit triumph over public benefit and safety. It is both a shambles and a shame.

On all society's evidence and all counts, the system is broken and does not do what is hoped. As we provide more mental health solutions, we have more mental health problems. The reason is that we have kryptonite in these solutions; and as we spread them, more people get harmed.

We have people who don't know that they are doing bad psych. And the institutions and businesses that allow and promote bad psych believe and perpetuate the myths they are entangled within. Some of this is a mistake, as in public health settings. In business settings and new career pathways, it is simply careless disregard.

If we peel away the myths, we find some clear facts, the inconvenient truths if you like. I've catagorised the myths into ten and given them names so you can remember to look out for them, also to help you see your way through them. Instead of the myths and lies, I want you to remember these ten commandments:

1. It is like the Wild West out there. Be diligent and seek out a good psychologist that will do good psychology with you. That means

seeking out an endorsed counselling or clinical psychologist with more than five years' experience.

2. Your doctor's or school's or institution's or best mate's referral is at best a guide to what you need. Remember that they actually don't know what you need. And you must let your good psychologist prescribe your therapy in partnership with you. That is so your personal input and preferences are taken into account. That means what therapy, why, how often, and how long for.

3. If you get referred to an institution, not a person, ask for that to be changed. Institutions tend to have few good psychologists, instead preferring to hire cheaper parapsychologists. So demand access to a good psychologist from the very start—no substitutes. And don't worry about hurting a parapsychologists' feelings. If they haven't met the psychology board's standards, then they are not competent. If they say, 'But I'm competent in CBT,' tell them you're competent in stacking bricks, but you can't build houses.

4. When you are told that some counselling will do, or that the telephone will do, or that a session each month will do, know that it is a weak dose. That may be fine if it is all that is available. But make it clear from the start that you know a little won't be enough. Then make plans to find a good psychologist and work with them face-to-face.

5. If you feel that your psychologist is very kind and caring—letting you talk all the session, avoiding topics, avoiding therapy, and never hurting your feelings—you have a bad psychologist. Ask for honesty and clarity. At the end of each session, ask how you made them feel.

6. Many, I think most, generally registered psychologists are incompetent to let work with your mind. I've not met one yet that isn't or wasn't. I know I wasn't. The general psychologist likely skipped the hard part of learning and used the lack of regulation to achieve registration. So check their endorsement and qualifications via the AHPRA website. You will be surprised who they let perform surgery on your mind.

7. At your first session, ask about your psychologist's notetaking and their protection of your privacy. Ask what gets written and what

doesn't. Ask who owns the notes and who has access to them. If it is the health centre, hospital, or insurance company, get out. Or ask your good psychologist to put ethics above their job. Yes, ask them to keep separate notes—their notes. Otherwise, your history, dilemma, and next visit will be stigmatised. Loud alarm bells please!

8. Ask for therapy and ask what form of therapy might be suitable for yourself. If they only offer the same therapy to everyone, then that is bad psych. If they offer you a brand of therapy, such as CBT or ACT or SFT, ask why and what would that therapy leave out.

9. When you are told they will provide you with a targeted treatment, be very careful. They don't seem to work very well at all. It is exactly the opposite of the scientist-practitioner model where you are involved in deciding the direction of therapy. Targeted means reduced, simplistic, procedural, and cookie-cut for the bland diagnosis. It will not sufficiently consider your particular, or even peculiar, personal complexities.

10. Remember that you can't take antidepressants safely. They have side effects and don't do much, if anything, measurable. If you want to take them, fine, but also remember that they don't change your patterns of behaving, thinking, feeling, and experiencing the world. Only therapy will do that.

Why do I tell you the 10 commandments? To keep you safe, of course! But also to guide you towards finding good psych. That is good psychology with a good psychologist. When you have that, you are in Box A, so settle in and work hard.

Meanwhile, remember there is no regulation. Our Australian Psychology Board has set world-class standards for competence and ethics in the delivery of psychological therapy. They are easy for you to find and praise. Despite that, the Australian Health Practitioner Regulation Agency has zero power or instruction to enforce those standards. In fact, they must allow anyone to prescribe and provide psychological therapy to anyone, regardless of how dangerous that is.

A man with a certificate cut out from their breakfast carton can provide psychological therapy even to the sickest and most vulnerable Australian. Major health centres hire people demonstrably incompetent in psychological therapy to provide that psychological therapy. Consequently, they provide cookie-cutter bit therapies that can't and don't work. Vulnerable, sick people, including children, are fodder for a growing cashed-up industry, riding the back of good psych and government ineptitude.

Did I tell you that following one particularly poor instance of demonstrable incompetence and harm, I wrote to the AHPRA and asked that they intervene? I asked that they instruct a major provider to ensure that their hired people be competent and meet the psychology board's standards. They wrote back telling me that they had no such power or mission. Their response told me that they were unable to ensure that psychological therapy providers were competent. The AHPRA explained that the health ministers would need to agree and then empower them to do so. And they suggested I direct my communications that way. So I did.

I wrote to the health minister asking if they understood the awful state of affairs. Did you know that ministers accountable for this dangerous shambles can avoid knowing what is going on? They simply have a department bureaucrat handle correspondence. She went around in circles with me; like a skilled football sweeper, she stopped the ball from reaching the goal. I think I tried four times; but each time that I asked for confirmation that the minister was aware of my account, she would not answer.

Her purposeful misdirection for me was to make a complaint about the instances of harm I notice to the providers. I had to explain that that job would be full-time because people are being harmed full-time. Still, the minister is safely in the dark, not having to do their job.

So I figure if the ministers won't tell you that your psychology health service has zero regulation, then I would. And I have.

It really would be a full-time job to make the daily complaints required about the frequent harm of bad psych. I made one, and the hoops and hurdles in your way drive you batty. Each complaint fails because the AHPRA has no regulatory power to ensure competence in the provision of this regulated health service. And the minister responsible is able to stay in the dark, avoiding accountability for the catastrophe they preside over. To close this part I, I'll give three quick current examples of likely harm because of bad psych.

On one Sunday in July, on the ABC radio was a programme where an entrepreneur was provided air space to announce his new product. His company was making a monitoring and recording 'device' that school-aged children would interact with frequently whilst at school. This device was going to collect environmental and personal, private, and emotional information of those children so schools and other watchers can know what is going on.

The lovely entrepreneur glowingly spoke about the good that could come from this, such as preventing emotional difficulties and identifying children in distress. But he never spoke of the harms of such a device, such as children being asked systematically about their mental state, the child knowing they are being constantly monitored, and children expressing emotional content to a machine instead of with a person.

He is not a practicing psychologist, has no equivalent qualifications, so can't know what he is doing. But he *knew* it is a good idea, and he is an entrepreneur. Now on their website, there were lovely words and pictures of happy children, all positive about the product. He had academic psychologists and such saying nice things too. As far as I can tell, none of the 'team' he had mustered had field expertise in mental pathology and therapy. Frankly, I'm disappointed that those psychologists seemed to endorse this product without investigating harm thoroughly.

JOSHUA THOMAS

You know me a little by now. You know I've worked with school-aged children and adolescents. You know I value good psych and loathe bad psych. So you've already guessed that I wrote to the radio host.

I noted my worries and my credentials, so she knew I was not a crackpot or something scary like that. I asked that she forward on my concerns to the entrepreneur and that maybe he would give me a hoy, and we could chat. After two months, no answer. Another letter, and she forwarded on my offer to the entrepreneur. But no contact from the entrepreneur. I think the entrepreneur really thought he knew what he was doing. He had good intentions if you like.

But do you really want your child to be 'inputting' emotional responses into a box recorder, even or especially if they have made it to look cute? Do you really want your child to have to continually appraise their body and mental state, a driver of anxiety? Do you really want your child to work through a machine instead of with their teacher? Do you really want your child to be closely monitored so they either behave or lie to please a system?

This is bad psych not because it is not a good idea for some children but because it is a bad idea for most children. And a very, very bad idea for some children. Children are not all the same, and many children would be harmed.

I did eventually get a response from the entrepreneur who reassured me all was okay. I'm not sure if I can ever be reassured by someone who has zero expertise. The response demonstrated that he had little appreciation for the ordinary but fragile development pathways of children. In any case, it seems that there is no regulation to prevent them from selling this stuff. So I'm hoping expertise and their ethics will. What would definitely stop them is hundreds of parents with harmed children angry enough to engage in lawsuits. But it should not come to that. It would already be too late.

Then we have a well-meaning large not-for-profit Australian organisation training anyone who pays in what they conveniently call mental health first aid. They proudly proclaim being evidence based. Well, I've read their research, and it tells them quite bluntly that their programme does not work. But that bit doesn't appear on their website and brochureware. The facts show that after the training, participants had little improvement in identifying mental health problems and that they did not help anyone. It seems that once participants get their certificate and leave the room, they steadily forget everything but still believe they know stuff. That is a dangerous combo!

These good but naive people are walking around large workplaces providing mental health advice and counsel, thinking they know what they are doing. But they don't. It's just crazy, worse, dangerous. But the 'feel good' branding means it is being taken up by many organisations as good practice. These organisations include not only big businesses but also your local school! Of course, the unsuspecting sick person does not know they might be heading straight to Box D.

And then there is the public system that is parapsychologist hungry. This month in Victoria, community health centres were advertising their mandate to spread further into the mental health industry. That means sending people into sick people's homes to provide psychological therapy. The job position says the person must be a nurse, occupational therapist, social worker, or clinical psychologist. I presume the managers of this institution also think that a podiatrist can do good physiotherapy. Odd, isn't it?

This new role is to provide therapy to our most vulnerable and seriously mentally sick people. Apparently, public health managers are serious in their self-perpetuated myth that these different professions can do the same job competently. But as I've shown, only one is competent. The others are at best parapsychologists. So who will apply and get the job do you think? Hint: the pay rate is better than nursing, occupational therapy, and social worker levels.

　　　　JOSHUA THOMAS

Well, I hope you can sense how worried, angry, and ashamed I am. You're at high risk of getting bad psych. And I worry. The government's and industry's acceptance of zero regulation provokes my anger. And I'm ashamed that my profession is sitting back knowingly, but carelessly, allowing the demise of good psych.

PART TWO

The Good Psychologist

True or False?

Just like medicines, the success of psychological therapies is due to their careful development and potent ingredients.

I want to say yes, do you?

FOR THOSE OF us who did the required learning as part of becoming a good psychologist, we found out something at odds with what we thought. We spent a lot of time learning therapies and about their development. We spent a lot of time learning assessment. We spent a lot of time learning the scientific method and how to make and consume research. We did lots on various theories of psychological constructs, mechanisms, and pathology. We even learnt heaps about brain parts, nervous systems, nerve cells, axons, dendrites, and neurotransmission. We did ethics too. But very little about who and what a good psychologist is in the therapy room.

That is an odd omission. It is odd because of the overwhelming conclusion from repeated research that all the other stuff matters less than half. That's right. More than half of the benefits of therapy are related to the person in front of you, the psychologist. Independent of what or which therapy they are doing with you.

Now most psychologists don't know that, and most public institutions seem oblivious to what evidence-based therapy is. They incorrectly know and promote that it is the therapy type, the procedures, the homework, the practices. But it isn't. It never has been and never will be. It is the person, what they bring into the room with them that you find useful and what they don't bring into the room that would defeat therapy. Can you think that way? Because it means that only a good psychologist can do good psychology.

This unexpected and unwanted revelation diminishes the focus on careful development of therapies into a small effect size. It hardly matters at all. It makes a mockery of poached-egg-therapy branding, targeted treatments, one-week training courses, and clinical procedures—the things parapsychologist can do. So what is it that the good psychologist is and does that provides the potency of therapy? Let's find out.

If you have children, are you a good parent? Likely, after all, you are reading this book; and we both really know this is about their future. But how do you know you are a good parent? Similarly, if you are a teacher, how do you know you are a good teacher? If you are a bricklayer, how do you know you are good at what you do? It is tricky, isn't it? Well, if you really are a teacher, then there are the obvious, the basics such as knowledge, techniques, and practice years. There are also your abilities to put that together and deliver. Things like smarts, physical capacities, and family supports. Then there are the attributes and motivations you bring as a person. They all kind of intermingle into an art form—and presto! You're a great teacher.

Well, it's like that for good psychologists too.

When you see a bad psychologist, something will be wrong with one or more of those areas. Either knowing and techniques might be poor, or perhaps their thinking and life experience might not be sufficiently fluent. Or perhaps they lack empathy and interest in you. Sometimes they just don't look right when they sit with you. Often, all are apparent! You will turn up twice and then quietly retreat, disappointed and quietly annoyed, and remain a statistic. However, if I'm going to help

JOSHUA THOMAS

you get good psych, I can't do the easy bit and just point out the bad things. I have to pass to you the figuring on what to look for, what makes the good psychologist.

I will explain the competencies and personal attributes that a person brings to the room that allows them to be a good psychologist. I will contrast those competencies and attributes with those of what a bad psychologist brings into the room with them. When I do this, I will cover the material regardless of the job title a person is given or gives themselves. For example, people you or your children end up in front of might be called *counselling psychologist, clinical psychologist, mental health clinician, general psychologist, occupational therapist, nurse, psychiatrist, social worker, counsellor, therapist, analyst, sage, guru, mindfulness facilitator, GP, marriage counsellor, priest, pastor, school counsellor,* or *life coach.* Without exception, all these people play psychology with your or your children's mind.

Except it is not play!

TECHNICAL COMPETENCIES

True or False?

Your psychologist is more technically skilled than your bricklayer.

I want to say no, do you?

LET'S FIRST LOOK at the technical competencies a good psychologist must be able to demonstrate and bring into the room with them.

Just like the bricklayer who knows his way around bricks, mud, plans, measures, angles, and gravity, the good psychologist must know their way around the mind. I won't reinvent the wheel here because some people have done such a great job, perhaps missing only a few but key technical competencies. Those people are the Australian Psychology Board. Their contribution insists that the good psychologist must be good within eight broad categories.

1. Knowledge of the discipline
2. Ethical, legal, and professional matters
3. Assessment and measurement
4. Intervention strategies
5. Research and evaluation
6. Communications and interpersonal relationships
7. Working with people from diverse groups
8. Practice across the lifespan

They also insist that this material be competent at a level commensurate with a master's degree in clinical or counselling psychology. That is six years of full-time study. Further, it must be then demonstrated under supervision for a further period of two years. This is eight years of learning and practice and is more than equivalent to becoming a medical doctor or MD.

So it is easy for you to know if your psychologist *can* be good. Simply ask if they are endorsed for counselling or clinical psychology. If they say no, you should assume they might not be technically competent. If they say yes, then they might be competent in the technical arenas of psychological therapy.

I say *might be competent* because, although the psychology board does a good job, they can't be 50 per cent sure. Now, this is a bit controversial, but the psychology board, just like all institutions, tend to know what they know and think how they think. And so, they tend to trust in the very institutions and profession they regulate. I've already explained that Cs get degrees, so university certificates are at least 50 per cent suspect. All through my honours and master's years, it astonished me how students wanted the questions to their tests and answers to their essays before they start. Questions of the assessors were often in the ilk of 'Will I need to know the DSM criteria for depression?' Hmm . . . I wonder what they thought they were reading and studying. I was more astonished when the assessors answered those questions. You see, if there are fifty questions in a test, and you know what is in and not in, you can easily pass that test without knowing much at all. Well, you have to know twenty-five things I guess.

Then there is the self-regulated buying of your counselling or clinical endorsement. Your ticket to the big money. Did I tell you that when I completed my two-year registrar programme to demonstrate my endorsed competencies, I paid another clinical psychologist to give me the ticks I needed? No? Oops, I must have forgotten. Not surprising given it looks like I might have paid for my credential!

Well, I did actually. I bought my most treasured credential: my clinical endorsement. And so has everyone else, one way or another. Honest direct buying like me, or maybe more hidden, like they got it as part of their terms and conditions of employment somewhere. But getting your biggest credential is very like a pyramid scheme, where the big mice are in charge of the cheese. They tick off that other littler mice can start eating. Yes, I was once a little mouse like that, running in their wheel, buying permission from a bigger mouse to get my cheese. *Squeak, squeak!*

And it is the expensive kind of cheese too. Some clinical and counselling psychologists charge obscene amounts to provide what is called supervision. It is not unusual that an aspiring psychologist will pay $10,000 to another psychologist to get their tick of approval. It really is a ludicrous—oops, I meant lucrative—system to learn and demonstrate competency. I know one clinical psychologist who tells me they are not a good psychologist. They enjoy their work, and it is a well-paid job with hours that work well for them. Their résumé is fine, and they paid very well for the registrar programme to gain board endorsement. Now endorsed, they can charge so much more and have fewer hours at work. It suits them, so maybe this system of buying your ticket is fine.

To be honest with you, many psychologists are like that. In the words of my insightful wife who rides a road bike, 'They have all the gear but no idea.' How come? They passed all the neuropsychology, ethics, cognitive behavioural therapy essays, statistics and research methods, and essays on assessment and diagnosis and completed their thesis, a massive project of personal choice. So how come when it comes to working face-to-face with real clients, they can't do a great job? Well, most of it comes down to three key technical incompetencies.

Firstly, they don't really understand what psychological therapy is and is for—that is, they simply don't get it!

Secondly, they have not done enough work on lifespan and the unique challenges and opportunities that people of different ages face.

Thirdly, they can't do analysis.

Let me give you three case studies.

Therapy and Its Purpose

True or False?

Your psychologist likely has no clue as to the purpose of therapy and what it is.

I want to say no, do you?

<u>Case of Beverly</u>

Beverly is a friend of mine, and she had a life-threatening experience of brain bleed. At the ripe age of 63, a small artery in her head had weakened. An aneurysm had formed and then ruptured, and blood was leaking into her brain. Beverly did not know that at the start. She said she had a bad headache and felt a bit drowsy, and her vision was odd. She took some painkillers to help, but they did little. All the while, the balloon of blood was getting bigger, ready to kill Beverly. After some hours, when the symptoms worsened, she went to hospital. It was not long before she was under anesthetic and skilled people were saving her life. For all intents and purposes, Beverly was facing and experiencing death. She was completely vulnerable, not sure if she would be coming back.

All of us that love Beverly prayed and crossed our fingers. When we could, we popped over to the rehabilitation area where she was to spend some time recovering, at least physically. And she has, so our finger crossing worked I figure. But what was her experience, her deepest instinctual fears and reckonings? Only people facing imminent and unexpected death from a reckless source can have an idea. Perhaps? Perhaps we all know that she must be damaged, blunted, or at least changed forever.

Worse, that strongest of all fears bound by trauma and the instinct for safety can become her most prominent drive. That hyped-up drive might diminish her characteristic propensity to explore and take on life as it comes. Beverly might project those fears on life's canvas, maybe painting a darker world than needs be.

Well, Beverly's good doctor was onto that. He knew that good psych will help a person's mind escape much of the damage. Much of the trauma can be healed quickly and other productive drives harnessed, even made stronger. Not only could Beverly's life continue, but she also has an opportunity, albeit undeserved, to work her mind with new discoveries of mortality and immortality. She could work her hero's story with a rare piece of life's jigsaw. I don't wish on anyone the experience of pain, fear, inability to not say goodbye to loved ones, and prolonged recovery. Not anyone at any time. But I am Jungian trained, and so instead, I wish it for everyone. The experience can and should be transformative. Minds need deaths as much as any other experience to become complete. And Beverly was one of the lucky ones to die an awful death, then to come back, and live. Wow.

Anyway, Beverly did what was advised, and she made appointments to see a psychologist. The doctor referred her to them, so it must have been a good psychologist (myth #2). What did Beverly get from her psychologist? Jack shit. Beverly told me that the psychologist asked superficial, expected questions like you see on TV. 'How are you feeling?' comes to mind. Beverly astutely pointed out to me that she felt she was providing therapy for the psychologist, and there is every chance she was. Beverly was having profound experiences; and 'How do you feel?' just isn't going to cut the mustard, is it?

I'm quite ashamed of my profession sometimes; and when Beverly described her experience, my heart sank. The psychologist was not competent. She might have been kind and enjoyed working with trauma. But she had zero competence in how to work with people who needed help with profound experience, in this case, the experience of death and life. I lied to Beverly a little bit. I guess I fibbed to make her feel good about it all. I told her that her best help would come from those that love and care for her, not a stranger that she meets on some professional level. It is true in a way, but Beverly deserved good psych, but she got bad psych. So I know that Beverly is still broken somewhere inside. I don't know where or how or how much. But Beverly knows, and it will be diminishing her life experiences.

There was an opportunity missed. Beverly is potentially in her best and most important stage of her life experience. She can look back and fit all the pieces of her jigsaw together using all the colours, especially the black pieces. Beverly can sew her tapestry of life and integrate all experience into her meaning. A good psychologist would have relished the chance to help in her endeavour.

What we can say from Beverly's experience is that well-credentialled psychologists can be very competent in psychological therapy but, unfortunately, often are not. Beverly's authentic feeling that she was the one providing the therapy, maybe even being better at therapy, is a common client experience. Can we ever say that about a bricklayer? It does my head in really. All that university study, all those marks passed, all that money paid to become endorsed. And they don't even know what therapy is and what it is for.

They somehow have missed the purpose and practice of therapy. They don't know the main, the key, the overarching competence of joining in with someone's mind and its complexes. A good psychologist is competent in working simply with the complex. For others, it is often too simple or too complex—and it fails.

Knowledge of the Lifespan

I meet a lot of health professionals; and often we chat about their subjects and mine, one of which is psychology. I've lost count of the times a person who should know better talk about a *child psychologist*. They know one, they referred to one, they admire one, and so on. Did you know there is no such endorsement, no such board-approved title? The psychology board identifies and promotes some specialisation in psychology; but a general psychologist can, and often do, work with children. So do clinical and counselling psychologists, so they should.

There is an endorsement for educational and developmental psychology, which makes sense. But most psychologists working with children enduring common psychological pathology are not educational and developmental psychologists. Educational and developmental psychologists have a focus on testing within educational environments. This focus means they have relatively lower competencies related to psychopathology and therapy. You can't learn everything in your two years' master's programme. It has to have some focus to achieve sufficient depth of knowledge.

Having said that, I expect every psychologist working with children and adolescents to be fluent in developmental psychology. How can you work with a child of 7 or an adolescent at 16 if you don't have a clue on how they work, what capacities they have developed, what challenges they are overcoming, and what is yet to happen for them?

I'm absolutely sure that you can't work with anyone of any age if you don't understand attachment theory. Attachment theory explains how we develop ways of building and maintaining lasting psychological connections, emotional bonds if you like. It informs us how these ways start at birth and develop rapidly during childhood. These ways predispose us to feelings of safety and fears in our relationships with others and ourselves. Think emotional development.

Then there are the theories associated with cognitive development such as Piaget's stage approach. When is it possible for a child to understand time? Some psychologists think it is when you give them a watch or a mobile phone. Really! And what about brain development, synaptogenesis, and pruning or lobe development? What implications does that have when we introduce various environmental conditions for our children and adolescents? If we don't ask them to practise quietness or patience, can that capacity develop sufficiently for adulthood?

Therefore, psychologists working with children and adolescents have to know more—a lot more than when they work with adults. But do they?

<u>Case of Tina</u>

Tina is a clinical psychologist who knocked on my door mid-2015. She worked down the street from me and had been working with children for some years. Tina was seeking some help for a 2-year-old girl she was working with, who had been diagnosed by a paediatrician with separation anxiety disorder. Separation anxiety disorder is a debilitating disorder that, as well as being a fearful experience, impairs much of a child's life. Parents are also affected, usually themselves becoming fearful in their parenting.

Tina had been working with the child and mother to solve the inevitable sleep problem. You see, the little girl was so afraid of being separated from Mum that she would refuse to sleep without her being next to her. Mum was very scared for her infant child

JOSHUA THOMAS

and was questioning what she had done wrong or if her child was being damaged through all the lack of sleep, tantrums, and crying. Anyway, to help, Tina had been teaching Mum the 'controlled-crying technique', which had not been successful after a month of practice. Tina had heard that I had helped parents and children before with sleeping, so she came for my thoughts.

Before I started on my thoughts, I asked about hers. What did she think was going on for the little girl and her mum? What might have gone astray that needs repair? What options were open to us to help them? Tina explained the behavioural problem of the little girl, how she had learnt to pull her mum's strings. And now, when Mum resisted, she used crying and screaming to get what she wanted. She said things had likely gone astray because Mum was too caring and responsive. The options open to us were to help Mum correct her overcaring, overresponsiveness and have her little girl become accustomed to the new way—kind of like exposure therapy—so the little girl would learn not to be scared and not to pull mum's strings.

Now, I would have expected those thoughts from a general psychologist. After all, I've explained that in my stubborn view, most of them aren't competent. But this is from a clinical psychologist, fully educated and fully paid up for her endorsement, having gone through two years of supervised practice. Anyway, I offered to discuss her thoughts in the light of my ideas.

Based on Tina's descriptions and the paediatrician's diagnosis, my ideas were that something had gone astray in the little girl's development in her capacity to feel safe, quiet, and calm with herself. She still needed the proximity of her mum to provide that security for her. She has missed some developmental opportunities or else had a setback.

Refusing to sleep on her own is likely a symptom of this underlying dilemma. After all, sleeping to a little girl is just like going away, being separated. And having to go away or Mum and Dad going away brings the fear of death to her. Mum is also likely parenting scared, lacking her calm assuredness, the very thing her infant needs to feel and internalise. What was open to us was to orchestrate more developmental opportunities for them—opportunities for them both to feel safe, calm, and quiet together and apart at various times, distances, and places.

You see, Mum needs help to firstly establish her sense of calm, security, and confidence and then transfer that to her infant girl. It can't be the other way around, which is what was being expected of everyone. When Mum can do that, her little girl might become okay to close her eyes and say good night to her mum and dad. And yes, to do that, the little girl will have to learn to fall asleep on her own too.

We discussed the little girl's life so far, based upon her mum's information. Nothing was standing out that was unusual developmentally. Some months back, Mum had hired a sleep nurse to help; but that had not worked. Mum had told Tina that her girl also cries and screams when dropped off at her three sets of grandparents. This was three times each week because both Mum and Dad worked, and so the grandparents helped out by babysitting. One other weekday was day care for the girl, where, apparently, she did fine. Anyway, I spent time with Tina helping her imagining the infant girl's life. How do 2-year-olds actually work? What kind of information do they work with? How do they experience life? What bonds matter to them? How quickly are they learning from things around them?

Well, she is 2 years old, time and days don't mean anything to her. She is still egocentric, and so she can't relate to another's point of view despite her seeming to happily agree in any particular moment. She works with information mostly symbolically, and her emotional state is her mirror of her mum's. And her bond with Mum had become entangled with fear. She has anxiety disorder, a disordered level of fear triggered by potential separation from Mum and Dad. Her rate of learning is so fast it is hard to comprehend, and she checks and learns about her life this and every day.

For example:

When Mum excitedly asks me if I want to see Grandma tomorrow, I might say yes. But I don't have a sense of tomorrow or yesterday. I just experience; I saw Grandma, or I will see Grandma, or I'm seeing Grandma.

Mum explaining that she needs to go to work just means she is leaving me behind.

When Mum says, 'I'll be coming back after work,' she is telling me that she is leaving me.

When I wake up, I'm not thinking about going anywhere, even if you told me last night.

When I have a bag, I'm going to be left behind.

When I get in the car, I'm going to be left behind.

When Dad says, 'I love you so much,' it means I'm being left behind.

And it's all true, proven more than one-half of the days of her life.

By imagining being the little girl, Tina was able to see how chaotic and fearful life was for her. Simply put, she is taken anywhere, any day, and left behind without warning. And she does not have the capacity to calm at the moments of separation. Her routine is not a routine for her because she does not understand or work with hours, days, and weeks. She works with what happened, is happening, and what happens next. Her life, from her perspective, was chaotic and scary.

I was able to help Tina imagine her life like that. She wakes up expecting to be at home but not today. She is taken to work. The next day, she expects to be at home; but no, she is dropped off at her husband's parents for the day. The next day, she wakes up expecting to be home; but no, she is taken to her parents for the day. No day predictable, ordinary, or repeated enough to understand life from a stable base.

We as adults would think this was ridiculous for us; and we would ark up, form a union, refuse, or develop a mental disorder. But we think a 2-year-old can do it. Worse, we think a 2-year-old should do it, and it is good for her. Crock of shit, isn't it?

Anyway, Tina and I agreed that we needed the help of the girl's parents to orchestrate more developmental opportunities for the girl—opportunities to experience stability, opportunities for her to learn she has a safe and enduring base to work from and return to, opportunities to take the sense of safety, security, and confidence from her mum (and dad) into herself. We did. We made a whiteboard of suggestions to be added to and worked upon with the little girl's parents. We also drew a simple model of parenting to work from, increasing care and authority over their little girl's life.

Tina came back to me a few weeks later appreciative of my help. She told me that the parents seemed to link in better with the formulation and direction. They had implemented a routine that their girl could build upon. Nothing radical. One main element was grandparents doing the moving about. They looked after their infant granddaughter on her home turf, with all the attachment items available to her. There was a dramatic increase in physical interactive (with parents) play formats such as chasey, hide-and-seek, and playground slides. Also, they had figured out that somehow shopping together and meeting nice strangers was good for this too.

To start all this, both parents had taken five days off work to get organised and let others know what was happening and kick off from an ideal situation. Pleasingly, their little girl, although still clingy around bedtime, had resisted but not refused to sleep on her own for quite a few days in a row.

After telling me that things were going well, Tina asked how I knew all that stuff. I told her that I'd learnt it at university, done the required reading, and aced my units in developmental psychology.

Tina really enjoys working with and helping children. I too think there is no greater privilege. Still, it is no accident or coincidence that the Australian Psychology Board especially notes general principle B.1.: competence. That means taking the years to study, learn, and practise developmental psychology, including therapy for young people.

Just like for the infant, good psychologists are technically proficient across the lifespan. That doesn't mean just 'enjoying' working with young folk or older folk. It means understanding the complexities, capacities, and challenges of the mind for that demographic and being technically competent in providing therapy that works with them and for them. If the psychologist can't do this, they often will revert back to generalised counselling or cognitive behavioural approaches as their go-to and often will be doing bad psych.

I'm sure you have examples in your work. But would you like to see a general nurse working in intensive care with inadequate skills and knowledge? Would you accept the metal-work teacher teaching your year 12 kids maths because he liked working with older kids? Of course not. Knowledge and competence matter more than preference and pay rates, and folk must do the required learning.

Analysis

It makes me both nervous and happy when I meet people for the first time outside of psychology. After small talk, or as a part of small talk, they eventually ask, 'Josh, what do you do for a living?' I'm nervous because people have the idea that psychologists 'analyse' people, like mind reading or something. In fact, they often ask if I'm analysing them now! And because I simply don't like answering that question, I always say no. I'm happy, though, because I'm proud of my strong professional capacities, and having the opportunity to say no suits my ego. The truth is that I can analyse people, but it takes time and effort. And mostly, I'm doing other things with my mind; or more accurately, my mind is doing other things with me.

But what is analysis anyway, and why is it a missing competency in most psychologists?

Well, analysis acknowledges and works with unconscious material as well as what is obviously apparent. Let's face it, if we were only conscious, rational beings, we would not fuck up half as much or behave irrationally so often. Oops, did I just swear? Um, that's right. Despite our intelligence and predisposition to logical thought, we still say things we really mean. We chase sex, can't stop ourselves sneaking a look at a man's arse, eat the whole large pizza, and feel guilty when we can't help someone. Hmm . . . I just found out I'm a bit gay. Cool! Ordinarily, very little of our core life drives; and avoidances are planned, countered, thought through, discussed, or spoken about.

JOSHUA THOMAS

In the inner world, we are simple human beings designed to survive, make our mark, and spread and advantage our genes. And conscious, civilised rationalities, niceties, and political correctness are not going to stop us. Or if they do, we will develop a neurosis, a mental dilemma! In fact, we all will from time to time.

Analysis is the way to investigate our dilemma. Remember Will in the movie *Good Will Hunting*? Analysis is the only way to heal and overcome your inevitable neurosis—yes, you too. And analysis is the path forward towards your full potential as an individual.

Convinced? I would not be. In fact, I was not at all impressed when this claptrap was first put to me. Sigmund Freud, the first explorer of the unconscious mind, is dead for a reason, right? But do you see bunny rabbits in the clouds? We all can unless you have some neurosis that prevents you. Why and how? Did you know they are not really there, just like the man in the moon is not really in the moon? Well, the answer lies in something called projection. You project those bunnies using the clouds as a convenient canvas, kind of like painting I guess. You can't do it if you have never seen a bunny rabbit, of course, because your mind needs to have the bunny before it can paint it.

Interestingly, importantly, and quite confronting, it's the same for everything. You constantly use the canvas of what you see, hear, smell, taste, and touch to paint your world. Really, how else could it work? Your mind does this for you or, more honestly, with you. It sees your little boy on the trampoline and 'paints' fun. For your husband, it sees your same little boy on the same trampoline and paints danger. Both might be reality, of course, but we are not talking about reality. It's all bunny rabbits, remember?

A real-life example and case in point: My mate across the road is a lovely man. We've done some cool things together like sail from Adelaide to Melbourne and canoe the Murray river lakes. He loves his wife and family dearly and is a real volunteer. Mike knows I admire him. Yesterday we were chatting outside his house, just chitchat, being nice to each other really. His eyes wandered across the road to the front of my car, and he noted that he could see that my car's wheels were badly out of alignment. I looked, and all I could see were good straight wheels. We are seeing the same reality, but painting up our modified reality, aren't we? Mike's mind paints risk on the canvas available to him, whilst my mind struggles to do that. I must frustrate the shit out of him because I have no problems, no worries, even when I'm shown them! Of course, Mike drives me bonkers too. You see, I don't want to see my world through the lens of risk anymore. Been-there-done-that kind of thing.

Now, Mike and I are both good, ordinary people. As such, we interpret and paint our world as we mix with it. So do you, and normally, it is entirely appropriate. This unconscious painting goes for our internal mental world too. Yes, our conscious thinking will become the canvas for our projections.

We can get ourselves into all sorts of knots that did not need tying just because we think. If we care a lot about people, the person in front of us can become a canvas for that care, even though they have not even asked for or needed our help. If later on we again think of that person, that projection can take off under its steam. Let's call that bit *worrying*. Do you know of anyone who can't sleep at night because they can stop the roundabout of thinking and worrying? Surely, not you! For that roundabout to stop, you might consider analysis to undo your neurosis of self-sacrifice.

So how does this unconscious stuff appear in therapy? Well, it appears as an invisible force, just like sunlight on your arm. Well, not quite like that, but it is invisible, undetectable by our five senses. So you have to have radar.

Have you ever sat with someone and felt awkward, even repulsed? Is that them or you? Or some other invisible force? Would you tell them?

JOSHUA THOMAS

Tricky, isn't it? One way to think about unconscious material is to appreciate that when you and your psychologist are in the room together, there are really four people in the room: you and the psychologist (yup, the ones you can see) and your unconscious self and the psychologist's unconscious self, the ones you can't see but feel when your radar is tuned in.

It looks like this:

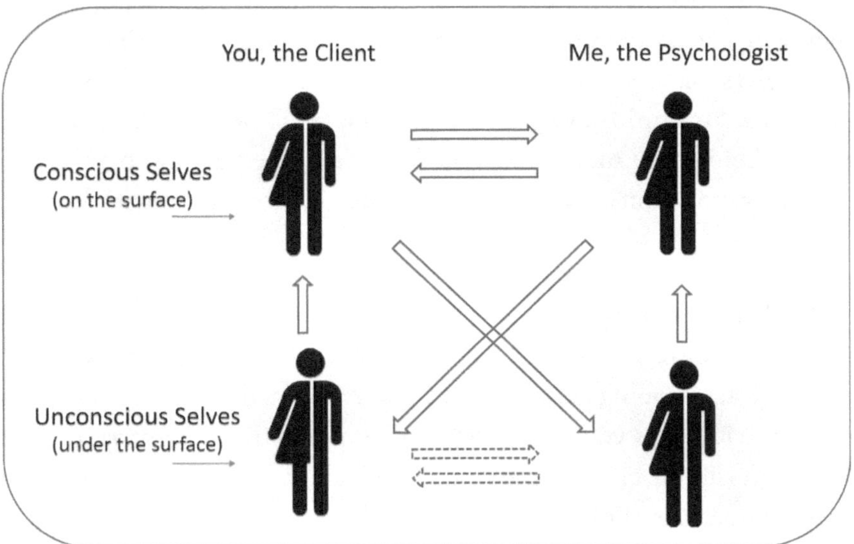

The surface is our conscious experience. You and I are observing each other and talking, along with our private thoughts and experiences. The interaction is mostly overt, although I've got my private thoughts and experiences that I'm maybe not communicating to you and vice versa. But much of your overt appearance, behaviour, and communication is being watched and interpreted by my unconscious self. I can't turn it off! Similarly, my overt appearance and behaviour is being interpreted by your unconscious self, and you can't turn that off, can you? Your mind is instantly both judging me and using me to project your neurotic inner world. Not only that, but that unconscious interpretation then flows through into your overt appearance and behaviour.

Let's take me for an example. If you mention abortion to me, my instincts, learnt gender role, and morality will interfere with my thinking. It is not a *may interfere*. It is a *will interfere*. I can't help it. I may blush or be quiet, may avoid my curiosities, or not answer your questions in a straightforward way. I may now use you as a canvas for my insecurities of being childless or defend my anxieties by intellectualising your difficulty.

Because an incompetent psychologist can't know why this is happening, they will put it down to some other substitute feeling, perhaps telling themselves once again that they don't like working with women's problems. Hmmm . . . yet you are the same good person asking for help now as before you mentioned abortion. You deserve good psychology, but likely, you won't get it there. Can you sit with a man with leprosy?

This never-ending series of unconscious effects and countereffects leads to both dilemma and opportunity. The dilemma is that my unconscious mind might spoil my efforts of therapy. For example, I may become nervous with little logical reasoning going on. Or I may say something with a slip of the tongue that upsets you or otherwise interferes with the therapy. Perhaps worse, my 'liking' or 'disliking' you may mean I avoid important enquiries or interpretations. This is called the transference effect.

This transference effect is your effect on me that can't be helped. All I can do as a good psychologist is to expect it, not allow it to defeat me, and, when I can and should, use it as an opportunity for us to build insight. You see, your unconscious content moves through you into your overt behaviour. It may be as simple as your slip of the tongue or how you project unconscious content onto me or others. Yes, you do that all the time. And during therapy, your defences are always there, always apparent. After all, you must resist therapy—resist observations, realities, and truths that provoke anxiety.

Working with this material is the most potent force of psychological therapy. Therefore, the good psychologist must be very technically

JOSHUA THOMAS

competent in this arena. Unfortunately, most psychologists are not. Most have never even completed analysis themselves or completed a single university unit on the unconscious mind. Yet they are exposed to its forces in each and every encounter such that therapy is defeated by the client's and their unconscious dilemma.

Case of Jack

Jack is an experienced general psychologist working out of private practice. He also works in the public system as a high-graded mental health clinician. He came to see me in 2019 to discuss a case that had affected him badly. Jack expressed loss of confidence and was considering if private practice was right for him.

A month prior, Jack had been providing therapy for a young man who had asked for help with anxiety, specifically social anxiety. Social anxiety disorder is the most prevalent disorder in adolescents, and Jack had helped others through this devil of loneliness. Jack told me that he was particularly worried for this boy because he was so sad, so lonely. He had scored 'extreme' on a common symptoms severity index, and he had checked boxes indicating strong experiences of feeling meaningless and of low worth.

Jack had started working with the boy. He had completed essential psychoeducation and initial practices in identifying avoidance behaviours. The boy failed to attend the third session. He had been in hospital following a period of intense suicidal ideation. The boy survived.

This case could have been any for Jack and most other psychologists. Jack was helping with the problem the doctor and boy described and was running the programme, as he had many times before. It had gone wrong; and now Jack felt a mix of fear, guilt, and shame. It was occupying his mind too much. It was interfering with his work with other clients, and he needed some help.

It would be obvious to you, the reader, the mistake that had been made. Jack had missed the overt and clear indications that this boy was also experiencing significant depression. And every good psychologist working with a person experiencing symptoms of depression checks thoroughly for suicidal ideation and intent. And that is what Jack told me too. He said that he had made a mistake, missed the obvious, and it nearly cost the boy his life. Jack was convinced that it was the private setting that set up the mistake. In his public job, there is much more support for the psychologist. Meetings take place and cases discussed with help forthcoming. That is my experience too, especially in the larger teams, not so much in community health settings.

Okay, what was Jack saying? I know what he was telling me, but what else was he not saying that was expressed through but not part of the overt conscious exchange? If you were me—sitting with Jack, listening, and tuning in—what is it that you 'know' that Jack must investigate and, if he chooses to, make some growth in?

When I was with Jack that day, I felt disappointed in him, almost dislike. It moved through me as if I were with a guilty person, even though he was admitting his mistake. Now, I like Jack. He is still a good friend of mine. So I knew it wasn't about me liking him or disliking him. What was it that poked me? It wasn't logical, at least not at first. It was an effect he was having on me; and after many years of study and practice, I know what to do with that intuitive information. I become very honest and straightforward whilst looking after the potential hurt I'm about to inflict.

I asked Jack if perhaps he was shifting blame from himself. I said it felt a bit like that because he hadn't mentioned being sorry and working through an apology or such. I told him that I knew him well and that he is a great person, but a boy nearly died. I was curious about contributing factors that lead to Jack missing the sadness and despair

JOSHUA THOMAS

in the boy. Or if Jack had noticed that despair but had not acted upon it. I was also curious if Jack somehow hoped that I was there to comfort him, to absolve him of sin, without the corresponding lessons being learnt.

We had an uncomfortable 30 minutes or so. But as everyone is, Jack is stronger than he thinks; and we took on and worked around his defences. Jack eventually got to the place where he was prepared to look at his frailties, fear of mistakes and lack of confidence of his obvious abilities, and his work ethic. He spoke about how he dismisses the risk of mistake because of overload of clients. How he takes on seven clients per day, even knowing that he can't be at his best for the whole day. Yet still not able to say no to new clients waiting in the queue. About any apology, Jack said he felt he should and had wanted to call the boy and say sorry, but he had been too scared to make that call.

Jack was happy to look at the public system as a way of avoiding his dilemma. In that system, they screen folk in triage, openly share personal and private information of their clients, and manage risk for you. So it is easier on the psychologist even if you aren't doing good therapy with them. After all, why are you talking about them and discussing *their* therapy behind their back? In private practice, you are on your own—you are everything. You are triage, risk manager, therapy provider, and self-care. The money is good, but you can't treat clients as material in your job. Working harder, longer is a mistake, even if it feels right and feeds your ego and brings the money in.

Doing things differently, growing independence, reducing crutches, owning mistakes, and finding out you are greedy are anxiety provoking.

Aren't they?

They are also very important!

Did you know that once upon a time, analysis was the mainstay of all psychological therapy? If you want an idea what analysis is like, watch the movie *Good Will Hunting*. Will is the main character who has various psychological dilemmas to overcome. Dread of failure and intimacy and loss come to mind. These unresolved dilemmas meant that he was not living the life he was otherwise capable of. His ego runs the show, making sure he is comfortable with his lot. But there was a dark deep chasm between who Will was on the outside and who Will is in the inside.

Unable to traverse the gap and terrain of his mind, Will was loved and guided by another human being, Sean, an expert in navigating that terrain. At the very least, Sean could shine light into the darkness of the chasm so Will could find his way across. Sean was a good psychologist.

If you can't watch that movie, then think of yourself. How far are you from who you are on the inside? Why is it that you don't live the deep simple life you can, instead living some shallower, busier, more neurotic, and less human version?

Feeling comfortable?

Consider this model of you and who you are. It was drawn with me, for me, by my analyst, Benjamin in Caulfield. I've made the squiggly line:

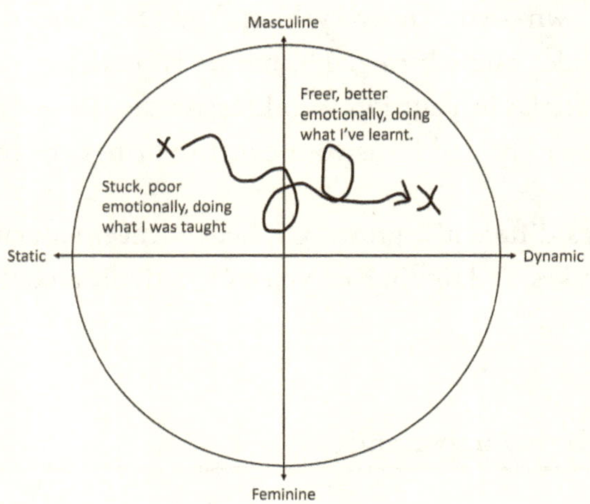

JOSHUA THOMAS

These days, I consider myself sitting somewhere in the top-right quadrant, but I wasn't always there. For much of my adult life, I was living in the top left: kind of stuck, being a man overly driven by security, a need to be loved but fearful of loss. Avoiding emotional content, I subjugated my life experience to others, second-guessing what they wanted, often being wrong.

On the outside, it looked like Josh was having a successful job in a great industry and a conflict-free marriage. But the distance between what I was on the outside and who I was on the inside was growing. Pauline, my loving wife of ten years, eventually became a victim to that distance. I loved her until my heart wept, but my broken mind refused to let her know. Instead, I broke and burned everyone that loved me until I was fully alone. Alone, I have no fears, no insecurities. I also have no love, no pride, and no life. A man safe but stuck, like many men and women become. Depressed and needing to die and become reborn.

So how would cognitive therapy work? How would any cookie-cutter therapy work? It's not my cognitions that are distorted. It's not some *DSM* diagnosis of clinical depression. I'm a broken man on the inside, and I needed someone who can help me across the darkness. An analyst. For me, it was Benjamin, whom I can't and never will forget.

That's how you learn analysis. You spend time—no, lots of time—with an analyst undoing your neurosis and, more importantly, allowing yourself to heal, become less fearful, die, and then grow. You work your way across your dark chasm, and you ground yourself deep in your granite. You build security, confidence, and spirit from within, where it always was, suppressed by your fears. And yes, you let parts of you die—some peacefully, some painfully—but you let things die that must be left behind. All the while, the analyst loves and guides you, like a good parent loves and guides their infant child.

When you watch that movie about Will and Sean, or if you think about your internal distances and dilemmas, how would you know *what* the psychologist was doing? How would you know *what* step they were at in the therapy? How would you know if *what* they were doing was right? How would you know *what* was being worked upon? Well, the best answer is that you can't know. In fact, you can't tell any of those things because in analysis, *what* matters much less than *how*.

How is the process, the dance of disclosure and interpretation. *How* is the movement between fear and safety, risk and learning, stopping and going, hurting and healing. *How* is the dance, and fencing, of two minds so that both grow, taking and enhancing the capacities of each. When this *how* is done well, it is therapeutic to someone in need, someone in trouble, someone whose mind needs help.

Just like when a good father puts his arms around his daughter when she falls, analysis is a series of moments of demonstrable love, vulnerability, and strength. And how can you put that into steps? How can you reduce that into bits without those bits becoming unhuman, meaningless, and ineffective?

Why would we try?

Well, in 1892, a tiny but powerful lobby group of psychologists decided that if you can't put it into steps, you can't call it psychology anymore. That lobby group became the American Psychological Association, the APA for short. With their mission to 'advance psychology as a science', they built a big protective wall of science around the profession. That's right. It's not just USA presidents who build big walls. You already know that most folk in charge of anything have big walls. Look at their houses. Anyway, the APA was headed and controlled by 'scientists' rather than 'practitioners', and they gained political control of the agenda.

Psychology was mostly studied and practised within arts and philosophy but not anymore. It is now studied almost exclusively within science. And progression within science is easier when you have *what*s that can be broken down, reduced, staged out, observed, measured, and repeated

                JOSHUA THOMAS

over and over. This is ideal for the development and advocacy of cookie-cutter techniques, which have become the mainstay of modern reductive therapies. But what are the consequences of the scientific method at all costs?

Unfortunately, analysis is a process that is different for each coupling of client and psychologist. Although the beginning and end are clear, as are the results, analysis can't be reduced into bits. If you can't reduce it into bits, they can't teach it in the science faculty. So no one is taught it anymore as part of their psychology credentials. A shame, isn't it? The most powerful technical competency a psychologist can aspire to apply is not available to them though the normal avenue of study and learning. Consequently, to learn, practise, and become competent in analysis, the psychologist has to take additional and alternate pathways. This takes time, effort, money, and, uncomfortably, intrapersonal risk. So most psychologists don't even try to become proficient.

The takeaway from all this is that as a potential client, you should be sure that your psychologist is familiar and confident working with the unconscious. The unconscious is where you will invariably travel, like it or not. And your good psychologist is your best guide.

> True or False?
>
> *Your psychologist is centred, grounded, and perhaps the most ordinary person you will meet.*
>
> I want to say yes, do you?

WE'VE HIGHLIGHTED THE three technical competencies that good psychologists have in spades, relative to the bad psychologist. This means you know what to seek out and look for. It also helps you to know what to sidestep and avoid. Firstly, good psychologists really understand what psychological therapy is and what it is for—that is, they get it! They have done heaps of study and work on lifespan and the unique challenges and opportunities that people of different ages face. And thirdly, they are proficient in working with unconscious material and can use that to complete analysis work, the most potent of all intrapersonal change processes.

But this is all worthless unless your psychologist brings certain personal attributes into the room and leaves others behind at the door. Remember the bricklayer who really knows his way around bricks, mud, plans, measures, angles, and gravity? Well, if he is interpersonally inept or unsuitable for doing that job, it counts for zilch. Maybe they have a busy mind and are overtalkative and under listening? If so, they will never settle zenfully into the zone required to concentrate on each and every brick. Or perhaps they are motivated in life more by the afternoon surf report than your presence at the building site. If so, they will be lazy with your walls, letting their mind drift to the green wall they will encounter at 5 p.m. Perhaps they have a hang-up, maybe they carry anxiety. If so, they will overworry and take ages. Perhaps they had a bad experience and are holding a grudge. If so, they will be frustrated, easily annoyed, and be difficult to talk to.

It's precisely the same for psychologists, and all of the above apply. But it is worse because you can't see if the bricks they are laying inside your mind are crooked or missing any foundation. Psychologists may be too straight, uptight, and anal. If so, they will create a tense or overly clinical atmosphere. Remember, just as psychologists, they paint their bunnies. They paint their lives too, including the therapy room.

And it's not uncommon for psychologists to have distressed minds. Neuroses, including depression and anxiety, are common within the profession; and psychologists are often on psychotropic drugs, hiding the symptoms so you don't know. But their projections are everywhere; and so they are harmful psychologists, full of mistakes and, more likely than not, really getting therapy from you!

Yes, you make these psychologists feel good at your mental expense.

At my first lecture in clinical masters, the lecturer asked us to write down why we wanted to be psychologists. The most common answer was to be helpful to others in distress. Fair enough. Seeing distressed people and painting helpfulness in our lives might be a good trait. Towards the end of that year, we were asked a different question, 'Why do you think you will make a good psychologist?' The most common answer was because we had experienced trauma or abuse and endured depression or anxiety. In other words, we were mostly all broken.

Only one budding psychologist said because they were content, generally happy, and well rounded. Interesting, isn't it? How do traumatised, sad, and worried minds paint? When they see you, how will they see you, and why do they need that?

The upshot is that you are more than likely to be referred to a psychologist that is interpersonally not suitable for the job. No matter what qualifications they have.

And of course, just like the bricklayer's motivations matter, so do those of the psychologists. Sure, most are wanting to help, perhaps give back, or prove something to humanity. But please don't forget the biggest motivations in any industry—and it is an industry—status, power, and greed.

There are six areas of personal attributes for you to identify and seriously consider if they affect your therapy.

1. Is their mind healthy?
2. Are they of good age?
3. Are they fluent with complexity?
4. Do they work to their limits?
5. Can they work with all of you?
6. Are they ordinary?

If they tick all those boxes, go for it!

JOSHUA THOMAS

A Healthy Mind

In one of my first jobs, I worked in community health. Around me were physiotherapists, dentists, nurses, and such. For a fair period, I shared an office with a diabetes educator, the health professional who worked with folk sick with diabetes. He was about 160cm tall and 100cm around. I guess he weighed around 85kg, which put him in the obese range of the body mass index. For lunch, he had sandwiches; but for morning and afternoon tea, he had cake and doughnuts. Every day. Hmm.

Now this person, in my opinion, has every right to provide good advice to his clients about healthy eating in the face of obesity and onset of diabetes. I'm confident their advice was sound, perhaps expert. But there is a problem, isn't there? The client can see that the expert is sick and doesn't follow their own advice and counsel.

Do you think that matters?

The first attribute to seek out and consider in your psychologist is a healthy mind. Psychologists do need to be quite clever in that they are doing a lot of thinking and joining of dots during therapy. They do that fluently, and it should be like a duck swimming on the water. Calm on the top, but underneath, they are doing heaps of work. Now, I'm going to tell you something obviously wrong.

All good psychologists are bright. Well, they must be, mustn't they? They have done all the hard yards of study and practice, likely more than your ordinary GP down the street; and they are all bright too, aren't they? But you and I both know that a bright mind isn't the same as a healthy mind or even a clever mind. Just like there are some smart, dumb folk, there are some dumb, smart folk.

Anyway, let's assume they are bright enough to do the required technical stuff. High IQ if you like. What slows or spoils a bright mind? You got it: a mental problem, especially a neurosis. I've alluded to this already, but why does it matter? How does the problematic mind and mental state of some psychologists cause bad psych?

<u>Case of Simon</u>

Simon is a clinical psychologist. Although having some private practice background, he is well settled in public mental health. He has good credentials and is especially proficient in his therapy of choice.

I'd been working alongside Simon providing individual and group therapy for adults with a personality disorder. During the very first group session with eleven clients, he told the group that he 'has depression' and takes 'antidepressants' to manage the symptoms. There had been no reason to tell the group. Self-disclosure was not a skills practice for the day, and antidepressants were not part of the therapy. In fact, for this demographic, antidepressants are contraindicated and quite unhelpful. Still, this top psychologist made that disclosure. Our clients were women with very severe difficulties in understanding and regulating emotions. That, along with skewed interpersonal capacities, meant that these women were liable to form emotional attachments too quickly in an unconscious attempt to feel a strong bond.

At this time, this psychologist was one of my supervisors. So aside from a quick check-in with him as to if he was feeling okay, I never mentioned it with him. I briefly discussed my options with another senior psychologist who told me it was common knowledge anyway.

        JOSHUA THOMAS

But I'm a big boy and decided for myself that it would be silly to broach the subject further within that organisation. Still, I did put the incident in my notes of the session. It did bewilder me somewhat. Can, and how can, a person with a mental disorder and taking psychotropic drugs do good therapy? He clearly thinks he can. I clearly think he can't.

I had no clue as to his inclinations and capacities at home; but at work, I did. This psychologist worked long hours and took extra work home. He voluntarily got involved in additional project work and was prolific in getting documentation done and attending management meetings. The word *dedicated* comes to mind. The other things that come to mind were *achieved, ambitious,* and *grumpy.* He was admired by many, and we accepted his occasional grumpiness as a small part of the deal.

To many, he seemed the ideal psychologist, and I'm one of those that learnt much by working in that team. It wasn't like that for everyone, though. Disagreements with Simon led to dislike, and a number of team members found themselves on the outer. Still, in many ways, he was very technically competent; and his clients would mark him highly on that.

But he wasn't, was he? Well, he was and he wasn't. His mind is problematic. If antidepressants work at all, which is unlikely, masking the symptoms does not fix his internal dilemma. Some part of him was not happy, craving for something. And he was getting some of it from his clients. My analyst interpretation is that he sought out admiration. Simply put, Simon was at his best when people looked up to him. It helped him feel pride. In itself, that is not a bad thing; our ordinary drives are there to help us develop and individuate. But a psychologist is at their worse when they are accidentally using their client's weaknesses to fill a need springing from neurosis.

Often during therapy, a psychologist will disclose something about themselves. They are not an empty book. But that disclosure must be in the context of resolving the client's dilemma, not our own. Are you able to see the unconscious motive for Simon disclosing his mental illness to the clients? Remember, these clients seek attachment and bonds and can't regulate their emotional content. Can you imagine what the clients felt with Simon's disclosure and their consequential reaction to Simon?

Well, of course, I was in the room, so I know. A number felt sorry for Simon, sympathy for his plight. Some even offered support from their (disordered) experiences. Most started to feel a bond, the start of admiration for him. Self-disclosure is the food for bonding, and it suited them. It worked their disability, and it promoted their disordered splitting of all-good and all-bad people. Simon was now one of the all-good people in their world. It was not helpful; rather, in my opinion, it set back the building of a good therapeutic relationship. The foundation of the relationship was corrupt and so therapy forever flawed.

I suspect Simon in some way understood this. After all, he is technically competent. But group feedback admiring your work is therapy for Simon. Not good therapy but therapy that keeps Simon rocking up to work.

For me, I regularly made a point of polishing his badges, making him stand out. It got me lots of easy brownie points, and hey, I needed the work.

What is the takeaway from this case? I suspect you already know. After all, without exception, all of us have sought admiration and bathed in its sunshine. It is definitely in me. Often in session, I have to remind myself that I'm more privileged than admirable and that plainness is underrated. In my rooms, I make sure there are no photographs of me or

JOSHUA THOMAS

my family. There are no certificates and diplomas on the wall to make me look good and reassure you—and me—that I'm clever. I don't even wear my wedding ring with clients. I try to be plain mashed potato and peas. Outside of the room, I live a life that keeps my mind clean. Oh yes, I have my neurosis and attributes that could defeat therapy, but I try to leave them at the door.

That's what you are looking for in your psychologist: careful plainness, someone who is happy knowing a lot more about you than you about them. But that won't be possible if they are carrying unresolved trauma, depression, or anxiety. By definition, mental difficulties are a disorder of the mind. How can that person then be trusted not to use you, the vulnerable client, to soothe or avoid their problems?

They can't.

Of Good Age

True or False?

Your psychologist has the capacity to work with you because they are well credentialled and have had five years of experience helping people just like you.

I want to say no, do you?

I wish you did not have to discriminate based upon age, but you do if you want to have a better chance of being with a good psychologist. Imagine you are 27 years old and have recently been in a car crash where your husband was killed and your promised future evaporated. You've incurred trauma that needs resolving but also lost your life partner, and dreams, to fate. Or let's imagine you are 35 years old with family dilemma. You are experiencing depression and perhaps drinking way too much. Just how is that 30-year-old man sitting in front of you going to help you? Well, he can if you believe in 'treatments'. But hopefully, I've put the idea of treatment into the same category as Santa Claus. That's harsh, isn't it?

We don't like to, and I'm not even sure if we are allowed to discriminate by age. It is possible that the 30-year-old has squeezed in a lot of deep life experiences. Perhaps himself being in a car accident or even having experienced prolonged depression. But that's not the point, is it? Psychological therapy is never about working with shared experiences.

The point is that your patterns of experiencing the world, and therefore appreciation of that world, take a lot of time and work. And it's the same for your inner world. Patterns of experiencing yourself deeply, and therefore deep appreciation of yourself, take time and work. Many folk never make it, never even get halfway on that quest, never really find the way to self-appreciation. I figure some get close by middle age, and that's a good starting point for you.

If a psychologist is really going to work well with you therapeutically, you need someone middle-aged or older, don't you? If you're older than middle age, you must seek out an even older person, so have to be even fussier.

<u>Case of David</u>

Life was going awfully wrong for David across a number of life domains. His doctor referred him to me for counselling and had prescribed antidepressants to help lift the depression. David was 60 years old.

Mental State.

David presented looking stated age of 60, tall and of ordinary weight. Dressed in jeans and a paisley shirt. Initially, he appeared casual, relaxed, and smiling. Good rapport, David willing to participate in an easy conversation about the weather, day, and busyness of the streets. Mood stated as 'mostly good'. Affect incongruent with stated mood as David became teary and upset. Speech normal, thought processes distressed, fused with feelings of loneliness and not belonging. Thought content mostly about questioning the meaning of life, especially in the context of his Christian beliefs. No evidence of perceptual abnormalities, nil delusion or hallucination. Memory not formally tested, but David able to recall recent and distal memories. Insight fair, recognises he needs assistance. Judgement impaired, suicidal ideation persistent.

Background

David explained that he is questioning who he is and how that works in his life. He said he left Surry, England, in his teenage years and feels that he belongs back there. David said he thinks about going home more than ever now, feeling disconnected from his life here in Australia. He told me that he lived here because he is married, has two adult daughters, and has built a career in IT. David explained that his dad had died three years ago. His mother is still alive but quite sick, living in a nursing home. Otherwise, David said that he is quite alone. David described having working relationships at the office but no close personal friendships. David said he attends church each weekend and reads the Bible for solace and direction. But that had not been helping recently, and he is also questioning his faith.

David described his childhood in Surry as ideal. He recalled the freedoms of growing up in those days, close to rural lands and forests. He told me that he knows that neighborhood like the back of his hand, and he has never developed that sense of belonging here in Australia. He put that down to his family moving around every few years because his dad was in the army. Still, he did well at school; and that, along with church, formed the basis of his life until he was 18 years old. After school, he got a part-time job whilst he went through university in a regional town in Victoria.

David said that he met his wife through church at the age of 22; and they settled into having a family, raising two girls and a boy. Their son died an infant from a blood disease, which set them back as a family. But with local support and their faith, they recovered and have lived an ordinary life. David told me that, until recently, he did not think that there was such a thing as a mental disorder. When he had hard times, he focused on his faith and the wisdom within the Bible.

David explained that things really started coming apart for him after his dad died. It was not unexpected, but it seemed to take away another family link to Surrey in England. Around the same time, his workplace started a programme to reduce costs because of government budget cuts. The consequential restructures were never ending; and although there was no obvious threat to his job, it was all done in secrecy. This process caused endless suspicion and distrust in the workplace, and the job satisfaction he used to feel had evaporated.

JOSHUA THOMAS

On top of all this, his mum had a chronic illness, and the family had decided to move her into a nursing home. David said that he understood the reality of the situation, but the decision had left him with feelings of guilt and shame. He could not see anything on the horizon to be optimistic about. David explained that he did all his emotional work alone and on the inside and that his family did not know how bad it was for him. He would not talk with his wife about all this or ask for her help because he already felt like a miserable burden to her.

David was on a week's sick leave, and his wife thought he was with me getting some general counselling about how to cope with workplace distress.

Okay, 30-year-old psychologist, go for it! Do your CBT or ACT and see how that works.

It can't be done, can it? In fact, David was first referred to a nearby 29-year-old psychologist. David told me he attended for three sessions, but it felt like 'them asking for the time, then me giving them my watch'. David can't be helped by someone who has a treatment for depression. His life is a wonderful long personal recipe, and what he needed was a psychologist who was seasoned.

During our first session, it became very obvious that David's actual life was in real trouble. Self, family, work, and faith all broken or at breaking point. No one can do that on their own. I know because I've tried, and I nearly died. Asking for help and putting your trust in another's capacities seems impossible, burdensome, and wasteful. Yet this was the first step for David.

He trusted a seasoned campaigner of life, and I made a life raft with him in the form of a safety plan. I then walked alongside him to emergency triage so they could also play a part in his turnaround. At triage, they called his wife, who came in; and within two hours,

David was standing up with others to lean on. He was enacting his faith. He had moved his relationship with the Lord from helper to helped, a place he needed to take his turn in.

I saw David again the following week, and we agreed that we would follow the protocols of acceptance and commitment therapy. ACT is another cookie-cutter therapy but had some very useful practices for David. And telling David that I know what will help, that I know the steps to recovery, and that everything is going to be okay was the most important thing I could do. Taking that warm but authoritative stance, I put my arms around this lovely, broken man. There, we must talk of life, death, God, family, lineage, love, belonging, meaning, and ourselves—and we did. None of that is in ACT, of course.

Look, I'm not a Christian but was brought up with church and praying until I got to maybe 12 years old. Mam thought it would be good for us kids, and she was right. As an adult, I've certainly taken the time to read the Bible and studied many of the major stories. It does not matter if you think they are true or not. The stories were written for mostly good reason. The book of Job comes to mind, which is an insightful Hebrew text.

Otherwise, I'm simply just old enough for David. After all, age must accumulate life. At some age, everyone has experienced the death of family, moved from their homeplace, fallen only to accept good help, and rebuilt a life from premature death. Everyone has lost their love and questioned their connection with others. All that stuff that comes with time is seasoning, and you get more seasoned as you age if you're living an ordinary life.

David was a tricky case. He was overtly suicidal, and his depression had no single precipitating factor. His predispositions made him susceptible to his inevitable fall. Too self-reliant, too concerned for others, too sensitive of his impact on the world, and too intelligent to not have

JOSHUA THOMAS

answers. Happy to self-sacrifice, he had not really appreciated the Good Samaritan story, which, if misread, fuels guilt and burden in ordinary folk. Everybody takes their turn on the side of the road, broken and dying, needing another to help.

This case illustrates the need for seasoning in the psychologist. Therapy is not about empathy based upon shared bad experience or trauma. Rather, the question to be asked is 'Does the psychologist wear their wrinkles kindly?'

If they do, then they have brought something special into the therapy room: their wisdom.

So just like in all the best stories, seek out the wise woman or the wise man. In many ways, they are the archetype sage, the seer of your path forward, your best parent and trustworthy teacher.

Works with Complexity

If you've seen iconic photographs of natural Australia, then you certainly know that those billions of grass termites living in northern Australia are very clever. Maybe you've been and stood next to them, amazed at their mud dwellings, which are often two metres high. During winter, you can enjoyably walk amongst their red or grey houses and take your photo snap and smile. But not in summer because within seconds, the scorching sun will beat you back into your air-conditioned car. In northern Australia, that sun is a wicked problem for life, or maybe it is the lack of shade. The latitude, flatness, lack of plant life above grass level, and clear skies make it too hot. Cause and effect make it all but impossible for such large biomass to exist. But it does.

If you were going to live and thrive there, you would need to think hard and long about that complicated, wicked problem. And of course, we have. Mostly, we decide not to live there; but when we do, we often solve that problem with technology: air conditioning.

We have studied physics and understand laws about the conservation of energy. You can't actually cool heat down. So we need to move the heat energy inside our home to the outside. We do that by generating electricity to power refrigeration compressors and fans. By forcing the hot air inside our house around pipes containing coolant, we move the heat into that coolant. Then we move the coolant to the outside where we squeeze it so tight that the coolant condenses and forces the heat out of it. A large fan then blows that heat away, and the coolant circulates back inside to start again. That system was a breakthrough design around 1930, and we haven't been able to improve on it.

But those clever grass termites don't need your air conditioning to thrive there. They have something that is even more complicated than our air conditioning and hard to replicate. Anyway, it seems they also understand the law of conservation of energy and know how to move heat around. Inside their houses, they have built a chaotically complex network of many thousands of corridors and doors that, if working together, keep their cool, so to speak. It really is chaos inside. Tunnels, flaps, and termites crawling apparently in any and every direction. We can't follow what is happening even when we concentrate.

Now I've been told I have the intellect of an ant, but I still doubt the conscious-thinking and problem-solving capacity of these termites. But they do build this lifesaving air conditioner and then run it on hot days. You see, nature has provided something we understand these days as complex adaptive systems. It puts chaos to work.

Thinking differently, we can see that the termites' chaotically complex system works with the simplest of actions: opening and closing hatches. As the termites get about their work, whatever that is, they open and close doors based upon the temperature inside their tunnel. As they do this, excess heat is captured and moved from the inside to the outside of their sunbaked houses. A supercomplex colony resolves a wicked problem by simply opening and closing doors!

Once we know this, it seems obviously simple. In fact, we should have known about this simplicity all along. It's just that we didn't. There are many examples of this distillation of the chaotically complex into the simple. Perhaps you have wondered how hundreds of budgies fly safely within inches of one another, swooping and dodging like a clever cloud, or how schools of fish move in unison within a blink of your eye. Perhaps you have sown the simple seed of kindness into your child to see it grow into complex interpersonal relationship capacities. Have you tried instilling that capacity in an adult who does not have that seed? Good luck with that!

Anyhow, good psychologists don't think like you imagine. Yes, they are connecting dots but not in the straight lines of cause and effect. Their mind can do that; they can do cause and effect really well. But in therapy, their mind is mostly working with your chaos, distilling that chaos into simple real-world models. We do that so we can work with you on the simplest of capacities such as kindness, honesty, forgiveness, acceptance, and taking a step forwards.

This ability to conceptualise complex, chaotic, unsolvable dilemma through distillation and see it through simplicity is an attribute of the good psychologist. But some people have it; others just don't and can't. It is imperative that you find the good psychologist who does.

<u>Case of Suzanna</u>

Good psychologists, bad ones too, are obliged to complete continuous development of their practice. It's an obviously good idea to keep ourselves up-to-date and learn and hopefully become good psychologists. One compulsory way this happens is through peer supervision and review. I'm a member of a small band of good psychologists that do this stuff together often over an evening meal at someone's home. I like to think I'm on the lookout for those small bits, those insights that make me better at my job. This is a case in point.

One evening, we had each discussed a case, seeking feedback about our practice and, of course, advice on how to proceed. Most had been about helping folk with depression and related symptoms. It is an awful, wicked, and common disorder and one that is well researched and studied.

The aetiology of major depression disorder is complex. No one can really work out the causes and effects, although we were having a good go at it. We were discussing predisposing, precipitating, perpetuating, and protective factors. Yes, we have our language, a bit like I imagine Martians would have, because no one on earth understands us! Anyway, we were talking about those factors that make some folk susceptible to major depression disorder. And we were relating that to how we best help people. For example, cognitive behaviour therapy is a complex multistage, multistep process aimed at undoing the complex and interconnected factors that maintain the disorder.

That night, there was much discussion, analysis, and suggestion. In my notes, I had written half a page, which is an awful lot for me. I had lists, boxes, and lines and arrows going every which way. I'd got myself into an analytical mode. I'm very clever, you know! Obviously, just like the disorder, contributing factors were very complex, hard to discuss and explain, even in Martian. I asked Suzanna, another good psychologist, what she thought. Suzanna looked at me with her all-knowing confidence and said, 'Gratitude.'

Suzanna had distilled every research paper ever written, every lecture, the Beck depression triad, psychoanalytical defence systems, protective attributes, and more. She brought it down from Mars into earthling language. One word, one idea, one experience, and one action. Gratitude.

Wow!

Can something as complex, personally experienced, and chaotically debilitating be distilled like that? Sure, it can! And it must be if we are to work with our clients outside of Mars. I've got my whisky for depression too. I often find myself asking clients what it is like being 'stuck' or 'fallen down'. Now, none of these distilled, simple, but provocatively useful truths are in our manuals. They come from within the good psychologist who is fluent with complex systems thinking.

Systems thinking is really quite new to people and is difficult to do because we are not taught it. Well, that is not quite true. In the olden days, systems thinking was ordinary thinking. They just didn't give it a fancy name. But it is new to new people because we are taught and love cause and effect and argument. In fact, often, problems are found just so we can argue our positions and stop the causes. It keeps us busy, I guess. Anyway, we know that wicked effects, like depression, are caused by complex mechanisms and processes. I'm still to be convinced of that, but perhaps they are. But if we use complex mechanisms and processes to solve them, we can't! Likely, we make it worse. Bad psych.

Our minds and those of our clients struggle to build those complex mental models because minds like real-world, earthling material. So our therapy must be a representation of the real world, not some reductionist explanation or micro step-by-step process hoping we can cause a different effect. By the time we've covered all the causes and explained all the steps, the client has died on us. Or at least run out of money. We need to get there quicker but in a way that the client understands as real, human, and easily shared.

I know that Suzanna's distillation to gratitude will work because I can work it backwards.

- If I'm thankful for what I have, I don't need much to feel good.
- If others are thanking me for my help, then I'm useful and worthwhile.
- If I'm thankful for having known someone, I can handle losing them.
- If I'm thankful for my privilege and opportunity, then I'm compassionate to people less fortunate.
- If I'm thankful for my vocation, then I can enjoy my work.
- If I'm thankful for my capacities and individuality, then I don't need admiration from others.

JOSHUA THOMAS

This attribute of being comfortable working in chaos and complexity and distilling that into simple earthling language, experience, and action is an essential ingredient in the good psychologist. Without it, the psychologist is stuck in the realm of Martian models and with the limited tools of cause and effect. Your life is not like cause and effect, is it? It is many, many causes and many, many effects. Attempting to work on one cause or one effect is like trying to connect just two distant stars in the sky together. You will get a little way and quickly realise you are lost in a futile process. Isn't it better to stare at a star that gets your attention and then allow your eyes to go where they may? Maybe feel like you belong to something simply magnificent?

So seek out the psychologist who can work with patterns and use their intuition. Maybe they will tell you that they are using detailed information and a step-by-step cause-and-effect process. But that will be to comfort you and help you feel safe whilst you both explore and distil your chaos.

Work with Their Limits

What do you think is the cause of most deaths when climbing Mount Everest? It's the altitude, lack of oxygen, jagged steep slope, deep snow, cold, and the changing weather. Well, most likely? No, actually, it is nothing to do with anything outside of the person. It's their psychological difficulty that kills them. Climbers that have died knew they might not make it, knew that they should quit and turn back. Only they didn't. They carried on, even understanding that it wasn't going to work out.

They are very dead, of course; it's both sad and tragic really. So we can't actually ask them about their psychological dilemma. But others who survived by the skin of their teeth have given an insight into the problem. One theory is that keen, competent, and motivated people have trouble accepting that they have gone as far as they should—that is, they are quite happy not to start or go a e bit and turn back. But once they have gone most of the way, they can't turn back. They would rather die than call it quits even in the face of, or better put, in-your-face obvious danger. My idea is that the theory holds up for psychologists too. If they go so far with you, a keen, motivated, and seemingly competent psychologist won't quit with you when they should. They don't admit that what they are doing is causing harm or at least wasting your time.

I'm not sure about mountain climbing. I can't and don't want to climb a big rock 'because it is there'. But I have been known to climb the occasional fence, ladder, and tree too high to steal some figs. Anyway, aside from the Everest syndrome, your psychologist is also invested for secondary gain: money. Imagine a good baker selling good bread for good money. Now, when they run out of good bread, they could sell you bad bread and take your money. But the good baker won't. She will tell you that she has nothing left for you. Best you go elsewhere, maybe save your money, maybe make your bread, maybe try the discount store if you really must have any-old bread.

The same for the good psychologist. She will tell you she has nothing left for you and be honest about your options. But there are very few psychologists that will do that. Psychologists need a special attribute for that. Let's call it humility. Humility, to me, in this sense, means being honest about what they can and can't do or should and shouldn't do—working with their limits.

Dangerous for you is the fact that most psychologists are quite happy to give you, and be paid for, bad psychology. Long after they have been useful to you, they will sit, passing your time and wasting your money. They know what they are contributing amounts to nothing, except maybe some company for an hour a week. But they aren't saying it. They are staying mum.

<u>Case of Kamali</u>

Kamali is a general psychologist that I hired in 2013. She did not do the hard yards of learning but took one of the shortcuts, the easier way to get her registration. I'm critical of that because of the lack of taught technical competence. Enough said! However, there is something crucial that Kamali does on a regular basis. This is one case example.

In 2020, Kamali came to my house to discuss some of her cases and get my thoughts on her practice and practice direction. She won't mind me saying that we both know that she lacked basic competencies when she attained her registration. Consequently, when I first hired her, I would not allocate anyone with a mental disorder to her. Only simple counselling and problem solving for Kamali.

Still, over the years, she has done plenty of professional development and has built a much better technical base to work from. Most importantly, Kamali only works with people she can help. Even so, Kamali could be a good baker, selling bad bread, and she knows it.

In 2020, a GP had referred their patient to Kamali for assistance with low self-esteem, poor mood, and ongoing patterns of self-sabotaging behaviour. Her client had recently been with the Barwon Health 'Access Team' following a crisis. The risk of deliberate self-harm was low, and this man would likely do well with practical, psychologically informed practices. Right up Kamali's alley so to speak, a good match by the GP.

Kamali charges about $160 per 50-minute session, which is on the lower side of the price scale. Of course, she works more than 50 minutes for each client. And considering administration fees, recordkeeping, and letter writing, her actual rate is more like $80 per hour. Likely less than your local plumber but still good money for good bread. And after all, Kamali is not going to do complex therapy or work with folk with very complex and risky difficulties, is she?

Well, yes, she is actually. GPs are often quite crap at directing referrals based upon the competencies of the psychologist. Often, the best you get from the GP is 'Thank you for seeing Ms Smith for opinion and management.' Kind of slim information, isn't it? Anyway, Kamali does get to see complex and risky cases. But once that is understood through her assessment, she lets them know she can't do that work and gives them options. Humble and honest about her limits.

Anyway, back to the client in 2020. This man really did not present with much risk or complication. Not dreadfully unwell, he simply needed practices to improve his state of mind, self-esteem, and productive routines. Kamali discussed this case with me and was seeking direction. She explained that they had completed four sessions that had gone nicely in terms of joint formulation, motivational interviewing, and introductory practices that would likely help. But after four sessions, he had not tried any of the beneficial practices.

Kamali said that her client believed that they 'would not work for him'. Now, I'm not a true believer in the Almighty; but if I was in a sinking ship and someone suggested I quickly learn to pray, I likely would give it a try. I'd be motivated by my discomfort! Unfortunately, this man was unwell enough to need help but not unwell enough to do much about it. He was quite happy to rock up for each session and spend time there.

Now don't be mad at this guy. He had seen psychologists before attending with Kamali; and whatever they did, it did not help much. So in a way, he has good evidence for his stance. He simply is not motivated to do any work, and therapy is always work. Sometimes easy work but often hard work.

You personally might not be aware that people avoid hard work and like to take the easier, less-effort option. Buying an e-bike whilst your legs work really well comes to mind. Or driving to the shops only 1,000 yards away. Or using car navigation instead of your memory to get from A to D. I'm not talking about me and you, of course. Other people! Still, he was happy to pay good money for any-old bread, and Kamali was asked by the GP for 'opinion and management', which is kind of like asking for white bread. Plus, Kamali, just like many of us, has bills to pay and a life to invest in. There is good incentive all around to keep having useless sessions. He wants to, the GP wants to, and Kamali is tempted to. Except that she isn't.

When we discussed the case, I was promoting Kamali to do another round of motivational interviewing with him, trying to build enough steam that he would do some simple practices and realise that it was helpful. Hopefully go on an upwards cycle. But Kamali explained that was what everyone else had likely done and that he would go through the motions but was quite disinterested. Doing more would be bad psychology, what others had done. Instead, Kamali decided to tell him she would not sell bad bread, not take money for nothing. She would tell him to come back when he had decided to do something about his life. Another option offered was that if he wanted bad psychology, he should go elsewhere, perhaps to the discount store.

That conversation with him might save his life. Wasn't it about time that a psychologist told him that it was up to him?

Too many psychologists were not humble and honest enough with him. They had been prepared to work outside their ethical limits, albeit on the slack side.

As you can see, this attribute of being honest and working in your limits can apply to not only technical competencies but also to ethical ones. And at both ends of the difficulty spectrum. Psychologists are frequently put in a position where the work is too hard, but they persevere because they 'should' be able to help. The Everest syndrome plays out such that after going so far with a client, neither is prepared to call it a day when they should. Very often, psychologists are working with malingerers and are quite happy to spend the time and take the money, providing only bad psychology or no psychology at all. Perversely, many well-credentialled psychologists refuse to work hard with complex or risky clients, preferring, like Kamali's client, to have an easy life and only do easy work.

What does this mean for you? Well, the risk is that the psychologist is either out of their depth or else not trying, not working hard enough for you. Dangerously, you won't know unless they tell you, and that is your trick. It is very wise to simply ask your psychologist, 'Are you any good at what we are going to do?'

The good psychologist will answer with 'Yes, but we will both have to work hard.'

                    JOSHUA THOMAS

Addresses All of You

Yes, it is rude because you're not overweight, are you? You probably don't drink too much either. And, of course, people should stick to their own knitting. Psychologists work with the mind; doctors work with the body. So the doctor should have told you. And anyway, *fat* is a bad word, and people have a right to any body size. Just ask a jovial fat lady who is still singing. So most psychologists will not notice or mention your weight. They won't engage in that judging and shaming.

On the other hand, many mental difficulties are related to weight gain or weight loss. Many of my clients have eating problems from mild to dangerous. Too controlled or poor control—perhaps that's the same thing? And navigating that territory over the years has been tricky for them. Not enough to be an eating disorder but certainly a mental dilemma and a cause of other mental dilemmas. And it affects both the mental and physical capacities required to engage in life, confidence and agility, for example. Still, most psychologists will not notice or mention your weight. I find that quite interesting, do you?

Is the psychologist scared? Well, yes mostly. Fear of breaking rapport, fear of being judged themselves because most of us are overweight, and fear of hurting your feelings. Perhaps even fear of having to notice their body and the lack of care for it.

Exactly the same dilemma is frequent when noticing and discussing alcohol use, cigarette addiction, and Valium use. Many psychologists will go out of their way not to notice such frailties, all of which are at least life sapping, if not life threatening.

<u>Case of Jessica</u>

Jessica was referred to me by her GP for 'counselling' with regard to her history of depression and borderline personality disorder. At 23 year of age, she had spent a year with Headspace and more recently four months with Jigsaw. Headspace is the public's attempt to provide early mental health advice and counselling for young people. Jigsaw is the public service for young people with more severe mental health problems.

Presentation

Jessica presented dressed casually in dark loose-fitting clothes, long-sleeved shirt, looking stated age of 23. Seemingly grossly overweight/obese. Rapport initially was patchy. Eye contact satisfactory and conversation avoiding subject of therapy. Affect normal range, facial movements expressive. Said her mood was 'depressed and stressed'. Speech, quiet otherwise normal prosody and tone. Thought process somewhat avoidant, attempting to stay closed to enquiry. Mostly about her referral from Jigsaw and seeking entry to my group therapy programme because they could not do that there. Nil sensory problems observed, alert, memory intact. Insight good, appreciative of her mental state and mood problems. Judgement fair. Intermittent suicidal ideation, persistent with deliberate self-harm, Jessica cutting herself on her upper legs majority of days of each week.

Background

Jessica told me that she experienced periods of depression where she would become very lethargic and withdrawn. She said that it had been like that since childhood following the time when her dad left the family. She remembered her dad promising that he would stay close and that he loved her more than anything. But over time, he stopped having her visit him; and by the time she was at high school,

JOSHUA THOMAS

they did not see each other at all. Jessica described liking school and her teachers but being teased and then bullied by her peers for not fitting in well and having no friends.

Jessica explained that it was at high school she started to cut her legs. Other 'rougher' girls were doing it; and when she first started, it was like having a tattoo, a bit of a taboo. She said that the bullying stopped, and she got some friends; but she kept up the cutting, now in secret. She told me that when she does not cut for a few days, time goes slower; and eventually it feels like she gets full of 'white noise', static in her head. When she cuts, it goes away again. Jessica knew it was a circle of harm but said it was part of her and was just what she did. She said that she has a special hairdresser's razor that she uses and keeps close by in her bedroom.

Jessica told me that earlier in the year, she had met a 'lovely man' who understands and loves her. They had been going out for around six months when he went to see a friend. That friend was a girl; and Jessica said she got very jealous, expecting her boyfriend to cheat and then lie about it. Jessica said they had a big fight, and they broke up. She then took an overdose of antidepressants and made some deep cuts in her legs. The overdose did not work, there was too much blood, and Jessica said she panicked. After crying out for help, Mum took her to triage, the Barwon Health Access Team.

Jessica said the access team was really kind; and on assessment for risk, they discharged her and made an internal referral to Jigsaw. Jessica explained that at Jigsaw she was allocated a psychologist, provided the diagnosis of borderline dersonality disorder, and started a programme called DBT. DBT is dialectic behaviour therapy, quite an impressive name I think.

DBT is a mixed behavioural style of therapy with as good-as-it-gets evidence to support its use in reducing parasuicidal and DSH behaviours. Remember our graphs about effectiveness of treatments? Well, it turns out that DBT makes a difference to parasuicidal and DSH behaviours of about $d = 0.6$. That's still not great in real terms, and most people don't get better, but some do. But hey, we understand targeted treatments have their problems.

Unfortunately, in terms of helping with depression, Jessica's main complaint, DBT seems not to help much at all. It seems DBT gets you safer but not happier. Still, helping folk stay alive is a worthy cause. And I can't complain because it was me who formalised the DBT programme for youth at Barwon Health and then at Jigsaw. It is a manualised programme; and my job was to make it fit into the public health system, which I did. It's been running there for around eight years now. I'm not sure if it is successful, though, because the outcome and process measures that I recommended were, as far as I know, never implemented.

Still, Jigsaw is an institution; and like all institutions, Jigsaw must promote cookie-cutter step-by-step therapies. I'm sure there would have been a sincere, although misguided, discussion about which therapy would be most helpful for Jessica. Remember how picking a targeted therapy is really the same as cutting out lots of potent therapy? Anyway, the manual says it is a treatment that works, so they picked DBT from their list for Jessica. I presume because they mistakenly thought she wanted to stop cutting her legs, which she didn't—yet.

I was very curious with Jessica about what she thought were the roots of her problems. The problems were easy to define; but they are the symptoms, not the reasons. I'd noted that through all what she told me, which was quite insightful and detailed, she had not mentioned that she was carrying way too much weight for her little body. I asked her about that. I can't remember my words, but I'm a kind man who knows kindness often goes best with courage and straightforwardness.

JOSHUA THOMAS

I likely said, 'Jessica, it's way too complicated by now, isn't it? You got set astray when you were little, and although you've tried, you've never found your way back. Maybe you'll keep cutting and stay sad until you do. Depression can sometimes be heavy sadness, and you do seem sad. Your body too is likely suffering because of all that weight. It is way too big for you. How did it get so big?'

Not elegant I know, and I avoided asking about it until the end, but it was said. *Phew!* I remember Jessica looking up at me, tearing up, and saying that I was the first person to ask that question. Not Mum, not friends, not her boyfriend, not the doctor, not Headspace, not triage, not Jigsaw.

She then said that it was the question she most wants answered.

I really do believe the scientist-practitioner model works best. If I'd just been the scientist, I would have gone with DBT, you know, cause and effect; and DBT is a 'treatment that works' for BPD. But that is like doing therapy to a label, not seeing the person, not working from the very start with what they bring into the room. And clients always bring a whole lot. In Jessica's case, she brought her story, insights, questions she wanted answers too, her sadness, and her broken body. We needed to get to work.

Jessica set some objectives for herself. Go back to university and pass a unit, allow her boyfriend to build trustworthiness, and lose half of her weight. I helped her set some psychological objectives too. They were to heal the wounds of her past and leave them behind, change her relationship with herself to one based upon gratitude (yes, I stole that from Suzanna), and reduce her avoidance of emotional pain. In the room, we had an understanding that we would not finish the work required to get all that done. But we would work hard to make big inroads, not wasting our time.

We did have measures of our work together. Some as simple as turning up and counting our efforts. Others were more peculiar to Jessica, for example, caring for her body. We made up an index that would not hold up to scientific scrutiny in terms of reliability. But it was personally valid for Jessica, and she seemed to like counting and rating her self-care actions.

What therapy did we do? Well, I told Jessica we were doing schema-focused therapy. But the therapy was therapy, wherever it goes. We started at the start, Dad leaving and the sadness and mistrust that he handed over to her. Yes, it was not hers after all! We moved on to loneliness, feeling alone and separate, then onto making emotions happen and working through them in a useful way. We discussed dreams, movies, sexual pursuit, play, and work, whatever she brought with her into our room. She was a young woman, and I treated her as a healthy, dynamic person so she could feel what it was like to feel free. We did not do one self-harm diary, not a single distress tolerance or emotional regulation skill. It was not DBT skills that she needed.

We timed our work to cross over the new year. That is perversely important because the Medicare system then doubles your available subsidy. Instead of ten sessions, we went to twenty, which gave us six months together. Plus, Jessica joined my group schema therapy programme, with a special emphasis for her on 'healthy adult' roles. Another ten sessions. She did do a lot of work, didn't she? So what happened?

Jessica stopped cutting the second week of our therapy. It was not even on our list; but she just stopped, saying she had finished with that. She went back to university but failed the units she took. So she got a job in a shoe shop for three days per week. She loved working there. She lost weight at an average rate of 1kg per week for 26 weeks. Jessica's boyfriend had to live in Melbourne, but the relationship continued even though much of the time he was out of sight. She wrote three songs and played one of them for me. Towards the end of our work together, she used to smile quite a lot.

JOSHUA THOMAS

Unfortunately, as a psychologist, we don't get to see much more, and I wonder what life Jessica made for herself. Working hard and making change to life patterns is easier with a psychologist—or anyone really—who has got your back and is helping. When we stop the helping, we really are praying and crossing our fingers for our clients. But Jessica had felt alive and well, and she had not experienced that since her childhood years. I hope she pushed on.

The attribute of wanting to work with the whole person before you decide for them what they need and should do is rare. 'Not knowing' what help to provide, what therapy is warranted, and what the answers are for the person is anxiety provoking. And it takes courage to not stick with your knitting and address issues that might not be thought of as 'mental symptoms'.

People bring all of themselves into the room for a reason. They hope you are brave enough to address their frailties whatever they are. Whether it be being 'fat' as for Jessica or living in poverty or cheating on partners or drinking too much or being abused or even showing off riches. The good psychologist will work with all of that with you. The bad psychologist will pretend to be a clever scientist. You'll have a diagnosed illness, and here is the correct treatment. What a crock of shit that is. No wonder people don't get better.

What does this mean for you?

Well, you know yourself the best. So make sure that you stay the expert on you and don't let them fix you. If they fail to ask 'Aside from your symptoms, what else about your life concerns you?' tell them anyway and see if they can work with you.

If not, get out and find a good psychologist.

Leaves Their Ego at Home

But that's your ego speaking. Do you really think that you are that important? Just have a look in their car park. See any Holden station wagons? More likely, urban SUVs, perhaps Mercedes? Does that matter? No, not as long as they don't bring them into your room, it would clutter up the session I reckon. But you know what, most psychologists do bring their Mercedes urban SUVs into your room, quite unaware that they drove it in so you can see it or at least clean it for them.

Do you know Narcissus? Well, not personally, of course, but the story. It is one of my favourite simple stories that tell simple truths cleverly. Try saying that quickly! There are quite a few interpretations of his story, and this is mine.

A young boy grew up never really looking at himself, so never learning to love himself. Instead, he got love from being adored by his mum and others that saw how handsome he was. Grown up, although he was handsome and strong, he had no real love of his own inside. And so it became that Narcissus was kind of stuck with only superficial love for himself and the need for admiration to fill the hole that was left. Anyhow, when one day he saw his reflection in a deep pool, he could only stare in self-admiration. He stared so hard and long, he fell in and died.

Does that sound a bit like you? Well, it sounds a bit like me, and I know everyone carries a bit of Narcissus inside of them. Certainly, most psychologists have their fair share of narcissism; but just as in the story, they can't see themselves, and they fear they will die if they look.

Narcissism can be one form of an overgrown ego, such that a person seeks to express their handsomeness and strength, so they feel admired. It is a brittle and superficial veneer, like a Mercedes badge covering a Renault engine.

Do people really think they are better because they have that badge? Yes, they do actually, They already admire that badge and like to stare at it themselves. Self-admiration if you like. And don't you admire that badge? Every time you do, you look after their ego for them. They will fail to see their frailties because then they will see themselves for who they are: ordinary, like you. This is important because a psychologist who can't leave their ego, or at least the problematic bits, outside the door, can't give you the love you will need. They are better than you, in it for themselves, and you're the fodder.

<u>Case of Jean</u>

Jean is a psychologist.

Well, that's all I can tell you in terms of a real case study. If I told you more, I'd be sued maybe. Anyway, glass houses and all that.

Instead, I can tell you what to look out for, what to notice, and what to hope for. It is important because all other things being equal, if their motivation is weighed heavily towards interest in and care for you versus interests in and care for themselves, you have a good chance of being in Box A, good psych.

Anyway, let's give these problematic egos common names just to help us differentiate.

The Workaholic Ego

This ego works and works just like the pet mouse in its little wheel: around and around and around, doing the same thing over and over, but getting nowhere. Tiredness is both the reward and the only thing that can stop this psychologist.

In a typical day, they will complete seven, eight, maybe nine sessions of therapy. Lunch is taken between one client booking in and the other walking out the door. If you could watch from above, it would look like a turnstile of cattle, each having a turn in the branding station. Like any production line, mistakes are inevitable; and the product is homogenised, bland. Yet the psychologist with this ego will not see the blandness and will not count the mistakes. If they did, they would be forced to slow down, work less, and they can't tolerate that.

These workaholics are not driven by monetary reward; rather, it is an internal drive where time doing work is converted into feeling secure and worthwhile. You may have a workaholic in your family. They are everywhere because we institutionalise this mistaken drive through our religions, schools, and workplaces. Working harder makes you better, right? Well, these psychologists are the same. They see their work by the hour; and if they are not working, they feel like they're not working. Yes, I meant to say that. So the more they work, the better they feel.

They actually attain their psychic energy from the busyness, a drug if you like. If they take fewer clients—say four or five—spread sensibly through the day, what would they do with the rest of their time at work? They would be bored. It would seem wasteful to them, even though the quality of their therapy would improve dramatically.

The Narcissist Ego

Well, I've introduced this ego to you already. Let's be clear. A little narcissism can be a good thing if you can turn it on and off. It can help your mood stay up when things are going astray for yourself. And it can help get you good jobs and present well to others. The problem arises for therapy when the psychologist can't see it and can't turn it off.

Anyway, this ego booster looks good, dresses up, intellectualises, and is better than you in so, so many ways. Their best days are when admiration comes through to them. Admiration sometimes delivered from their reflection in the mirror, noticing the badge on their car or spending money they have more of. Otherwise, and on a daily basis, it's up to you to give them it. How you give it will be a surprise to you. You might think that it's when you say thank you or when you tell them you found the session worthwhile. But no, they expect that ordinary applause. What they get out of therapy is the added reinforcement of their betterness. Yes, that's a new word. Betterness is when they notice looking down on you, notice your inadequacies, frailties, and sickness—all the things they reject and feel disdain in themselves.

This betterness interferes with their—uh, sorry—your therapy. You are at best a foil for their expertise and flair. Unexpectedly, they appear very empathetic, interested, and concerned for you as if to ensure you are in your place in their room. They will sit in a big chair, stand up in front of you, and use whiteboards to act as if they are *the* teacher or to make sure you see their shined leather shoes. Their tissues that you apparently need will be strategically placed aside of you, just making it clear that you're the one in need of a good cry. If you do cry, don't expect them to move towards you or sit close to aid your comfort. They will be welded in their position, confused as to whether they just watch or say something they don't really mean.

It's not their fault they can't feel and respond to your emotion in an ordinary way or even pick it from your cues and act a response out. Their emotional life is empty and lonely; and although they will make themselves appear attractive, they don't know what to do with your emotional material. It is like a different language to them with syntax and morphology just beyond their grasp. Consequently, their therapy normally comes in a structural or behavioural form, where your inner world need not be explored. You are likely to be doing skills practice; form filling; ABC charts (antecedent, behaviour, consequence); and intellectual analysis that you did not ask for.

Meanwhile, the psychologist with this overgrown ego defence will be getting therapy too. Where else can a person find others so obviously worse than them and then be able to rise above and heal like a god? The ultimate elixir of betterness!

The Greedy Ego

From the good psychologist's thinking, wanting more can be a good thing if you have little or enough. It can provide security for that rainy day, perhaps even become a gift later on to someone in need. So you should have some 'greed' in you if you are going to have a full life. After all, you're not a Buddhist monk on some mission that means you can't have more than enough. In an ego sense, greed is a drive related to narcissism but focused primarily on taking wealth where it is available. And unless you print your money, that wealth comes from other's territory. It can be various forms of territory. Some examples are professional territory, business territory, and geographical territory; and it is not fairly dispersed. My suggestion to you is to find some greed and then learn how and when to turn it on and off within your moral grounds.

Yep, learn to make greed suit yourself and your citizenship roles. Still, many psychologists can't see the excess greed in themselves; and that inevitably leads to poor therapy, what I have called bad psych.

Two main greed territories are rife in psychology. By far the largest that I've already elaborated upon is within professional territory. Making and dreaming up therapies and calling them treatments is plain stealing. It steals territory once taken up by good psychology and in doing so has

JOSHUA THOMAS

made fortunes on the back of cookie-cutter therapies and cardboard-cutout credentials. You already know to identify them and steer well clear.

The second territory for greed is business territory. Psychologists and parapsychologists, with the greed ego, are happy to take over the business of good psychologists. They have successfully carved away at the territory once cared for by good psychologists and made it their own, so much so that in many towns and localities, good psychologists are hard to find, maybe even extinct. Think of the Indian minor displacing our beautiful honeyeater. Again, I have elaborated on much of this in part I of this book. Public health organisations march over and trample the business of good psychologists, not only taking the money but also ruining the reputation of psychological therapy in the process.

But a new wave of private businesses, mostly headed by psychologists enacting their greed ego, is ruining your access to the good psychologist.

During the recent pandemic, folk needed a way to retreat from even short travel and face-to-face therapy. Many became part of a holding pattern, stitched together by the allowing of bulk-billed telehealth, the weak alternative to proper therapy. According to the Australian Psychological Society, the APS for short, this telehealth was a revolution in health delivery. By the way, the APS is the union for psychologists of all ilk's, not just the few good ones. Their representative said that about 95 per cent of their members have taken up telehealth and that it had become popular for psychologists to consult with their clients electronically. The APS wants it available to their members permanently.

I promise you that I'm not really mean, but I know I can turn it on in spades. And so I should because this telehealth 'revolution' is a manifestation of the greed ego and needs burying, doesn't it?

Firstly, you can't do therapy if you're not in the room. The ordinary first step during every session of therapy is to complete a mental state examination, at least in your head. This means careful observation of the person's interaction with others, their walking and movement, their body and function, dress, self-care, hand gestures, and other nonverbal cues. I'm not clairvoyant, so I have to see the whole person, not just a bobbing head.

Much of good therapy involves multi-axial, nonverbal experience such as language cues, hand gestures, change in proximity, and such. Let's call it the prosody of the therapy interaction. Have you ever moved closer to, or farther away from, a person to change the kind of, or intensity of, your verbal and nonverbal interaction? How would you ordinarily work emotional content with your family? Perhaps move farther away from a greater distance? Rubbish! You'd move closer and get very close if it was tough stuff to work through.

And then there is the demonstration and practice of beneficial psychological exercises that must be done. But over telehealth, they become a waste of time because the client really can't see much, and you can't see anything they don't show you. You are reduced to talking in turns, perhaps at best solving today's practical problem but unable to work on life patterns, engrained psychological dilemma, and unconscious content.

Frankly, that's enough to ban the practice of telehealth except in emergency or for general counselling, where you're just talking. Therapy is not talking. That's just what people who are not educated might think, but talking is the weak link in the therapy chain. Can you imagine talking about your most important experiences and emotional content over the phone? Well, yes, you can because you've tried it. But it did not work well enough for you, and you have learnt that being with the person you are talking with somehow is a much richer experience. Simply better. That's because you are human, and any less than being next to the person degrades the experience. At best, mistakes and misunderstanding are common.

And what is the experience of the psychologist during telehealth? The same, of course. I've had a crack at it myself, you know, and it is at best supportive, like Lifeline could be I guess. Remember, this is not some kind of Zoom business meeting between two healthy-minded folk. At least one mind is having real problems, not working well, deteriorating, perhaps about to crash and burn. And the psychologist is working with broken radar. Just dumb and dangerous practice. Remember, the psychologist can't assume that the client is safe, especially in the early stages of therapy. Remember Jack?

I've spoken with a number of good psychologists and bad psychologists about telehealth. Their description of therapy and their opinion about its effectiveness, as a standard approach, are opposites. The good psychologists unanimously experienced gaps in their ability to do their best therapy. Interesting not all because of client engagement difficulties. Much was due to their ability to maintain a focus within the telehealth environment. They report finding their mind wandering more, perhaps even doodling on some paper, just out of camera shot. Some noted they felt a little bored, being somewhat detached from their client, even flipping screens, and scanning emails. All the things even a healthy mind might do when not being stimulated. It's normal and ordinary.

Again, unanimously, the good psychologists told me telehealth is not good enough as a standard approach. They told me that they would only use telehealth in an emergency if no alternative was available to their client, such as a good local psychologist.

Unsurprisingly, feedback from bad psychologists was that telehealth was quite effective because it made it easier and convenient for their clients. These psychologists did not report any problems in doing their work. And they told me telehealth was an efficient, low-cost method for them too. I presume because of the cheap overheads.

Hmm . . . you have noticed that both sets of feedback are true, of course. Remember how we paint our reality on the canvas in front of us? Now you're seeing things like a good psychologist. But what do you think greedy-ego psychologists are painting on the convenient canvas being laid out? What are they promoting and doing?

Remember the greed-based rush to the free money that happened with the Primary Health Network's Psychological Therapy Services programme? Yes, the one that can put you in front of the cheapest and poorest provider possible. Well, with the advent of the government throwing free money at telehealth, we see greed egos emerging everywhere. Why not become the centre of telehealth, steal client bases, and start taking up the territory of good local psychologists? After all, you can be in Melbourne or your backyard in Kangaroo Island and now do psychology to anyone anywhere.

This stealing of clients is not fanciful. I know of a good local business that has lost clients to a telehealth business that hires parapsychologists for goodness' sake. And because clients give them their Medicare rebates, they can charge a big ripe fee! Such a telebusiness—yes, that's another new word—will charge you $90 out of pocket, plus your Medicare rebate, a total of $210 for talking to you for an hour. Yep, today you can find this kind of telehealth service as easy as your next mass-produced hamburger. It's probably just as good for you too.

Can you hear the *kaching, kaching, kaching* of money moving around? Over the internet, of course. In the meantime, telehealth destroys access to good psych provided by good psychologists. And it's becoming a race to the bottom. Ordinary psychology businesses and now public health are also expanding telehealth to collect and keep even local clients. Remember, psychology has become an industry! And dumbed-down client convenience is driving its direction.

Telehealth for everyone? Whilst the good psychologist wonders why, the greedy ego says, 'Why not?'

Unless you live remotely, perhaps in smaller towns, your good psychologist works nearby, has a room, and charges you what they are worth.

> True or False?
>
> *The most important thing to look for in your psychologist is that they have a blend of technical competencies and personal attributes that have become more an art form than a technique.*
>
> The answer is yes.

THERE IS A little model that I found in the 1990s that still works today to help you figure out how expert someone is or you are. It assumes that when we start on our job of providing therapy, we are incompetent, naive. These days, I think that is very true. To be honest, I thought I might know most of what I needed to know before I started my master's program. I get that arrogance from my dad, remember? And I did find much of the content easy to assimilate and add to my knowledge. Following my master's, I was sure I knew all I needed.

Boy was I wrong. I was naive, unconsciously incompetent. What I mean is that I did not know I was incompetent; my mind did not think that way. Only when I started with real-life clients, face-to-face with people's lives and dilemma, I realised I was incompetent. Like a brand-new day, it dawned on me that the amount I knew was far less than the amount I did not know.

	Unconsciously	**Consciously**
Incompetent	First Stage	Second Stage
Competent	Final Stage	Third Stage

JOSHUA THOMAS

In effect, for years, I had been sitting in the first stage of competency, unconsciously incompetent. Blissfully and arrogantly knowing what I needed, only I didn't. I'd done all the learning. I'd aced exams and gotten awards for research, even been published. But I was unable or unwilling to face my incompetence and impotence. What forced my hand was trying to do therapy with real people, with real lives with real mental dilemma. Nothing from my coveted textbooks seemed useful anymore.

Still, at least, I'd been told, so to speak. And now I knew I had to get a lot better. I had moved to the second stage of competence: consciously incompetent. That doesn't sound very competent, does it? But it is a big step to take, coming to grips with how little you know or can effectively do. That's when I had to work harder than I ever worked during my studies. I was no longer content to regurgitate the subject-based matter that I'd been fed over the last six years of formal study. I decided that I needed to become a good psychologist, whatever that meant and whatever that took.

Being able to sit uncomfortably in that second stage, consciously incompetent, allowed me to develop and grow as a person and then a psychologist. I am sure that you do it in that order. First, you continue the work on yourself, and then you grow and develop the attributes of a good psychologist. Slowly, over the next few years, you become competent, good at psychological therapy.

The avenues of adult learning must suit the person; and for me, it was the search for meaning and connectedness. Identifying the connections across therapy styles and protocols, for example, allows me to see why many therapies are the same for the client. That's despite psychologists arguing in Martian and politicising various theoretical standpoints. It also lets me see what does not connect—what is, in fact, nonsense—bad-psych myths made up to suit institutions and the drives of individuals.

I needed to find meaning and purpose in my work beyond the temporary resolution of symptoms. People don't like to hear that symptoms of neurosis tell you that something is wrong with your life or the way you are using your life. But it is 100 per cent true. For me, symptoms are there to tell you something about yourself, if only you and I could listen. So my work became more about a person's healing, leaving behind stuff that keeps them stuck, and adding stuff that moves them along. My Jungian experience would say helping people further individuate, become the person of their potential.

For myself, making meaning and purpose forced me to leave the supportive public setting and establish my practice, a little small business providing good psychology. There, I'm allowed and free to understand our evidence for therapy and be honest with my clients that therapies don't work. I certainly would not have fitted in the public psychology team if I was to tell my clients that the therapy we are providing is missing many potent ingredients and that, although the brochure says it is a treatment that works, the best evidence is that it won't for you. In fact, for many of you, it will make you worse. Nope, that message would not be welcome at all.

So freed from the myths of psychology, I worked and learnt. For me, this book is difficult to write because I'm forced to think and explain how psychology works differently. If I told you that psychology is seven-parts art, two-parts technique, and one-part arse, what would you think? How could you use that information despite its succinct accuracy? Whilst consciously competent, it would be simple to explain what I do and how. In explaining driving your car, you're able to say how to steer, how to change gears, how to navigate, how to start and stop, and how to watch others through mirrors. But you don't actually do that, do you? When you're driving, you get in the seat and go. All the other stuff melts away into your expertise of driving. You are unconsciously competent and no longer need all the parts. That is why it is hard to teach your kids to drive. You could teach them all those parts, but they still would not be able to drive on real roads, would they? If they did, it would be very messy, and it often is.

Well, it's the same for explaining therapy. Experts have long forgotten all the steps and parts. In fact, according to the model, until they are forgotten, the psychologist is, by definition, not an expert. When you remind them of a part or bit, they, of course, have assimilated that part and gone further by changing and enhancing it. Don't tell an artist how to make the colour green by mixing proportions of blue and yellow. I promise you, they stopped painting by numbers many years ago.

If your psychologist is still doing it by the numbers, then it indicates what? Well, it indicates that you could do it yourself. You can paint by numbers, and that is what self-help books are for. So just read a book maybe? But if you want good psych, seek out a real person who will spend good time with you in person, a psychologist technically competent but has forgotten more than they remember.

Your first check on the psychologists should be browsing the AHPRA register of psychologists. Click on their name and review their credentials. If they have endorsements for counselling or clinical psychology, then that is a good start. It means they did not take the easy route to play with your mind. If they don't, then unless you know otherwise, assume they are incompetent in anything other than cookie-cutter therapy. It is imperative that you remember that if they are not endorsed, then they *did* take the shortcut. They can argue the point, but they must lack technical competencies. They might not even know how medications work or rather don't work. Or even how memory happens or how the parasympathetic nervous system works or how emotional content gets expressed. On the other hand, they likely can talk quietly just fine and can explain what a negative thought is.

Your second check will have to be done during your first session with them. Your psychologist will think they are assessing you. But it is much more important that this step be you assessing them. Your therapy should wait until you have gotten your good psych assured. That is a good psychologist who can do good psychology with you. How can you be assured? Well, I've made a table and a rating scale and put it at the back of this book.

Work your way through it like a checklist or scoresheet. Remember, there are no perfect psychologists. In fact, that would be an oxymoron. Still, you will need to be able to complete a rough mental state examination (MSE) of your psychologist. We Martians are good at MSEs. It's a word we throw about like the Spanish do olé at the bull killing!

In completing the MSE of your psychologist, all you are doing is observing them and their response to your enquiries. It takes less than ten minutes, and you're seeking ordinariness. Anything other than ordinary is a flag to consider. You've been reading my rough MSEs in each case example I've taken you through so far. So it will feel familiar to you. Let me give you a case example:

<u>Mental State Examination, Joshua Thomas</u>

Josh presents in casual dress, short tidy hair, kempt but looking as if unshaven for a few days. Looks younger than stated age of 63, ordinary build and weight, no striking features. Rapport satisfactory. After some chitchat, Josh willing to start work with me, open to questions, seemingly relaxed and tuned in. Affect was relaxed but focused, obviously working hard to listen to my story. Speech ordinary, a bit quiet. Ordinary prosody and tone. Mild accent. Thought processes mostly curious, also logical and goal orientated. Thought content mostly about why I think I need help and why psychology might help. Nil obvious ego problems. Collaborative, insight good with assured judgement.

That interaction and assessment would indicate that it is worthwhile you putting effort into working with Josh. Whoever he is, Josh is ordinary.

Contrast that with this MSE with another Josh:

Mental State Examination, Joshua Thomas

Josh presents smartly dressed with jacket and dress shoes. Well-groomed hair, kempt, and looking fashionable with a two-day growth of whiskers. Looks stated age of 63, ordinary build but underweight. Rapport satisfactory. Josh informative, confident, and engaging. Affect focused, obviously trying to explain what is wrong. Speech expressive and paced. Mild accent. Thought processes: intelligent, logical, and goal orientated. Thought content mostly about educating me on CBT and how it works for me. Mild ego problems—superior and betterness. Leading me, insight good with assured judgement.

That interaction and assessment would indicate less than good psych could happen in that room. Likely, bad psych will happen. Josh is simply not ordinary enough, and there is a distinct sense that he is already knowing what therapy you will do and why. You are the expert on you! Yet he is not really thinking that way at all.

That is not the balanced scientist-practitioner model of engagement, and you are working with too much of a scientist and not enough of a practitioner. You will be doing lots of evidence-based practices, logical step-by-step sessions, challenging what you already know to challenge. It will seem to be on the right track; but it will fail to get to the bottom of your internal and external dilemma, at best offering some temporary relief from symptoms.

This Josh is also a little odd, not very odd or odd in the sense that he is strange. But he is too flashy and too skinny. Whether you like it or not, your mind will use that canvas as material for you to project your insecurities on. And Josh does not work with unconscious material, so it will also affect his ability to complete good therapy.

What comes to your mind when you see some well-dressed guy? Is that an attractive look? Do you think of yourself as being too plain? Do you feel pride in your tradie presentation? Do you have an idea that he is well-off, successful? Do you feel more comfortable because you dress up too? Personally, I'd get the idea that he is a show-off or too formal or something like that. Somehow false. He might not be any of the above, of course. Those thoughts, feelings, and ideas are our bunny rabbits. Josh, of course, is blissfully unaware that we are painting our rabbits on him.

Because Josh does not know we are projecting our inner material onto him, he has no radar on the effect of that on him, never mind on you. Are you being extra polite? Are you holding back? Are you nodding when you wish you were saying no? Do you have an urge to flirt with him? Do you think he is showing off to you? Or are you planning to leave and not come back?

This Josh hasn't got a clue. Clueless! He is not ordinary, so can't see ordinary or not ordinary when it sits right in front of him. I guess that you will both carry on, complete CBT, tell kind fibs about how it worked well. Josh will not get the feedback he needs, so he can't correct his mistakes. Meanwhile, you think it was a load of shit, a waste of time, and you can't be helped.

Should have searched and found the first Josh I guess. Nothing really special about him, though. He just seemed to sit comfortably in the room with you. Now, his ordinariness does not mean being the same as you. You might like to think you're ordinary; but remember, it took that first Josh many years to get rid of his specials. You might just be starting down that path after years of thinking your life recipe was special, maybe a Master Chef version. But you will inevitably find that you and your life are not special, just a little unique. And that is plenty.

Still, in this part II of my book, I hope I have provided you insight into the attributes of a good psychologist. Although it is very true that a good

JOSHUA THOMAS

psychologist can do bad psychology, they are less likely to, especially in private practice. Importantly, only a good psychologist can do good psychology. So you can only be in Box A, when you are in front of your good psychologist. That's a good start, isn't it? Isn't it worthwhile trying to get good psych and preventing bad psych?

Your life might depend on it.

CONCLUSION

True or False?

Mentally, when you are at your most vulnerable, you are likely to get help that simply does not work. Rather, it will make you worse, make it your fault, and make it more complicated than it was.

The answer is yes.

Your mental health system is a kaleidoscope of public and private services, acronyms, job titles, institutions, and funding programmes pulling apart good psychology. Knowing who to see and determine if you are getting good psychological therapy is impacted more through myth, funding models, and convenience than assessment, diagnosis, and provision of good therapy. If your access to psychological therapy is governed more by chance than by informed choice, then you are very likely to get worse, not better.

This whilst you, the trusting client, believe *you* are the problem rather than the inconvenient truth that you have been getting bad psych.

My name is Joshua.

I am a well-credentialled and practiced clinical psychologist. I've worked within community health, hospital triage, and public primary mental health. I've led and supervised master's students and established a youth-specific programme run out of Jigsaw. In 2012, I established a busy private psychology practice. Being the principal psychologist there, I've hired, coached, and supervised others. I've spent years providing counselling and psychological therapy to clients experiencing mild to severe psychological disorders. I developed and ran the only schema-focused group therapy programme that works within the context of

Medicare. I work with people of all ages with moderate to severe mental disorders.

Prior to my psychology career, I have been a senior organisational development consultant in large to very large organisations. Through that career, the focus was on creating and sustaining people systems that were both effective and reliable.

I am in a better-than-fair position to see through the myths and mistruths and to let you, the client, know how to recognise bad psych and how to find good psych.

During my studies towards clinical psychology, I faithfully learnt and practised how to best help people of all ages with mental difficulties and disorders. I completed four-year undergraduate, then two years' master's, then two years' clinical practice under supervision. I meet the highest of competence and ethical standards set out by the Australian Psychology Board. I am well prepared to do this difficult and rewarding work we call psychological therapy.

But my work is bewildering.

- More than half of my clients have seen another psychologist or a mental health clinician but report that they did not get any benefit and that their difficulties endured.
- More than 80 per cent of my clients come with a wrong label or inadequate diagnosis.
- Many of my clients say they have gotten worse after accessing help.
- More than 80 per cent of clients cease therapy for financial reasons before they are well.
- Despite psychology being a regulated health service (AHPRA), anyone can prescribe psychological therapy.
- Despite psychology being a regulated health service, anyone can deliver psychological therapy.

There is good psych out here in the real world. But equally true, there is so much bad psych that it is actually rare that a person seeks help and gets well. Mostly, people experiencing mental difficulties languish relatively unharmed within junk therapy. But many are harmed by this bad psych; and it is getting worse by the day, not better.

This is my profession. I'm so ashamed and frustrated by what I see and our society's scorecard on mental health that I decided to write this book for you hopefully to change the balance in your favour, so the door to therapy you choose is based upon informed choice, not a badly weighted game of chance.

Having read back on this book myself–from the start to here, the conclusion—I've realised two things. I've noticed that I might be a good psychologist but that I'm definitely not a good writer. So I hope you have been able to get past my ordinary grammar and stuff. Perhaps smile and forgive me? But as you will have noticed too, this book is very critical, isn't it? The book says that, in the crucial field of psychological therapy, things are awful and are getting worse. It lays the blame at the feet of our leaders, institutions, and my fellow psychologists for not standing up for our profession and doing the hard yards. Instead, they're idly watching it get trashed and turned into efficient but cheap junk, not worth the private or public purse.

I can't tell you if anyone is actually lying barefaced to you on purpose. But leaders, institutions, and psychologists are lying to you. They leave out important truths; and instead, they misunderstand or misrepresent what therapy is and who is competent. They press on with making and providing cheap junk that you will trustingly consume. But like cheap-powdered mashed potato, it will stick in your gut and just be filling. So you won't heal, you won't grow, and you won't develop. Yet they will spruik evidence and statistics and invoke science as if it's on their side. You will be told that their offerings are based on knowledge, applied science, and good practice. Only it isn't. If they ever recognised good science and good practice, they have long forgotten or decided against it.

It is not like that knowledge, applied science, and good practice are not available in the field of psychology. To the contrary, we really do know how to make top-quality good psych and how to get it to you. You know, the psychology that works, lasts for ages, and makes you well. The psychology you deserve. But instead, you get sold cheap, disposable, poorly made, low-dose psychology off production lines. Being nostalgic, I can compare it to the junk Australians got sold from Japan before they, the Japanese, got their act together and decided that quality wins out. Interestingly, quality means less 'industry' and a smaller workforce because you don't get all the repeat repair business.

But in our case, psychological therapy, less repeat repair work is better, right?

Your answer to that question might depend on what side of the provider fence you sit on. Perhaps you are part of the bureaucracy that makes the junk. If so, you won't even see the junk because you can't, can you. And if you did notice it, you would look the other way, stay quiet. If you spoke up, you would have to backtrack, apologise, and make good the harm you have done. You might even have to close institutions and programmes, maybe lose your job.

Maybe you are a parapsychologist wanting your union to build an even bigger career path and access to more money. In that case, you might be happy to ignore the junk because it offers promotion and more money.

Maybe you're a GP, referring on, and you can't admit that you're a part of the damaged system.

Maybe you're the psychologist or client who, despite all the real evidence, would rather stick to the myths.

Whoever you are, it is tricky because we are all invested in more despite *more* meaning more damage to more people.

Look, I can't be sure if the people in charge of this chaos or those participating in the chaos know any better. I actually think that they believe their myths. But what I have demonstrated repeatedly throughout this book is that there is a kryptonite in the system. Not a little but so much that our therapy rooms glow green when you turn off the lights. That means your chance of getting good psych is quite awful. Just like in the game of chance at the start of the book, you must change doors, change your mind.

Obviously, being passionate about good psych, I completed a submission to the royal commission into the mental health system. This book is much more comprehensive and informative than that and, I hope, empowering to you, the client. But I did try to help them by drawing them pictures to tell it as it is.

Picture 1 represents what you think or hope will happen:

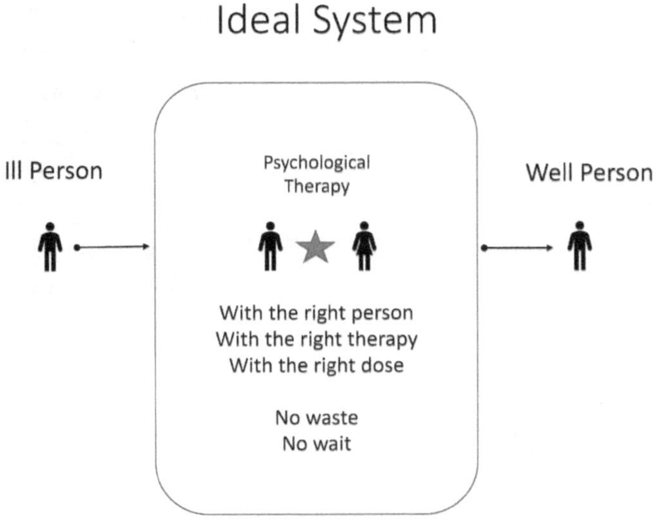

You're on the left. Then, you work with a good psychologist doing good psychology in the middle. On the right is the better you—healed, symptom free, with increased capacity. 'You're well', even 'weller'.

In picture 1, you don't stay crook. You move on and grow and do your life stuff. As more people are provided help, more people get better and fewer people remain crook. The system works.

The graphs of psychology spend and mental difficulties would look like this:

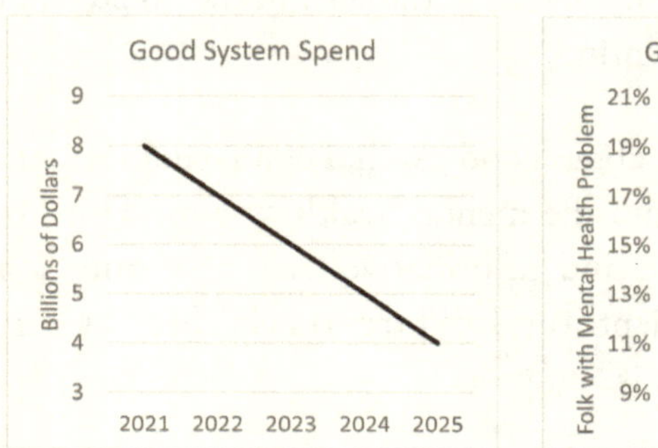

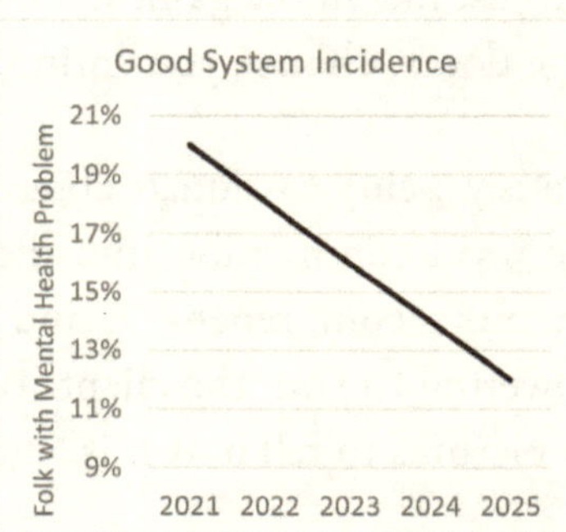

As we help more folk—and I mean really help them with good psych—fewer folk need repeated help. They get well, and so fewer people are staying crook or getting crooker. In terms of resources, there is less of the wasteful rework, so our costs go down dramatically too. This is one case where less is more. Get it? The other way of thinking about this is that the more well people we have, the less system we need.

We just need a good system like in picture 1 or as close to that as we can get! And we can have it because it is simpler and cheaper than the one we have now.

But what is the actual system we have now really like? Let's use the same picture format. And it looks like picture 2:

Actual System

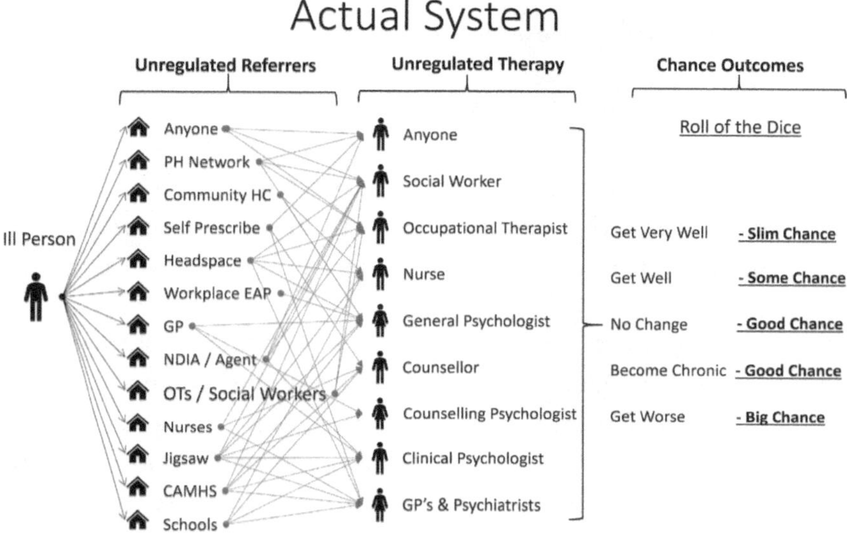

The plethora of referrers, most of which have never studied psychological pathology and therapy, means we have chaos at the very start. It is sold as choice; but really, it is just chaos. Each door is a potential pathway to bad psych. Which door would you choose? If you were 17, is it your GP or Headspace or your dad or triage or your school or social worker that sets you off to a good psychologist? I promise each can, and each would, send you somewhere else! Chaos!

This is not the good natural chaos, where solutions emerge. Rather, it is the man-made chaos, the kind that is confused and mistake ridden. Once through that door, most likely, you're not on the path to good psych. The odds were always against you.

Worse, the prescribers get to print and give out the money to whomever they feel: OTs to OTs, institutions to institutions, GPs to their darlings, and the primary health network to their contracted parapsychologists. It is mostly a marketplace, where the incentive is not good psych but easy cash, jobs, prestige, and feeling of worth. Yet what these referrers are doing is prescribing the most potent of all mental health elixirs—therapy—which, if in good hands, is a potent healer but in other hands a terrible poison to the mind.

In picture 2, if you look under who provides the therapeutic practice, the actual psychological therapy, it can be, and is, anyone. I've mostly only added people that are supposed to be on your side. I've not added the thousands of those that provide therapy for their gain, usually fuelled by the need for affinity or overly fueled by narcissistic or greedy egos.

Still, it is a mess, isn't it? Obviously against what we know is best practice. It is the reductionist scientist-only model where science has been badly used. The influence of a good psychologist is all but missing in the model. I guarantee none would design such a model because we know it will mostly deliver bad psych. This is despite the scientist-practitioner model being known as the best we can, and should, do. The model that puts a good psychologist at the centre so that your nuances, frailties, and strengths are truly valued ingredients in therapy. But with the bad-science-only model in vogue, you, the person, are ignored.

Ignored means you become fodder for programmes and reductionist practices that are not working. If you're emotional, you end up going to a DBT clinic and get DBT. If you're anxious, depressed, and suicidal, you go to a parapsychologist or poorly credentialled general psychologist and get some bad CBT or IPT. If you're a young woman, you go to a Headspace and get low-dose therapy. If you go to a private hospital, you get programmed or be CBT enhanced. And in all these circumstances, you keep going back for the rest of your miserable life. Crock of shit, isn't it?

And to assure you, we have a new language to teach you. There is so much Martian language out there even the Martians have forgotten what it all means, and so they make it up as they go along. In *Wikipedia*, there are 170 therapies listed. Yes, 170! Are we really that loony? Yes, actually. Many psychologists, and all parapsychologists, have become loony part players in the Willy Wonka psychology factory. In that factory, just like the door game of chance at the start of the book, some doors do open to good psych. And you may have the golden ticket. But you will need lots of luck, especially as the game hosts are running the factory. But mostly, your ticket won't get you to the door that leads to good psych and Box A. Rather, you will end up in some mix of counselling, repeat problem solving, or some mistake-ridden process or just really bad psych.

Why is it that you get bad psych? If you were to break your wrist, and bones needed careful pinning, would you accept the well-trained theatre nurse doing all the cutting, chopping, and fixing? There would be lots of chopping but little fixing I can tell you. He is a well-trained nurse, not a well-trained surgeon. No, you only go to the surgeon who has done the hard yards of study and practice. In fact, you can't get anyone else. It is not allowed. It's regulated, you see.

But psychological therapy is not regulated; so anyone can do the chopping—actually, anything—to anyone else. And they do. We are not talking trivialities here. There are so many mistakes made during therapy that kids get broken forever, episodic depression becomes permanently depressed, addictions get worse, worried folk become anxious folk, and people die or at least decide to die.

Disposable psychology for disposable people? In Australia, very few people get well and fewer get very well. It's simply a shame on our society that we won't do better.

And that is why we don't have the graphs in the right direction. Instead, we actually have this:

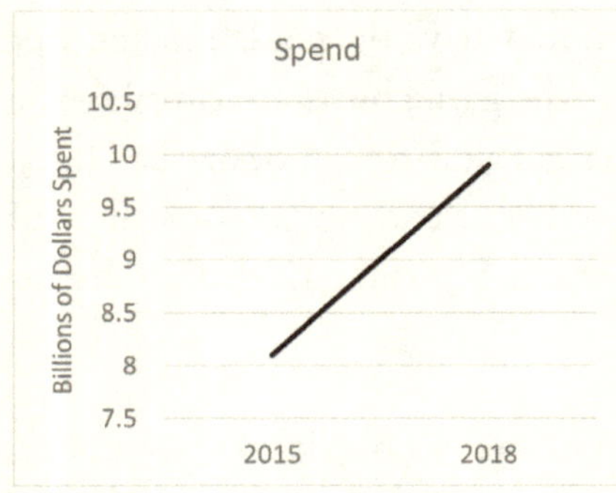

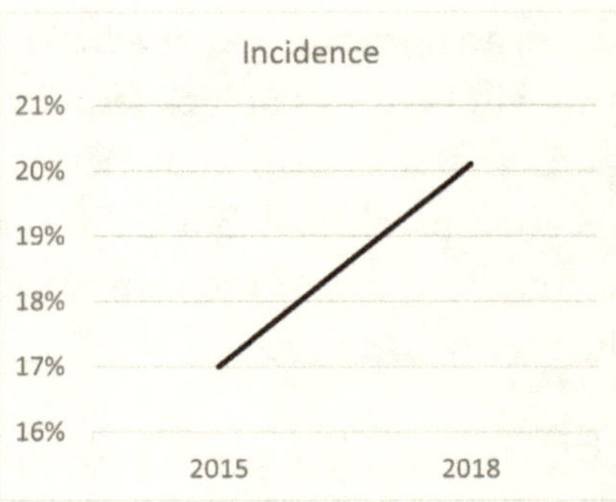

That is, the more mental health we do and the more we spend on it, the sicker the people get in the system. That means people are staying sick and getting sicker. The opposite of what we want and the oppositive of what we are promised if we are the client.

On every societal measure, bad psych trumps good psych and our scorecard is shocking: 5 million people suffering every year, 3 million living with depression, and 65,000 attempts at suicide each year. And 5 million of ordinary Australians popping pills that can make them worse. This despite over $10 billion per year investment into stopping all that. Often money down the drain because it is paying for cheap, junk psychology—bad sych. It's programming that does not work sold in a free-for-all shanty town market. It should make us all both ashamed and angry.

We often look across the sea and scoff at countries with poor unregulated healthcare that has no standards. Yet, not only do we have poor mental healthcare here, but we make it worse, not better. It is true that psychological therapy is officially a regulated health service in Australia. Yet that accounts for nothing because it is in name only. I can provide therapy for money. But so can you, and so can the butcher down the street. They don't need one, but they can buy a CBT certificate for $50, and they do.

Why is it that you sit there accepting this crock of shit when you would walk placards down the street if anyone could perform surgery, diagnose cancers, prescribe antibiotic, and pull out your child's tonsils? Well, it's because you are, just like I was, well indoctrinated by and involved in perpetuating the myths of the industry, the industry that would rather mental health was a marketplace and a place to build empires rather than a genuine pursuit of well-being.

You feel assured because our leaders have put in place regulation agencies to oversee this critical health service. I know you trust your GP, teacher, or hairdresser to provide a referral, you know, to point you in the right direction for psychological therapy. You're happy to take money from Medicare and the NDIA or free sessions from your workplace's EAP, or the primary health network's cheap therapy services. It is convenient to not do therapy at all but rather rack up each two or three weeks for a chat, you know, do a bit. You're most at ease with a kind psychologist that makes you feel better each session, and you don't mind paying to feel good.

You're also happy to accept that somehow all psychologists are the same, average, like homogenised milk or white bread. You don't care that your most private moments get written down for others to read. After all, they're all trustworthy. You're happy to know that you're getting good therapy because it has a brand name like CBT or ACT or EMDR, you know, just like it matters to pick iPhone over an Android phone. And your therapy is targeted to your difficulty, keeping you blissfully ignorant that the research says it will not work. Then, if all else fails or if it gets too hard or too inconvenient, you can take a pill that's never cured anyone.

That's why you're not marching on the streets. These are your myths, aren't they?

Well, they were mine too, and I've enacted every single one of them. But wake up from the cosy slumber of ignorance because the facts don't stack up for any of them. It is time for you to wake up and get a grip!

If you're a client, ask for what you want. And that is a well-credentialed psychologist who is prepared to do good psych, someone who has done the hard yards and did not take the easy route because it takes less brain effort and less time. You want a good psychologist because only they can do good psych, you know, the stuff that works and gets you well. And when you first sit with that good psychologist, you are going to participate confidently in your formulation, assessment, and direction for therapy. You will start that by quietly assessing that psychologist to make sure they stack up.

If you are a psychologist, then step up to the mark and your responsibilities. Don't be swayed by your workplace, union, or market forces into poor and unethical practices. You are in charge of your practice, not your boss and not the union. Learn the numbers. Yes, multivariate statistics are hard, but at least learn what *it works* means. It obviously does not mean what you think! That $d = 0.5$ statistic does not mean it works 50 per cent; so if you do twice as much, it works. Far from it. It means that statistically it worked a bit for a few, less than even one standard deviation. It also means it did not work much for most and made some folk worse.

If you're doing made-up, cookie-cutter therapies, stop it. You're hopefully fully educated and trained. You don't need to impose a simple procedure on your complex client. Think integrative, think with expertise, and be human. If you're still a general psychologist, do the study towards endorsement. After all, your clients are paying for your expertise, not your averageness.

You might be a person who can influence a provider organisation. If you are, it is time to stop doing all this so very wrong. Please find your courage to get better advice than you will get from heads of departments and established leaders. Learn those numbers and allow them to influence your decision making. For example, if DBT has research showing $d = 0.5$, then also remember that half of that gain is the psychologist anyway. You are left with $d = 0.25$, which becomes a triviality. That's not to say I would not work with DBT. It has, along with a good psychologist, saved women's lives. But it isn't a panacea. It isn't good therapy for all women with emotional problems. If you're running eating disorder programmes, stop them. Just engage good psychologists to work with your good clients and stop programming them into junk psychology. Let them do good psych instead.

If you are an elected member of any government, perhaps also if you are a journalist, campaign to have our regulated health services regulated. It is simply not good enough to have our AHPRA impotent. They must be capable of insisting that psychological therapy be provided by folk who meet the standards set by our Australian Psychology Board. The current mirage of regulation is both a mistake and a big fat lie that provides false assurance to our citizens.

If we must have parapsychologists, then have the psychology board establish its standards of competence. Without this basic citizen right being engaged, we will continue to get cheap, junk psychology. Junk psychology is in all public and larger private business offerings because of the simple formula of finance.

Their programmes can be bigger and serve more people if they are cheaper and efficient. And incompetent people are always cheaper to hire, and efficiency is at the expense of quality. But in the case of mental health, cheap and efficient equals junk psychology, more and more bad psych that sends people backwards and keeps them coming back.

Lastly, if you are a doctor, take what are wrongly called antidepressants off your front-line treatment for people coming to you for help. If you did not like my graphs, do your own. You will see that those pills have little efficacy, perhaps mildly helpful for those with severe symptoms of depression. For anyone else, they can become a worsening factor. Then, if you do prescribe them, please take 10 minutes to explain how they mostly don't work at all. And if they do magically work for your client, tell your client that therapy is still the only process we know that can help a person change from the inside out and get a better life. Lastly, get to know your local psychologists. Go and meet them, chat with them, and upgrade your partnership with the good ones.

Let us leave it at that. I've bashed your ears until they have bled. Well, I would have if this were an audiobook. Hopefully, I've helped. Hopefully, you've felt more informed about psychological therapy. Hopefully, I've left you with a job to do.

Your next job is to read my psychologist rating scale and have a practice rating a psychologist, you know.

Thank you for reading.

Cheers and best wishes,
Josh

PSYCHOLOGIST RATING SCALE

Part of being a good psychologist is being able to operationalise complex constructs that you would like to measure. I'm offering the psychologist rating scale (PRS) to you, the client, or perhaps the psychologist to use freely.

You will have needed to read my book first to understand and appreciate what makes good psych. Obviously, it is some combination of accessing both good technical competencies and good personal attributes whilst avoiding incompetence and poor attributes.

In fact, there are three main factors that the PRS covers. Yes, competencies and attributes. But also the freedoms to work well for you. Even good psychologists able to do good psychology are prevented by institutions, programming, workplaces, and funding models.

In any case, I commend my scale to you. Use it wisely. It is more akin to a screening measure than a guarantee of good psych. It is, if you like, an aid to choosing that best door for you.

Attribute	Your Rating	Score
Endorsed by the Australian Psychology Board (counselling or clinical)	Yes / No (0 or 6)	
Knows what therapy is	0 - 1 - 2 - 3 - 4	
Competent in lifespan	0 - 1 - 2 - 3 - 4	
Competent in analysis	0 - 1 - 2 - 3 - 4	
Has a healthy mind	0 - 1 - 2 - 3 - 4	
Of good age	0 - 1 - 2 - 3 - 4	
Works with complexity	0 - 1 - 2 - 3 - 4	
Works with limits	0 - 1 - 2 - 3 - 4	
Addresses all of you	0 - 1 - 2 - 3 - 4	
Ordinariness (balanced ego)	0 - 1 - 2 - 3 - 4	
Works independent of institution	0 - 1 - 2 - 3 - 4	
Can do maths	0 - 1 - 2 - 3 - 4	

Good Psych Rating Scale, Thomas 2021.

Instructions:
(Write in pencil so you can remove for next time.)

Rate endorsement via the AHPRA search.

The score is either 0 (not endorsed) or 6 (endorsed).

Each other element is rated subjectively. Score from 0 to 4. It's 0 if the attribute is unavailable. It's 4 if the attribute is fully available.

Tabulate to attain a score of 50.

Score 0 to 20	= bad psych
Score 21 to 30	= good-enough psych
Score 31 to 40	= good psych
Score 41 to 50 (max)	= very good psych

Example on the next page.

<u>*Example 1*</u>

The best way to complete this table, of course, is by reading the book. Each attribute is described well enough. However, I've rated a psychologist that I know quite well.

Attribute	Your Rating	Score
Endorsed by the Australian Psychology Board (counselling or clinical)	(Yes)/ No (0 or 6)	6
Knows what therapy is	0 - 1 - 2 -(3)- 4	3
Competent in lifespan	0 -(1)- 2 - 3 - 4	1
Competent in analysis	0 - 1 -(2)- 3 - 4	2
Has a healthy mind	0 - 1 - 2 - 3 -(4)	4
Of good age	0 - 1 -(2)- 3 - 4	2
Works with complexity	0 - 1 - 2 -(3)- 4	3
Works with limits	0 - 1 - 2 -(3)- 4	3
Addresses all of you	0 - 1 -(2)- 3 - 4	2
Ordinariness (balanced ego)	0 - 1 - 2 -(3)- 4	3
Works independent of institution	0 - 1 - 2 - 3 -(4)	4
Can do maths	0 -(1)- 2 - 3 - 4	1

Good Psych Rating Scale, Thomas 2021.

Total score is 34/50, which puts this psych into the good-psych bracket. I would happily have this person work with me on my difficulties.

In doing so, I would be mindful of their understanding of what actually works. Their math and therefore balanced consumption of science is suspect. So they will have been unduly influenced by industry and sales. I like that they are healthy, balanced, and independent, unimpaired by an employer or third party.

<u>*Example 2*</u>

This is another psychologist that I know quite well.

Attribute	Your Rating	Score
Endorsed by the Australian Psychology Board (counselling or clinical)	Yes / (No) (0 or 6)	0
Knows what therapy is	(0) - 1 - 2 - 3 - 4	0
Competent in lifespan	0 - (1) - 2 - 3 - 4	1
Competent in analysis.	(0) - 1 - 2 - 3 - 4	0
Has a healthy mind	0 - 1 - (2) - 3 - 4	2
Of good age	0 - 1 - 2 - 3 - (4)	4
Works with complexity	(0) - 1 - 2 - 3 - 4	0
Works with limits	(0) - 1 - 2 - 3 - 4	0
Addresses all of you	0 - 1 - (2) - 3 - 4	2
Ordinariness (balanced ego)	0 - 1 - (2) - 3 - 4	2
Works independent of institution	0 - 1 - 2 - 3 - (4)	4
Can do maths	(0) - 1 - 2 - 3 - 4	0

Good Psych Rating Scale, Thomas 2021.

Total score is 15/50, which puts this psych into the bad-psych bracket. I would not entertain the idea of this person working with me on my difficulties.

I like that they are independent and unimpaired by an employer or third party. They are also of a good age for me. But there are just too many gaps. The psychology will be mistake ridden, and they have no idea what therapy is really about. They are not endorsed, so I have to assume that they never did any deep university study in psychological pathology and therapy. They have an ego type that is problematic too and would mean that they would be at best very underprepared to work with me. Worse, though, they don't know their limits; or if they do, those limits are ignored.

Loud alarm bells please!

9 781664 105041